The New Americans
Recent Immigration and American Society

Edited by
Steven J. Gold and Rubén G. Rumbaut

A Series from LFB Scholarly

Undocumented Immigrants and Higher Education: Sí se puede!

Alejandra Rincón

LFB Scholarly Publishing LLC
New York 2008

Copyright © 2008 by LFB Scholarly Publishing LLC

Library of Congress Cataloging-in-Publication Data

Rincón, Alejandra.
  Undocumented immigrants and higher education : sí se puede! /
Alejandra Rincón.
     p. cm. -- (The new Americans : recent immigration and American
society)
  Includes bibliographical references and index.
  ISBN 978-1-59332-292-2 (alk. paper)
    1. Illegal aliens--Education (Higher)--United States. 2. Universities
and colleges--Residence requirements--United States. 3. Higher
education and state--United States. 4. Tuition--Law and legislation--
United States. I. Title.
  LC3727.R56 2008
    378.1'98269120973--dc22

2008015987

ISBN 978-1-59332-292-2

Printed on acid-free 250-year-life paper.

Manufactured in the United States of America.

Dedication

To all the undocumented immigrants who day by day build the country that denies their children educational opportunities.

Dedicatoria

A los estudiantes inmigrantes que me han confiado sus historias y me han permitido colaborar con ellos en su lucha por la educación. Deseo manifestar mi admiración por su perseverancia extraordinaria ante la adversidad que les impone este país. Espero, al igual que ustedes, continuar la lucha para la legalización y una vida digna en este país.

Contents

Preface

This book began when I set out to chronicle events in Texas that culminated in the June 2001 passage of an in-state tuition law—the first in the United States. I was a participant in efforts that led to the passage of this law and was able to work directly with the affected community of students and parents. I had the proverbial good luck to be in the right place at the right time in two school systems in Texas—the Houston and Austin Independent School Districts. There I worked for several years to implement the new legal mandate for in-state tuition, which opened the door to college for the first time to all students, regardless of their immigration status.

This hands-on experience provided daily lessons in the multiple obstacles faced by the undocumented parents and students desirous of attending college. I learned of the devastating personal impact of draconian anti-immigrant laws and virulent attacks in the media and by politicians. Parents told wrenching stories of their efforts to reunite their families after years of separation, of deportations of family relatives, of being denied the opportunity for a final visit to dying loved ones by immigration authorities, of being swindled out of thousands of hard-earned dollars and losing immigration petitions by unscrupulous agents, about never cashing federal tax refunds or seeking necessary medical care out of fear and, inevitably, about their struggle to help their children pursue an education increasingly denied them by more than just the cruel realities of economics.

As an educator working within school districts, I regularly encountered support but also some school officials who acted to obstruct immigrant and Latino students, either out of cynicism, indifference, or worse. Upon learning of my efforts, a local business woman indignantly called to decry educational opportunities for the undocumented, arguing: "Let's suppose all those people go to college—who will pick up the trash?"

These conditions prompted a small number of teachers, counselors, and administrators, admissions officers from local colleges and universities, myself, and others within the Houston educational community to organize in the late 1990s and form the Coalition of Higher Education for Immigrant Students to advocate for in-state tuition. The Coalition's membership expanded to include teachers, counselors, principals and school district employees, college administrators, staff members and professors, members of community organizations, immigration activists, lawyers, representatives from chapters of the Chamber of Commerce, consular officials, health care providers, and members of state and national professional organizations. I found the breadth of support to be instructive as to the actual fault lines on the issue of undocumented students and the tangible support to be found for immigrant rights, as opposed to the overwhelmingly negative portrayal of attitudes towards undocumented immigrants. In particular, the receptivity within the Black educational community was particularly instructive.

In 2000, I met Jay Pennywell, an administrator from the historically Black Prairie View A&M University (PVAMU). At the time, a colleague and I were searching for opportunities in four-year universities where undocumented students might be able to enroll. When we described the diversity of the pupils in the district where we worked, including the undocumented, Mr. Pennywell did not hesitate to invite the students to pre-college summer camps and gave me some forms to fill out—forms that required a Social Security number. I explained that it would not be possible to bring the students, since many were undocumented and thus had no Social Security numbers. Mr. Pennywell politely reiterated that he wanted us to bring the students anyway. I was quite moved. At that time Texas did not have an in-state tuition policy, and most universities in the state did not admit any undocumented students under any circumstances, much less encourage their participation in any of their academic programs.

A few months after the program ended, we met again, at a meeting of the Coalition of Higher Education for Immigrant Students, an advocacy group I had co-founded and coordinated for four years. I asked Mr. Pennywell why he had allowed those youngsters to attend the program. He began to respond, and then he paused, apparently remembering something. He then explained that his parents and grandparents had been sharecroppers and had been denied the opportunity of a higher education. Misty-eyed, he added that he was not about to let a "piece of paper" get in the way of an education for these young people. During the seven years that I collaborated and worked with PVAMU, I heard similar sentiment and opinions expressed many times and in many ways. While the conditions of Blacks and immigrants are very different, certain common elements and experience can draw them together.

In 2004, during the fiftieth anniversary of *Brown v. Board of Education* (1954), the university sponsored a group of summer program participants on a tour through the Southern states where many of the most important battles of the Civil Rights Movement had taken place. About a fifth of the 150 high school seniors in the program were undocumented students. The summer program organizers had tracked down some of the civil rights activists who had participated in the famous Selma march across the Edmund Pettus Bridge on March 7, 1965. During a visit with the students, one activist described how the police had attacked the peaceful demonstrators with clubs, tear gas, and bullwhips, driving them back into Selma. As she recounted that experience, I observed anguish and consternation in the faces of the young immigrant students. Having been born in another country and having received little or no information in high school about these events, most were unfamiliar with this important aspect of U.S. history. However, they quickly recognized certain similarities between the conditions of discrimination faced by Black people and their own reality as second-class citizens of this country. Significantly, the students became aware that as they enrolled in this historically Black university or in any of many other campuses across Texas, they would be the direct beneficiaries of those Blacks who, fifty years earlier, had fought for equal access in many spheres of life. Such experiences and perspectives of shared interests are all the more important as nativist forces today seek new ways to sow divisions between Blacks and immigrants.

***

I wrote this book to document the history of the struggle to secure immigrant students' access to higher education because I believe that an accurate understanding of this movement for equal rights is important for its advocates, for policymakers, and for others seeking to understand and document this aspect of life for the undocumented and this reality of the educational system in this country. I believe that by offering a context and an accurate presentation of the origins and implications of in-state tuition laws, readers will be provided the best basis for understanding this struggle for equal application of the law and access to higher education.

It is my hope that this book may serve to inspire others to write their own. While we are fortunate to have a growing number of articles and now dissertations on this subject, this may be the first general book on this historic change. More are necessary and undoubtedly on the way, especially since the issue is far from settled. Participant accounts by students, parents, educators, and supporters would help to document and provide greater understanding of the protagonists. An examination of in-state tuition from an educational framework in the context of many issues such as resegregation and continued attacks on the existence of public education, would be worthwhile. More in-depth analysis of the economic background to the issue, the constitutional arguments, or the situation in other countries would also be important contributions.

It is also my hope that addressing and correcting some of the seemingly limitless disinformation concerning undocumented immigrants will provide a modest contribution to counter the malignant demonization of undocumented immigrants, youth and their parents, and help to broaden support for equal access to higher education. Thus far, the number of immigrant youth in the United States who have availed themselves of in-state tuition policies remains negligible. Even so, as this manuscript goes to the publisher, attempts continue to repeal in-state tuition laws, such as a February 2008 vote in the lower house of the Utah state legislature. Even without these challenges, the states do very little, if anything, to inform educators, students, or parents of this new opportunity provided by the law. Still, the students continue their struggle to gain and defend equal access to education and to regularize their immigration status. They are undaunted as their cruel condition leaves them few alternatives, and their sense of dignity demands it. The main motivation for this book is their remarkable tenacity that has proved to us that they can succeed—*¡Sí se puede!*

Acknowledgements

This book documents the struggle to make in-state tuition available to undocumented high school students wishing to pursue a higher education. Logically, I begin, by thanking those who made this law possible in Texas. This list is by no means comprehensive as there are hundreds who made this possible and who have advocated for fair treatment of immigrants within U.S. society. Acknowledgments by their nature are characterized by who they leave out, as the author struggles with time and space, and in the end—utter exhaustion. As such I beg the indulgence of those whom I fail to mention.

In Texas, I begin by thanking those who in the late nineties joined David Johnston and me in forming the Coalition of Higher Education for Immigrant Students as we tried to explore opportunities, financial and otherwise, for undocumented students. They include, among others, Parvin Bagherpour (Houston Community College System), Charlie Galindo (Society of Hispanic Professional Engineers), Art Murillo (then with the University of Houston-Downtown), Jay Pennywell (then with Prairie View A&M University), and Patricia Rojas (then with Congressman Ken Bentsen's office). Others who supported the coalition work during those years included Rose Marie Avelar, Leonel Castillo (former INS Commissioner), Jacqueline Crespo Perry, Cecilio Molina, Anna Nuñez, Javier Parra, Sergio Montelongo and Felipe Reyes among many others. Special thanks to Robert Bernal, Juanita Elizondo, Joyce Jones, Jessica Moreno and others in the business community who buttressed the coalition's goal to expand higher education access.

My most sincere gratitude to those who, as they have become involved in this issue through their jobs, have reaffirmed their commitment to equality for the immigrant community: Ed Apodaca and Cynthia Santos (University of Houston-Downtown), Vangie Orozco (Austin Independent School District), Ruby Rivera (University of Texas System), Ray de los Santos (LULAC-League of United Latin American Citizens), Lorenzo Cano and Rebeca Treviño (University of Houston), and professor and colleague Angela Valenzuela (University of Texas at Austin).

To the educators who, like David Johnston, related to the plight of undocumented students in their own institutions and understood their powerful roles as advocates: Ruth Burgos-Sasscer (Chancellor Emeritus, Houston Community College System); Lynn Herrera; Irene Porcarello and José Salazar of the Houston Community College System; Diana Flores and Julia So from the Dallas County Community College District; Frank Jackson; Mark Pearson; Lettie Raab; Anita White and Nicole Woods with Prairie View A&M University; and Tito Guerrero and Mayra Gonzalez from Texas A&M University. In Texas I also want to thank those who assisted with disseminating information on the law, including Juan García (previously with University of Houston-Downtown), Manuel García y Griego, and Jaime Nisttahuz (both formerly with the University of Texas at Arlington).

I thank the various organizations in Texas and across the United States that have provided me a venue to speak about the in-state tuition laws. These include the Houston Hispanic Forum, the Texas Association of Bilingual Education (TABE), the Texas Association for College Admission Counseling (TACAC), and the Texas association of Teachers of English to Students of Other Languages (TESOL). Nationally, I want to acknowledge the invitations by the American Youth Policy Forum (AYPF), the National Association for Bilingual Education (NABE), the National Association of State Directors of Migrant Education, the National Council of La Raza, and the National Association of College Admission Counseling (NACAC). I also want thank my colleagues from the College Board, especially Adriana Flores, James Montoya, and Rafael Magallán, for their advocacy.

Across the United States, I wish to thank the hundreds of educators, activists, and legislators who have made these in-state tuition laws possible. First of all, I want to express my sincere appreciation and admiration to the undocumented student pioneers in California who fought for this right and its implementation since the mid-eighties with the Leticia "A" case: Irma Archuleta, Alfred Herrera, Dennis Lopez, Ramón Muniz and Betsy Regalado, among many others. A few other individuals also deserve an acknowledgement for the work they have conducted in their respective communities across the United States: Angelo Cabrera in New York; Ricardo Sanchez and Phyllis Gutierrez Kenney in Washington State; Melody Rodriguez in Georgia; and Mateos Alvarez, Ricardo Martinez, and Mariana Velasquez in Colorado.

***

This past year has reaffirmed my understanding that most accomplishments in the life of an individual are not possible without the help of many others. When I mentioned to Emilio Zamora, who has become like a mentor to me, that I had received an invitation to submit a manuscript for publication, he generously took the time to provide invaluable advice and cheered me on. He also introduced me to a wonderful editor, Katherine Mooney, who has patiently molded the various revisions of this manuscript—and who has helped me strengthen many of the arguments. Jackie Estrada copyedited, proofed, and indexed this book to bring it to its final form.

I want to extend my gratitude to my former professors and now colleagues at UT-Austin who have encouraged and supported my interest in these issues: Pedro Reyes, for his continuous guidance and for stressing the importance of the timely publication of this work; Barbara Hines for assisting me to better understand the legal aspects of the topic; and Jaime Chahin at Texas State University, for planting the seed about the importance of publishing this work. Special thanks to Rubén Rumbaut, co-editor of the LFB Scholarly Publishing series *The New Americans: Recent Immigration and Changes in American Society*, whose review of the manuscript and subsequent enthusiastic offer to publish it provided the final encouragement to complete this project. I also thank Leo Balk at LFB for patiently answering my multiple questions during this process.

Special thanks to those who provided me with copies of their dissertations or forthcoming articles and those who granted me permission to reproduce pictures from their personal archives. I want to acknowledge Sylvia Mendez for allowing me to include pictures from her family's fight to desegregate schools in California.

Finally, I am indebted to my husband, Aaron Ruby, for being my strongest bastion of support and pushing me to undertake this project, for going through several drafts, and for helping me to refine my arguments. This book would have not been possible without his help, support, and encouragement. *¡Gracias por tu apoyo, dulzura e inmensa paciencia!*

Above all, my thanks go to the immigrant students and their families, because their tenacity and drive for dignity are, no doubt, my main inspiration to write this book.

CHAPTER 1

Introduction

In 2002, Jesús Apodaca, the son of undocumented migrant workers, graduated with honors from Aurora High School in Denver, Colorado. Apodaca's story made the local (and later national) news after he was interviewed about the difficulties he would face in seeking to attend college as an undocumented student.[1] He had enrolled in a local public high school thanks to a 1982 Supreme Court decision known as *Plyler v. Doe*, which held that undocumented students have the right to a public education. The majority ruling noted the importance of this right by pointing out that "without an education, these undocumented children, already disadvantaged as a result of poverty, lack of English speaking ability and undeniable racial prejudices . . . will become permanently locked into the lowest socioeconomic class."[2] Moreover, the High Court decision underscored the contradictory nature of the anti-immigrant argument: Undocumented immigrants are "encouraged by some to remain here as a source of cheap labor, but nevertheless denied the benefits that our society makes available to citizens and lawful residents."[3]

The enduring validity of the justices' observations is vividly demonstrated by two aspects of the response to Apodaca's story, both involving U.S. House Representative Tom Tancredo of Colorado. When

---

[1] Mr. Apodaca had been accepted into the University of Colorado's computer engineering program, but he and his family were unable to afford the out-of-state tuition fees imposed because of his immigration status (Riley, 2002; Selyee, 2002).

[2] See *Plyler v. Doe* (1982), p. 208.

[3] Ibid., p. 219.

Tancredo, founder of the anti-immigrant Congressional Immigration Reform Caucus and one of the country's most virulently anti-immigrant politicians, saw the story, he called the head of the Immigration and Naturalization Service (INS) to demand that Apodaca and his family, which included two permanent residents, be arrested and deported. During the public debate that ensued, Tancredo's anti-immigrant tirade prompted a group of undocumented drywall workers to approach local media. These workers explained that they had been hired to build an entertainment center in the Congressman's basement. Tancredo asserted that he had been unaware of their immigration status.[4] Cheap labor clearly remains indispensable.

Today, it would seem that the Court's opinion, that access to education is essential, is even more compelling than it was twenty-five years ago. Now there are thousands of *Plyler* high school graduates. But most of these young adults cannot continue on to attain college degrees. In most states, their immigration status—and the poverty that such status imposes on them—makes postsecondary education unattainable. This book is about the long struggle by education advocates and immigrant students to widen access to public colleges and universities nationwide. Specifically, it chronicles the efforts to bring about changes in the legal framework regarding access to higher education. Events in Texas, the state that passed the first law guaranteeing undocumented students eligibility for in-state tuition at postsecondary institutions, provide a starting point for understanding changes elsewhere.

The question of broad public access to college is complex. It raises major economic issues involving labor and the U.S. and world econo-

---

[4] See Blumenthal (2007). This situation recalls the Zoe Baird and Kimba Wood scandals. Each woman had been nominated for attorney general in 1993 by then-President William Clinton; both nominations were withdrawn after it was learned that the nominees had employed undocumented workers (Johnson, 2004; Associated Press, 2001). Cases like these are vivid reminders of a long-standing contradiction whereby a significant part of the economy is built on the backs of undocumented workers, yet their children are denied the opportunity to attend college at nondiscriminatory rates.

mies.[5] It also raises important legal issues in the area of constitutional rights and the relationship between state and federal laws. And, perhaps most important, it brings forward issues related to human dignity and rights that accrue to each of us simply because we are human beings. The story of undocumented students' access to postsecondary education can neither be told nor understood apart from its context—the historical, social, economic, and political circumstances surrounding the debate. This chapter is a brief introduction to some key aspects of immigrants' overall experience in the United States in the late twentieth and early twenty-first centuries.[6] Later chapters shift the focus to a more specific level, examining significant legal battles over education and the environments in which they took place.

The central issue of access to education also poses fundamental questions that go to the core of democracy. Is education a right? Does the Constitution apply to all within the United States? Do undocumented students have the right to attend college at the same tuition rates as other high school graduates from the same state? Or does their immigration status justify discrimination that would otherwise be unconstitutional? Why are immigrants here? Why are they undocumented? Arguably, the answers to these questions have implications not only for undocumented students but also for the rights of all citizens and residents of this country.

THE ECONOMIC REALITIES BEHIND IMMIGRATION

The Jesús Apodaca case epitomizes nearly all the elements of the countless human tragedies whose backdrops are the growing international and domestic economic crises involving cheap labor, anti-immigrant scapegoating, civil and democratic rights, and public educa-

---

[5] For an analysis of issues surrounding the immigration debate, see Chomsky (2007).

[6] There is a large literature dealing with the immigration debate. For a general discussion, see Portes and Rumbaut (2006) and Jonas and Thomas (1999). For an in-depth account of the history of immigration laws and their impact on immigrants, see Martin and Schuck (2005). For coverage of the struggle of political refugees from Central America, see Coutin (2003). For a general discussion on immigration and education, see *Harvard Educational Review*'s Special Issue on Immigration and Education (2001).

tion. The influence of the U.S. government, both today and historically, and the role of its trade policies in creating the economic conditions that year after year force the exodus of thousands of persons from their countries of origin, are rarely the factual starting point in the debate over undocumented immigration.[7] Thus, in addition to contending with grueling economic exploitation and the unpredictable tyranny of Immigrations and Customs Enforcement (formerly the INS), undocumented workers and their children must bear the burden of continually being demonized for their presence, as if being in the United States were simply the result of a whimsical or selfish choice on their part.

Ultimately, neither Jesús Apodaca nor his family were deported. The significant reporting on his case and strong support from a public offended by Congressman Tancredo's callous and hypocritical response resulted in a unique, temporary reprieve.[8] Apodaca's experiences, though, do more than expose the speciousness of a debate that simultaneously encourages politicians' anti-immigrant stance *and* supports the country's continued dependence on cheap labor. His case also underlines another important reality. The debate over immigration inevitably begins with the "illegality" of millions of workers. Yet, it also invariably ignores the facts that economic hardship has compelled the overwhelming majority of these individuals to leave their homelands to seek work in the United States and that their efforts to obtain visas are routinely denied. A more accurate term for large numbers of immigrants in the United States, both documented and undocumented, would be "hostages," not "illegals." The majority are not free to return to their countries and families. Their paychecks are their families' sole means of support—a stand-in for the now-gutted Social Security and health care insurance systems, housing programs, public works, and the educational budgets of their homelands.[9] Past and present policies deliber-

---

[7] For a discussion of the historical origins of migration and the role of the U.S. government and employers, particularly in the case of Mexico, see Portes and Rumbaut (2006).

[8] In 2002, soon after Tancredo targeted Apodaca and his family for deportation, Colorado Senator Ben Nighthorse Campbell introduced private legislation designed to allow Jesús Apodaca and his family to become legal residents.

[9] In 2006, "migrants from poor countries sent home $300 billion, nearly three times the world's foreign aid budgets combined" (DeParle, 2007).

ately pursued by the United States and other highly industrialized countries have created enormous levels of debt in Third World countries. As increasing percentages of their national budgets are taken in payment of foreign debt, these countries' economic and social infrastructures have crumbled.

Foreign debt payments are the largest and most notorious aspect of the harsh economic realities most Third World countries face, but this is only one of the burdens today's global economy pushes onto less developed states. Specific policies, such as the North American Free Trade Agreement (NAFTA) in the case of Mexico, create both direct and indirect hardships; more general trade policies, tariffs, and formal and informal types of protectionism imposed by the United States and Europe all contribute to the upturn in poverty and unemployment and worsening social conditions in the Third World. In many cases, these dire outcomes come as no surprise to those who created the policies and signed the agreements.[10]

Beginning in the last quarter of the twentieth century, workers have streamed out of their poverty-stricken countries of origin in record numbers, looking for jobs abroad. Although many find work, few gain a legal foothold, either for themselves or their families. The result is the economic, social, and political pressure cooker we see in the United States today. There are no signs that these trends will do anything other than increase in the foreseeable future.

Immigrant labor, including the contributions of the undocumented, is indispensable to the U.S. economy.[11] Today, one out of every twenty

---

[10] In the NAFTA negotiations, for instance, the United States demanded the breakup of Mexico's traditional communal land holdings (known as *ejidos*). Meeting this ultimatum required an amendment to the Mexican constitution, a halt to subsidies for corn farmers and the urban consumers of this fundamental staple, and a dismantling of Mexico's protective tariffs on foreign corn. The inevitable ruin of corn farmers' livelihoods created rising rural unemployment. These worsening conditions in turn fostered a rural-to-urban migration that soon, just as inevitably, increased migration to the United States. For more on this topic, see Fernández-Kelly and Massey (2007), Hu-DeHart (2003), and Stuart (2002).

[11] The literature on immigration and the economy is wide in scope. For a discussion of immigrant taxation, see Lipman (2006). For information on the impact of labor legislation on immigrants, see Calderón-Barrera (2003).

workers is undocumented.[12] Entire sectors—construction, agriculture, meatpacking, garments, and service industries ranging from hospitality to janitorial services to landscaping—depend significantly on immigrant workers. Indeed, immigrants generate billions of dollars through their labor and their tax contributions.[13] Employer demand for cheap labor and the federal government's commitment to ensuring increasing profits will continue to shape immigration policy now and in the future, much as it has over the past century and a half.[14]

One of the most common charges nativists level at the immigrant population in the United States is that these newcomers are freeloaders who evade taxes while draining social services. This portrayal is inaccurate. Taxes paid by these workers boost rather than deplete government tax coffers.[15] Since taxation is not dependent on immigration status,[16] undocumented workers pay the same taxes as the rest of the

---

[12] Current data show 7 million undocumented workers in the United States (Lipman, 2006).

[13] For a discussion regarding the taxation of undocumented immigrant workers, including their high contributions to Social Security, see Mehta, Theodore, and Hincapié (2003).

[14] See Portes and Rumbaut (2006). Examples of efforts during the Bush administration include Congressional proposals to set up "guest worker" programs whereby laborers would be brought to the United States temporarily, under conditions established by their employers. One bipartisan proposal filed in 2007 is the Security Through Regularized Immigration and a Vibrant Economy (STRIVE) Act. This act and other similar proposals are strikingly like the Bracero program, a misnamed guest worker program that was instituted in 1942 as a response to the labor shortages created by World War II. "Braceros were the perfect exploitable underclass, willing to work for low wages and in deplorable conditions" (Garcia, 1995, p. 4). Recently, this program (which remained in place until 1965) has been portrayed as a shameful, distant, and never-to-be-repeated chapter in U.S. history, similar to the Japanese internment camps.

[15] American Immigration Lawyers Association (2004). Also see extensive discussion by Lipman (2006).

[16] The Internal Revenue Service does not require taxpayers to supply a Social Security number when filing income taxes. Since 1996, the IRS has made available individual taxpayer identification numbers (ITINs) which allow un-

U.S. population.[17] They have paid sales taxes and payroll taxes for decades; now, they are increasingly paying income and property taxes as well. These payments fund state and local expenditures for education and the other social services immigrants are said to be draining. In addition, the income and payroll taxes paid by immigrants contribute to Social Security, Medicare, and unemployment taxes, as well as to federal, state, and local budgets.[18] The undocumented who are forced to use false Social Security numbers in order to be able to work pay into the system just like other workers, but, ironically, they reap none of the benefits available to others.

They contribute funds to unemployment insurance, workers' compensation, retirement, disability, and survivor benefits, but they cannot file claims for any of these. According to the Social Security Administration, from 1937 to 2000, the amount of wages reported under the Earning Suspense File (ESF) reached $374 billion.[19] Recent figures show that, as of 2005, the total ESF is $519 billion.[20] In addition, undocumented workers provide an annual subsidy of up to $7 billion a year, representing about 10 percent of the 2004 Social Security surplus.[21] These figures do more than provide evidence of the sizable eco-

---

documented workers to pay taxes. An estimated 11 million ITINs have been issued to undocumented workers since then (Bernstein, 2007a).

[17] Lipman (2006) provides various examples regarding the multiple tax contributions by undocumented workers. Quoting another author, Lipman reports that "in 2003 the Small Business Administration (SBA) reported unposted earnings of $421 billion due to mismatches of Social Security numbers and names likely from undocumented workers, as well as some clerical errors, representing $64.4 billion of employee and employer contributions to Social Security and Medicare trust funds, including approximately $14 billion for 2003" (p. 4).

[18] The IRS reports that between 1996 and 2003, those tax contributions totaled $50 billion. In 2005 alone, the amount withheld from undocumented workers' paychecks totaled more than $5 billion (Bernstein, 2007a).

[19] See Mehta, Theodore, and Hincapié (2003). The ESF was created to temporarily hold Social Security earnings collected from filers whose names or Social Security numbers do not match the Social Security Administration's files while staff members try to determine the filers' true identities. Immigrant workers are believed to have earned a significant portion of these wages.

[20] Bosworth (2006).

[21] Porter (2005).

nomic contributions undocumented workers make at all levels. They underscore the grave inequity of taxation without representation. To deny undocumented immigrants equal access to education and social services by arguing that they are not contributors is plainly fallacious.

In the ongoing debate over undocumented immigrants, a fundamental fact is often obscured: it is not the presence of the undocumented per se but rather the conditions of their presence that provoke controversy. The wholesale removal of the nation's estimated 12 million undocumented immigrants would be so economically devastating to the United States that it is rejected out of hand by all but the most extreme elements. As President Bush has put it, "Massive deportation of the people here is unrealistic. It's just not going to work."[22] At the same time, providing legal status to this population would undercut some of the conditions that make undocumented immigrants so valuable to employers and to the U.S. economy as a whole. Their exploitative living and working conditions provide substantial profits. Meanwhile, the enormous risks they undertake in crossing borders, and the poverty they endure despite long hours of work that is often physically exhausting, go largely uncontested in political discourse and largely unmentioned in the media. In fact, such conditions are rationalized through the casual use of the dehumanizing term "illegals," and attacks on this population are justified on the grounds that they are present "illegally."[23]

CIVIL RIGHTS, IMMIGRATION, AND EDUCATION

Although the children of undocumented immigrants are, like their parents, denied access to many services and opportunities, their right to a primary and secondary public school education has been legally pro-

---

[22] See Dinan (2006).

[23] Petronicolos and New (1999) argue: "It continues to seem natural to large portions of the U.S. populace that these individuals and their children are entitled to few legal protections and have no right to the same benefits as other residents" (p. 402). As they note, the justification for what is done to undocumented immigrants, "requires that members of the society who are deprived of opportunities be viewed as outsiders, as 'domestic foreigners,' rather than as associate members to whom one has ethical and practical responsibilities" (p. 403).

tected since the Supreme Court's 1982 decision in *Plyler*. Thus, for thousands of young people like Jesús Apodaca, the first direct experience with the crippling impact of their immigration status is felt upon high school graduation, as they attempt to enroll in college, seek a job, or apply for government identification. As the Apodaca case demonstrates, these students' efforts to participate more fully in society have spurred a nationwide discussion regarding their right to a genuinely equal opportunity to gain a college education. This book tells their story.

Since 2001, when the Texas legislature approved the first law extending in-state tuition eligibility to undocumented students, nine states have followed suit, modifying their higher education rules to allow undocumented high school graduates to attend college. Anti-immigrant forces have responded by repeating their arguments regarding immigrants' lack of economic contributions, asserting that the laws allowing undocumented students to attend college constitute a subsidy and reward unlawful behavior. In rebutting those arguments, some have limited themselves either to pleading for recognition of the economic value and usefulness of this population or to portraying uneducated immigrants as a potential menace. Allowing these students to attend college, it is argued, will benefit businesses and the economy. Likewise, the economic and fiscal contributions already made by the parents of these young adults directly and indirectly help support public education at all levels. In the controversy over equal access and opportunity, however, such economistic arguments can be self-defeating.

Debates limited to immigration statistics, financial worth, and various economic indicators tend to reduce undocumented immigrants to chattel while at the same time surrendering the moral high ground and ignoring more fundamental issues. Comparing such arguments with the approaches taken by Blacks and other activists during the civil rights movement is instructive. The Black struggle for equality was not ignited by economic rationales that promised more productive servitude. Blacks did not demand access to the same schools as whites, equal employment opportunities, or an end to segregation by offering the promise of increased tax bases or profits or by threatening mass criminality and burdening social service systems. Instead, their compelling arguments were based on their inherent human dignity and their fundamental human and civil rights. As the signs carried by protesters during the 1968 Memphis Sanitation Workers' Strike reminded others,

"I am a man." A similar message from the undocumented community is clear in a slogan found on many of the signs protesters have carried during immigrant rights marches: "No human being is illegal."

This is the perspective from which undocumented students' efforts to attend college is best understood. These efforts are the current expression of past civil rights struggles and may have broader implications for the population as a whole.[24] The ongoing attempts to secure eligibility for in-state tuition can be characterized as a human and civil rights struggle based on the fundamental premise that no group should be subjected to discrimination. Undocumented students seek equality under the law. Just as important, they are also affirming their humanity and thus their rights as human beings. Like Blacks who struggle to overcome racist stereotypes, undocumented immigrants seek to overturn government and media images that portray them as "aliens" and "illegals," devoid of all rights simply because they happen to be living in a country other than the one in which they were born. The placards and banners on view in the many activities undocumented students and immigrant workers have organized around the country telegraph this message, proclaiming "Full equality for all"; "We all have the right to a future"; and "We belong here."

RIGHTS AND IMMIGRATION

Immigration opponents argue that the undocumented cannot assert any rights since they have been denied legal status in the United States. Some courts and legal writings also assert this. However, in weighing the significance and validity of such legal arguments, it is important to recall that at one time in this country's past, the Supreme Court and the majority of legal writings upheld slavery, and even after the Fourteenth Amendment was passed, women were still denied the right to vote.[25]

---

[24] For instance, given that most undocumented immigrants are people of color, their fight may have a positive influence on current struggles by U.S. minorities in areas such as affirmative action.

[25] See Petronicolos and New (1999) for an insightful analysis. Regarding the dissenting opinion in *Plyler v. Doe*, they point out that arguments that the undocumented have no rights because they are not here legally "can be made to appear 'natural' and rational, but within the psychological world in which Jef-

Furthermore, under the Jim Crow system, the majority of Blacks were disenfranchised by law and thus denied the protections of the Fourteenth Amendment, again with the imprimatur of the legal system and scholarship. The second sentence of Section 1 of the Fourteenth Amendment states,

> No State shall make or enforce any law which shall abridge the privileges or immunities of citizens of the United States; nor shall any State deprive any person of life, liberty, or property, without due process of law; nor deny to any person within its jurisdiction [emphasis added] the equal protection of the laws.

The deliberate wording "nor deny *to any person* [emphasis added] within its jurisdiction the equal protection of the laws" clearly extends such protections to citizen and noncitizen alike. Indeed, the crux of the *Plyler* case was the ruling by the Supreme Court that the Fourteenth Amendment's equal protection clause applied to undocumented children, thus guaranteeing this population equal access to public education. This was the first time that the High Court had applied such constitutional protection to undocumented immigrants.[26]

The U.S. Constitution contains no specific provision for education as a right. Nevertheless, many persons here and around the world believe such a right does exist, and such sentiment is manifested in the United Nations Universal Declaration of Human Rights of 1948, which states under Article 26 that "Everyone has the right to education." The popularity of the belief in such a right is also illustrated by the vehemence with which it is attacked by opponents of public education. Yet, even the courts, which have refused to recognize such a right, have been obliged to give a nod to such strong public sentiment. Justice

---

person lived, for instance, classifications based on skin color were equally natural and rational" (p. 402).

[26] See Olivas (2004) and Pabón López (2005). In *Plyler*, the High Court rejected the argument that because of their immigration status, undocumented children could not be considered "persons within the jurisdiction." Instead, the Court stated, "Whatever his status under the immigration laws, an alien is surely 'a person' in any ordinary sense of that term" (*Plyler v. Doe*, 1982, p. 210).

Brennan, writing for the majority in the *Plyler* case, made it clear that the Constitution extended equal rights to undocumented youth as they sought access to public education. One observer noted that Brennan "suggested a putative right to education," thus making the compelling argument that "education cannot be characterized as just another government benefit."[27] *Plyler* extended a right that does not exist, education, to those who ostensibly have no rights—the undocumented. This epitomizes the contradiction between de jure rights, which are codified in law and precedent, and the broad popular sense of rights and what is right, which has its own weight and bearing on the law and in society.[28] These rights or proscriptions for undocumented immigrants may be further extended or denied by the courts and legislatures as the law of the land at any given time. However, the actual outcome will be determined in momentous social and political struggles to which we are witness today and likely will continue to occur for some time.

THE RECENT EXPANSION OF ANTI-IMMIGRANT POLITICS AND POLICIES

Since the mid-1990s, with the arrival of 13 million new immigrants, the United States has experienced unparalleled demographic changes.[29] In 1990, there were fewer than 20 million foreign-born persons in the United States. A decade later, according to the 2000 Census, the foreign-born population had increased to 31.1 million (11 percent of the total population)—double the percentage of the 1970s. Asians and Latin Americans represent a large proportion of this overall growth.[30]

---

[27] Yates (2004), p. 591.

[28] Another case (discussed later in this chapter) that illustrates this contradiction was the inability to enforce California's anti-immigrant Proposition 187. In addition, many are surprised to learn that it was legal and common for noncitizens, including undocumented immigrants, to vote in elections in the United States. It was only in 1996, under immigration law signed by President Clinton, that voting in federal elections was made illegal and a deportable offense (Tienda, 2002).

[29] Portes and Rumbaut (2006).

[30] According to the Pew Hispanic Center, "Immigrants and their U.S.-born offspring accounted for 55 percent of the increase in population since 1966-67. Within this group of 55 million, Latino immigrants and their offspring were by

For the latter group, researchers project an increase from the nearly 44.7 million Latinos now in the United States to 74.2 million by 2050, making that population one of the country's fastest growing.[31] This rise in immigration has been accompanied by substantial growth in the undocumented population, currently estimated at some 12 million people, or 26 percent of the total foreign-born population.[32]

This rapid demographic change has been used by the government, the media, and nativist forces to promote anti-immigrant hysteria.[33] The past decade has brought more and ever-harsher measures, including raids at job sites and private homes, passage of state laws attempting to regulate immigration, threats to fire 8 million workers who could not verify the authenticity of their Social Security numbers, local ordinances banning the rental of housing to undocumented immigrants, and the physical as well as verbal harassment of day laborers.[34]

---

far the largest, representing about 29 million persons, or 53 percent of the addition due to immigration . . . About 12 million Asian and Pacific Islander immigrants and their offspring were added to the population, representing about 22 percent of the increase due to immigration" (Pew Hispanic Center, 2006a, p. 3).

[31] Murdock et al. (1999). The U.S. Census bureau estimates an even larger growth by projecting that the Latino population will quadruple its 1990 size (estimated at about 22 million) by 2050 (see http://facfinder.census.gov).

[32] Pew Hispanic Center (2006b). An estimated 57 percent of the undocumented are from Mexico, while 23 percent are from other Latin American countries.

[33] Examples of the use of undocumented workers and their families as scapegoats abound in the media, with nativist commentators such as CNN's Lou Dobbs taking the lead. For a sample of Dobbs' opinions, see Navarrete (2007b).

[34] In August 2007, the Bush administration announced a new measure "aimed at getting employers to fire illegal employees whose Social Security numbers cannot be immediately verified." The measure required the Social Security Administration to send out "about 141,000 no-match letters, covering more than eight million employees . . . Of those records with errors, [an estimated] 12.7 million belonged to native-born American citizens." In October 2007, a federal judge ordered an indefinite delay on the measure, reprimanding the Bush administration for "making policy changes with 'massive ramifications' for employers" (Preston, 2007c). The Bush administration has announced its intention to reissue the rule in 2008 (Preston, 2007f).

The ultimate goal of these attacks is to further criminalize immigrants' presence, and even their use of public space. For instance, vigilantes and paramilitary groups such as the Minutemen, who have for some time focused their attention on undocumented immigrants entering along the U.S.-Mexico border, now visit day labor centers. Their aim is to provoke and intimidate workers already present in the United States.[35] In cities such as San Diego, Phoenix, and Houston, to discourage the employment of undocumented immigrants, Minutemen have taken pictures of workers as they wait for work; allegedly, they send these photographs to Immigration and Customs Enforcement (ICE).[36]

---

[35] Internal "defense" tactics are increasingly common. Nativist groups, such as Save Our State (SOS) in California and Sachem Quality of Life (SQL) on Long Island, use strategies similar to those of the Minutemen. SOS was founded by Ventura resident Joseph Turner in 2004 and was deliberately named after the group that sponsored California's Proposition 187, ten years earlier. The organization's website invites others to engage in what they term "aggressive activism" against what they refer to as "the illegal alien invasion," which they claim has turned their communities "into a Third World cesspool" (http://saveourstate.org/index.php, 2004). Despite claims to the contrary, SOS has been increasingly associated with neo-Nazis, skinheads, and other white supremacist groups (Southern Poverty Law Center, 2005). SQL was founded in the late nineties by Farmingville resident Margaret Bianculli-Dyber and others, particularly homemakers. The organization's mission is to "stand up for the rights of middle-class suburban communities it says are being inundated by thousands of undocumented, mostly Latino, immigrants. To do that, it calls for expanded enforcement of immigration laws and expulsion of all immigrants not here legally," particularly those living in Farmingville (see Baker, 2001). One of this group's many activities was to organize protests in front of local day labor sites and verbally assault the immigrant laborers as they waited to be hired for the day (Sandoval and Tambini, 2004).

[36] During summer 2007, Minutemen "picketed a suburban church northeast of San Diego and held up an effigy of a priest depicted as the devil . . . used bullhorns to hurl invective at parishioners and taunted Latino children who were on their way to make their First Communion, telling them their parents were in the country illegally" (Navarrete, 2007a). For additional details, see Sifuentes (2007). The attacks, prompted by the pastor's decision to permit the use of the church as a day laborer pickup site, underscore the intersection of race and

These and similar activities make the undocumented easier prey and cheaper labor for contractors. On Long Island, anti-immigrant forces have staged a multiyear campaign against the day laborers who serve the area's housing and construction industry. Nativist and racist harassment there has ranged from legal maneuvers (e.g., passage and enforcement of ordinances against "loitering" and multifamily rentals) to physical assaults.[37] These kinds of immigrant scapegoating, racial profiling, and physical and verbal harassment are not anomalous occurrences. In fact, such actions, once the province of nativists and other extremists, are an increasingly normalized response to tacit (and in some cases explicit) support provided by politicians and mainstream media.[38]

---

immigration. Navarrete notes that these civilian patrols "have morphed from being anti-illegal immigrant to anti-immigrant and just plain anti-Latino. And now, anti-Catholic?" (ibid.). White supremacist groups also have stepped up their attacks against those perceived as foreigners, including Latinos. A 2007 lawsuit filed by the Southern Poverty Law Center involves the physical assault of a 16-year-old boy of Panamanian descent by members of the Imperial Klans of America (see Southern Poverty Law Center, 2007). For information on other cases reported by the Anti-Defamation League, see Associated Press (2007).

[37] As explained later in this chapter, recently passed measures in some cities are blatantly discriminatory and punitive. But some seemingly "neutral" changes in city codes actually are thinly veiled anti-immigrant tactics. For example, outlawing "loitering" targets laborers who wait on street corners or in parking lots for contractors who hire them by the day; and restrictions on rentals target these same men, whose very low wages force them to share apartments. In the Long Island town of Farmingville, home of SQL, the passage of city ordinances to criminalize and limit immigrants' physical presence created a hostile environment that, in 2000, led to the beating of two Mexican men. The workers had been lured by the promise of work offered by two white supremacists posing as employers, who then tried to kill them. Surprisingly, given the local atmosphere, the attackers were eventually charged with attempted murder, convicted, and sentenced to 25 years in prison. For more on the Farmingville attack, see Jones (2003).

[38] In 2005, for instance, Representative John Culberson (TX) filed the Border Protection Corps Act (H.R. 3622), which would allow governors to establish citizen militias to patrol international borders. This measure proposed to authorize the use force against people whom militia members suspected were

At the federal, state, and local levels there has been a growth in
legislation designed to intimidate immigrants, whether legal or not, and
to create a more subservient sector of the working class.[39] This anti-

---

undocumented, thus inviting racial profiling, among other acts. Such legislation, even when it does not pass, encourages the vigilantism of rightist groups,
including the Minutemen. Although this organization makes a point on its website to disassociate itself from racist groups (asserting that "it has no affiliation
with, nor will we accept any assistance by or interference from, separatists,
racists, or supremacy groups or individuals . . ."), there is evidence to the contrary (http://www.minutemanproject.com/). In Texas, the head of the Minutemen Civil Defense Corps resigned, explaining that he had been "unable to
overcome the racism" within the group (see Hegstrom, 2005).

[39] The National Conference on State Legislatures reports unprecedented activity on the issue of immigration at the state level: "As of July 2, 2007, no fewer
than 1404 pieces of legislation related to immigrants and immigration had been
introduced among the 50 state legislatures. Of these bills, 182 bills became law
in 43 states . . . State legislators have introduced roughly two and a half times
more bills in 2007 than in 2006. The number of enactments from 2006 (84) has
more than doubled to 170 in 2007 . . . Many states have focused on employment, health, identification and driver's and other licenses, law enforcement,
public benefits, and human trafficking" (National Conference of State Legislatures, 2007, p. 1; see also Preston, 2007b). For a discussion of preemption issues that arise with state attempts to regulate the area of immigration, see
Olivas (2007b). His analysis compares these state laws to the "pigtail" ordinances levied against the Chinese in the mid-nineteenth century. Pfaelzer
(2007) provides an in-depth historical analysis of that same period, offering a
powerful reminder of the history of racial exclusion in this country. In San
Francisco, laundry ordinances passed in 1880 made it illegal for Chinese to
have washhouses in wooden buildings (even though most dwellings at the time
were made of wood) and required laundry owners to secure a permit from the
Board of Supervisors. The board granted permits to all non-Chinese owners but
did not approve permits for any of the 200 Chinese applicants. In *Yick Wo v.
Hopkins* (1886), the Supreme Court overturned the conviction of a Chinese
laundryman who had operated without a permit, ruling that this discriminatory
application of the ordinance violated the Fourteenth Amendment. The case is
enormously important because it marks the first use of the Fourteenth Amendment "to protect aliens from unfriendly state regulation" (Aleinikoff, 1989, p.

immigrant legislative shift sharply intensified in 1996, with the passage of the Illegal Immigration Reform and Immigrant Responsibility Act (IIRIRA), legislation championed by then-President William Clinton. Even before the IIRIRA was signed into law, a pronounced increase in border enforcement began. In 1991, the U.S. Navy used military equipment to build a seven-mile, ten-foot-high wall between San Diego and Tijuana. In 1993, the Clinton administration authorized a costly lengthening of the wall to fourteen miles. Now, a decade and a half later, President George W. Bush requested $1 billion from Congress to build a 700-mile fence. Border Patrol personnel have also increased.[40] In addition, in the summer of 2006, President Bush authorized the deployment of 2,500 National Guard troops along the U.S.-Mexico border, announcing that they would remain stationed in the area for up to two years. These border activities have resulted in a dramatic increase

---

864). Just as important is the fact that "*Yick Wo* becomes precedent for the civil rights cases in the 1960s that seek to strike down statues that selectively discriminated against African Americans" (Pfaelzer, 2007, p. 282).

[40] "During the last thirty years, the overall size of the Border Patrol has increased sixfold, with full-time employees jumping from 1,746 in 1975 to 11,106 in September 2005. It is clear that in a broad way Congress and a long line of presidents have favored the expansion of the agency. And a recent White House analysis of the FY 2007 budget restated the Bush administration's previous statements that it was fully committed to providing the resources required to build "smarter and more secure borders" (TRAC Immigration, 2006). In October 2007, the Senate approved an amendment to the Fiscal Year 2008 Defense Appropriations bill to provide $3 billion for increased border security and interior enforcement measures. The measure passed 95-1 (see Graham, 2007). Senator Lindsey Graham (SC), one of the bill's sponsors, stated, "There is no doubt we need better border security at our *southern* border including more boots on the ground, more miles of fencing, better technology which acts as a force multiplier, additional detention beds, and unmanned aerial vehicles" (ibid., italics added). Co-sponsor Senator Jon Kyl (AZ) added: "This amendment provides an additional $3 billion in emergency funding for FY2008 to protect the border, *enhance interior enforcement*, including *at the workplace*, and detain more illegal immigrants who have either committed crimes or who are in the process of being removed from the U.S. for immigration violations" (ibid., italics added). For information on the use of military contractors to build the wall in the Southern border see Lipton (2006).

in the number of deaths as immigrants take alternative and more peril-ous routes into the United States.[41] The militarization of the border has also led to an increase in the number of apprehensions. Immigrants are now the fastest growing prison population in the United States, with courts having processed 350,000 immigrants in fiscal year 2005.[42]

While many of the apprehensions occur at the border, an increas-ing number of ICE operations focus on interior enforcement. One of the largest such offensives, begun in May 2006 and dubbed Operation Re-turn to Sender, allegedly targeted criminals and those who had ignored previous deportation orders. What evolved, though, was a massive and indiscriminate sweep through work sites and homes, proving that the real aim was to intimidate the undocumented community, whose mem-bers had protested en masse during the spring of that year.[43] Under this operation, federal agents arrested, detained, and deported thousands. Agents relied on surprise raids, most of which turned into illegal searches, conducted late at night or in the predawn hours, without search warrants.[44] Hundreds of families with undocumented parents

---

[41] The U.S. Border Patrol reported that in 2005, more than 500 people died along the length of the U.S.-Mexico border, double the number of yearly border crossing deaths since 1995 (Lomonaco, 2006).

[42] See Fernandes (2007).

[43] As it has done throughout history, the U.S. government uses immigration enforcement to quell political dissent (see next chapter for historical back-ground on the use of these tactics). The best examples of this tactic are the Palmer raids at the beginning of the century (Johnson, 2004). Efforts to intimi-date noncitizens continue today, as exemplified by the inhumane Operation Return to Sender.

[44] As part of its "accomplishments," the Department of Homeland Security reports that through Operation Return to Sender, "ICE arrested, closed the cases of, or otherwise removed 14,356 aliens from the fugitive/illegal popula-tion between May 26 and September 30, 2006" (http://www.dhs.gov/xnews/releases/pr_1162228690102.shtm). A few months later, the figure had in-creased. From May 2006 to May 2007, the number of deportations as part of Operation Return to Sender exceeded 18,149 people, destroying immigrant families and spreading fear throughout immigrant communities (Espinosa, 2007). By the closing of fiscal year 2007, "the number of immigrants deported

and U.S.-citizen children were broken apart, prompting at least one federal lawsuit accusing ICE of constitutional violations and racial profiling.[45]

In the past, adults detained with children were released on bond; now they increasingly face long-term incarceration. This shift toward criminalizing immigrant parents and their children is exemplified by the Department of Homeland Security's establishment of a privately run facility, the T. Don Hutto Residential Center in Taylor, Texas.[46] Immigrant families with children as young as nursing infants are imprisoned in this center, which used to be a detention facility. The Hutto

---

has risen to more than 261,000 . . . up from about 177,000 two years ago" (Gorman, 2007).

[45] In *Aguilar v. ICE*, 15 plaintiffs (including seven U.S. citizens), charged that ICE agents "unlawfully forced their way into the homes of Hispanic families in the New York area without court warrants or other legal justification . . . [the suit] accuses the immigration agency of conducting the raids in violation of the Fourth Amendment's protection from unreasonable searches, harming citizens and legal residents of the United States as well as foreigners here illegally [and] describe[d] abusive predawn raids on their homes this year by armed immigration agents" (Bernstein, 2007b). The impact of these raids on children is severe: as many as 13,000 U.S. citizen children have seen one or more parents deported (Preston, 2007d). One child, Kebin Reyes, a seven-year-old U.S. citizen who was seized with his Guatemalan father during a raid in San Rafael, California, was held in ICE custody for 10 hours, provoking widespread outrage in the local area. Immigrant rights activists are focusing increased efforts on stopping this trend toward forced separations of parents and children (http://www.aclu.org/immigrants/detention/29526prs20070426.html). In late 2007, ICE again provoked outrage when agents separated an undocumented mother from her nine-month-old nursing baby. The agency "rushed to issue new guidelines on the *detention of nursing mothers*, allowing them to be released unless they pose a *national security risk*" (Preston, 2007e, italics added). For a comprehensive study of the impact of draconian immigration policies on U.S.-citizen children, see Capps et al. (2007).

[46] Williamson County, where the facility is housed, earns $1 per day for each inmate if the facility is at capacity, a policy that can only encourage the long-term detention of families. Some adults have already been held there for two years, estranged from relatives, including their U.S.-citizen children (Women's Commission, 2007).

Center's poor conditions, reports of abusive treatment of the 400 prisoners, half of whom are children, and knowledge that children were forced to wear prison uniforms prompted protests. In March 2007, various organizations sued the Department of Homeland Security and, after a settlement in August 2007, won the release of some the children housed there.[47]

The increasing number of incarcerated foreign-born citizens is a direct result of the enactment of the IIRIRA. This 1996 law severely and retroactively restricts the rights of immigrants. The IIRIRA permits detention of asylum seekers, children, stateless persons, and long-term permanent residents.[48] Due process infringements include double-jeopardy violations involving mandatory detentions of immigrants with former criminal convictions, even if these sentences have already been served; similarly, asylum seekers who lacked documentation on their initial arrival face mandatory jail time.[49] The IIRIRA's retroactive enforcement provisions also affect legal permanent residents. Individuals guilty of nonviolent offenses—such as driving while intoxicated—which were not punishable by deportation when they were committed are now retroactively subject to deportation, as well as to detention, trial, and conviction based on secret evidence. This vast expansion of the type and number of offenses that are subject to deportation accounts for the spike in the number of detentions. The Office of Detention and

---

[47] The original lawsuits were filled by the ACLU, the ACLU of Texas, the University of Texas School of Law Immigration Clinic, and the international law firm of LeBoeuf, Lamb, Greene & MacRae LLP on behalf of 26 children housed in Hutto whose ages ranged from 1 to 17.

[48] According to the Department of Justice's Bureau of Justice Statistics, in 2005 state and federal correctional authorities held 91,117 non-U.S. citizens (6.7 percent of all persons then incarcerated in the United States). Since the passage of the IIRIRA, "when new criminal deportation provisions were enacted . . . more than 650,000 immigrants—both undocumented and legal noncitizens—have been deported as criminal aliens, many after serving substantial prison time. In both FY 2004 and FY 2005 more than 90,000 immigrants were deported as criminal aliens" (Capps et al., 2007, p. 10).

[49] Under immigration law, asylum seekers are automatically detained on arrival in the United States and must pass "credible fear" interviews before being released (Walth, 2001).

Removal (part of ICE) estimates that in fiscal year 2007, some 605,000 foreign-born individuals, charged with various offenses, will be admitted to state correctional facilities and local jails. Of this group, an estimated half (302,500) will be subject to deportation. In short, the IIRIRA establishes a system of dual liability that punishes the immigrant first with incarceration under the criminal court system, then with deportation under the immigration system.

In addition to the harsh provisions of the IIRIRA, immigrants in the United States face further restrictions from Public Law 107-56, commonly known as the PATRIOT Act.[50] Passed only 45 days after the September 11, 2001 events, this legislation gives the Department of Homeland Security additional power to detain immigrants, and it legalizes procedures that directly jeopardize some of the nation's most fundamental, constitutionally protected rights, including presumption of innocence and due process. Sanctioning the use of noncitizenship as a vehicle for the denial of due process has had devastating consequences, particularly for Arab, Muslim, and South Asian immigrants and detainees in the post–September 11 era. Ultimately, the vast majority of those detained under national security provisions are never charged with anything more than immigration offenses. The government has justified various practices, such as the use of secret evidence, on the grounds that as noncitizens, detained immigrants do not have the right to the same protections and guarantees afforded to U.S. citizens. The fact that these practices not only encroach on immigrants' rights under the law but also undermine the democratic and civil rights of all U.S. citizens is often overlooked.[51]

---

[50] The law's full title is Uniting and Strengthening America by Providing Appropriate Tools Required to Intercept and Obstruct Terrorism (USA PATRIOT) Act. It was signed into law October 26, 2001.

[51] A case in point is that of José Padilla, a U.S. citizen who was detained in a military prison for three and a half years. For the duration of his imprisonment, the government refused to charge Padilla with any crime and denied him access to a lawyer. His detention as an "enemy combatant" was possible under a PATRIOT Act provision that authorizes indefinite detention of noncitizens suspected of terrorism (see Johnson, 2004; Hernandez, 2005). This case exemplifies the impact that anti-immigrant legislation allegedly targeting noncitizens has had on the constitutional rights of U.S. citizens.

Anti-immigrant legislation at the federal level also includes limitations on the access and use of public benefits. The 1996 Personal Responsibility and Work Opportunity Reconciliation Act (PRWORA), passed during the Clinton administration and commonly known as the Welfare Reform Act, creates disparities in access to health care. The act's provisions have increased the number of immigrants and U.S. citizens who remain uninsured, despite eligibility, because of their inability to secure all required documentation.[52] PRWORA also reinstates a feature of old federal immigration laws, the use of "public charge." This term is applied to immigrants the government designates as likely to become dependent on public assistance.[53] This designation limits the likelihood that low-income immigrants will qualify for legal permanent resident status; it is also a threat to those who are already permanent residents, since they face deportation if they become a public charge within five years of entry. Under current immigration law, legal permanent residents and U.S. citizens sponsoring their relatives must prove that these newcomers are not likely to become a public charge. To do so, the sponsors must demonstrate that their own income is at least 125 percent over the poverty level. The concept of "public charge" thus functions as a method of exclusion that disparately affects low-income noncitizens, the majority of whom are immigrants of color.[54]

Federal legislative proposals reached their most extreme expression of anti-immigrant fervor in December 2005, with the filing of the

---

[52] The Center on Budget and Policy Priorities estimates that in the decade since this law's implementation, between 1.2 million and 2.3 million low-income U.S. citizens have delayed seeking care or may lose Medicaid eligibility altogether due to the onerous documentation process (Sonfield, 2006). For more information on the impact of these laws on eligible U.S.-citizen children, see Hallums and Lewis (2003) and Kandula et al. (2004).

[53] For an in-depth discussion of the origins of this aspect of immigration law, see Johnson (2004).

[54] Immigrants disproportionately occupy the lowest economic strata and thus are the most susceptible to layoffs, plant closings, and other vicissitudes. The devastating frost that swept through California in the spring of 2007, for instance, killed the crops normally picked by migrant agricultural workers. Reduced harvests resulted in many layoffs (Widess, 2007).

Border Protection, Anti-Terrorism, and Illegal Immigration Control Act of 2005 (House Rule 4437) by U.S. Representative James Sensenbrenner of Wisconsin. Following the framework established by the IIRIRA, this proposal sought to further criminalize undocumented immigrants by classifying them, and anyone who helped them enter or remain in the United States or had other dealings with them, as felons. While proponents of the bill argued that this provision was intended to target only smugglers, the charges of felony by virtue of harboring undocumented immigrants extended to those providing assistance such as food, clothing, or shelter. With the threat of five years in prison for aiding and abetting undocumented workers, HR 4437 cast a wide net of "would-be felons," including charities, churches, and even the U.S.-citizen relatives of undocumented immigrants. As with many other immigrations bills, HR 4437 was allegedly directed against undocumented immigrants, but it violated the rights of all U.S. citizens by infringing on various Constitutional guarantees.[55] For instance, under the premise of employment verification, the Sensenbrenner bill would have helped pave the way toward a mandatory national security card both for immigrants with work permits and for U.S. citizens and would have served as what was labeled a Department of Homeland Security "permission slip" for work.[56]

In addition to federal laws that restrict legal permanent residents' access to public benefits, laws in many states seek to prohibit undocumented immigrants' use of state-level publicly funded benefits and facilities (e.g., health and emergency care, education, and access to parks and housing).[57] Perhaps the most notorious of these emerged in

---

[55] The bill sought to impose background checks on citizens sponsoring their immediate relatives, including spouses and minor children.

[56] The counterproposal offered by President Bush made explicit mention of a national ID card as part of a nationwide program designed to impose sanctions on employers for hiring undocumented workers (Casillas and Punongbayan, 2006).

[57] In Jefferson Parish, a suburb of New Orleans, local councilmen have "outlawed rolling Mexican-food kitchens, calling them an unwelcome reminder of what Hurricane Katrina brought" (Bustillo, 2007). The motivation, the politicians said, was "strengthening zoning standards that have deteriorated since the storm, not racism." Latino immigrants, however, strongly disagreed, "It's racism; they're basically saying that we are dirty." A U.S. citizen who works in

California, where voters passed Proposition 187, a 1994 ballot measure. This initiative was championed by then-Governor Pete Wilson, under the banner of Save Our State. It was the first of many similar measures proposed at the state level and aimed at denying undocumented immigrants access to public schools, health care, and social services. Implementation of Prop 187 was immediately blocked by court challenges and also appeared untenable in the face of demonstrations involving over 70,000 people, walkouts of some 40,000 high school students, largely in the Los Angeles area, and the threat of civil disobedience by public sector workers ranging from teachers to librarians and health sector workers, who vowed not to enforce some of the more odious aspects of the proposition.[58] Ultimately, the measure was found to be unconstitutional.

Anti-immigrant forces in California remained undaunted and, slightly modifying their nativist message, promoted Proposition 227 in 1998. This ballot initiative, which was approved by 60 percent of those voting, eliminated bilingual education in a state where over 40 percent of students in the public school system are considered English Language Learners. Proposition 227, known as English for the Children, was sponsored by businessman Ron C. Unz, who sponsored a similar measure, Proposition 203, in Arizona two years later. Implementation of the voter-approved Proposition 203 the following academic year yielded unacceptable results, leading many school districts to request waivers to continue their bilingual education programs. Still, anti-immigrant sentiment regained enough strength statewide to support Proposition 200, Protect Arizona Now, a ballot measure that passed in 2004. This law denies noncitizens access to all nonfederally mandated social services, requires proof of citizenship to vote in local government and school-board elections, restricts undocumented high school graduates' access to in-state tuition, and deputizes local and state officials to report violations of federal immigration law. In 2007, the Arizona Legislature passed the Legal Arizona Workers Act, now known as the Employer Sanctions Law. The act, signed into law by Governor Janet Napolitano, requires employers to verify their employees' identi-

---

New Orleans and who had "secured all needed permits before officials changed the rules," wondered, "Why are we treated differently?" (ibid.).

[58] See Migration News (1996).

ties against a federal database maintained by the Social Security Administration and the federal Department of Homeland Security.[59]

Although Arizona unquestionably has led the charge in terms of the volume and range of state-level anti-immigrant legislation, by 2006, many other states had filed bills with language similar to that of Proposition 200. One of the most common provisions in these new state laws deputizes city police departments to enforce federal immigration law. For example, Georgia's Senate Bill 529, which became law in 2006, does that, and more.[60] It also strengthens laws against hiring undocumented workers by codifying into state law a mandate that contractors verify the employment eligibility status of new workers.

In addition to coercive state laws aimed at intimidating undocumented immigrants, a new trend toward punitive measures is emerging at the local level. Some cities are now passing ordinances that prohibit employers from hiring undocumented workers and that prevent landlords from renting to these workers and their families.[61] As court challenges are demonstrating, these vindictive actions by state and local governments are unconstitutional in their attempt to deny fundamental and civil rights. For instance, in dismissing one such ordinance in Pennsylvania, a federal court judge reminded the city of the protections in the Fourteenth Amendment: "Even if federal law did not conflict with Hazleton's measures, the City could not enact an ordinance that violates rights the Constitution guarantees to every person in the United

---

[59] The law goes into effect January 2008. For information on a federal appeals court decision not to block the law, see Pitzl and Hansen (2007).

[60] The Georgia Security and Immigration Compliance Act passed in 2006 mandates that law enforcement officers investigate the immigration status of anyone charged with a felony. The law has given a green light to racial profiling and increased the attacks against the undocumented by those who prey on them because of their lack of legal status. See Jarvie (2007) for one account of the impact of this policy.

[61] In July 2006, the town of Hazleton in northeastern Pennsylvania passed its Illegal Immigration Relief Act Ordinance (Ordinance 2006-10) seeking to prevent undocumented immigrants from being employed and also to restrict their ability to rent a place to live. Another ordinance established English as the town's official language.

States, whether legal resident or not."[62] Citing *Plyler v. Doe* (1982), the judge's decision noted, "Whatever his status under the immigration laws, an alien is surely a 'person' in any ordinary sense of that term. Aliens, even aliens whose presence in this country is unlawful, have long been recognized as 'persons' guaranteed due process of law by the Fifth and Fourteenth Amendments."[63] Regarding the anonymous plaintiffs, many of whom were undocumented, the judge ruled, "[they] are persons, and they seek to vindicate rights guaranteed them under the federal constitution."[64] Such decisions asserting undocumented immigrants' rights as persons are unusual in U.S. courts. As has been true for others who have been systematically denied their rights, immigrants have met with greater success by seeking to affirm their humanity in the court of public opinion. Nowhere was their humanity more evident than during spring 2006, when tens of thousands of individuals poured into streets across the country to remind the government, and anti-immigrant forces, of their humankind.

IMMIGRANT ADVOCACY

The rising tide of dehumanizing anti-immigrant rhetoric; restrictive city, state, and federal legislation; denial of rights; verbal harassment; and physical attacks did not go unanswered. Since the passage of the IIRIRA in 1996, immigrants have mounted organized protests.[65] How-

---

[62] See *Lozano v. Hazelton* (Case 3:06-cv-01586-JMM, p. 188). The plaintiffs (a group that included legal permanent residents as well as the Hazleton Hispanic Business Association, the Pennsylvania Statewide Latino Coalition, and Casa Dominicana de Hazleton, Inc.) sought an injunction to keep the city from implementing these punitive ordinances. The judge's decision that the measures were unconstitutional potentially affects as many as "100 other towns that have passed similar measures" (Hurdle, 2007).

[63] *Lozano v. Hazelton*, p. 45.

[64] Ibid.

[65] The public backlash and legal rulings that gutted Proposition 187 contributed to a greater sense of immigrant resistance and entitlement that saw its climax with the October 12, 1996 march in Washington, the nation's first pro-immigrant march (Migration News, 1996). The march drew an estimated 25,000 participants who supported a seven-point agenda that included "human and constitutional rights for all; equal opportunities and affirmative action; free

ever, much of this activism has been sporadic and relatively small scale. It was not until the House passed the draconian HR 4437 in December 2005 that immigrants and their supporters organized en masse. Undocumented workers and students, members of advocacy organizations, and immigrant supporters took to the streets in what became historic and massive protests against the increasing criminalization of immigrants. Beginning on March 10, 2006, in Chicago, 100,000 to 300,000 people demonstrated against HR 4437. During the following weeks, demonstrations took place in 76 cities and involved nearly 1 million people. Over the single weekend of April 8–10, more than a million and a half immigrants and their supporters were estimated to have participated in protests against HR 4437. These actions culminated in massive demonstrations on May 1, 2006. As many as 2 million protested against the Sensenbrenner bill and called for amnesty for the nation's estimated 12 million undocumented immigrants. Many immigrant workers also chose not to report to work that day in order to send a strong message about their economic indispensability.[66] This large-scale mobilization signaled a turning point in the history of immigrant activism in the United States. This was the first nationwide mobilization of immigrant protest on a massive scale. The marches confirmed the enormous importance of the immigrant presence in the United States as well as the weight of this group's activism.

The 2006 demonstrations were evocative of the civil rights movement. The size and scope of the protests surprised even the organizers. After decades of attacks that went largely unanswered, the immigrant community is now signaling a willingness to take a more combative stance. The massive size and intergenerational and multinational character of the demonstrations, along with the peaceful and confident tone of the marchers, have sent a loud message to anti-immigrant forces in Congress, state legislatures, and elsewhere: Immigrants are workers,

---

public education for all; expansion of health services; citizen police review boards; labor law reform and a $7 per hour minimum wage; a streamlined citizenship application program; and an amnesty for immigrants who illegally entered the United States before 1992" (ibid.).

[66] For an in-depth analysis of the spring 2006 immigrant rights marches, see Cano (2006). The May 1 activities, labeled the Great Boycott of 2006, incorporated a strong labor message within the overall protest against federal law targeting undocumented immigrant workers.

not criminals, and this country is critically dependent on the economic contributions of this component of the working class.

Although economic issues were part of most of the demonstrations, the larger issues of basic human and democratic rights were a focal point. The spring protests also brought together a cross-section of supporters from the wider community. The latter included representatives of the labor movement, educators, churches, and businesses that employ immigrants and those that offer services to this community, all of whom had played important roles in earlier struggles as well as in this most recent blossoming of protest. Among the supportive labor organizations was the Service Employees International Union, which, since the late 1980s, has been working with immigrant janitorial workers as part of their "Justice for Janitors" unionization campaign.[67] The high representation of immigrant workers in key areas of the U.S. workforce has also prompted major AFL-CIO unions, such as the United Food and Commercial Workers Union (UFCW), to take a more inclusive approach toward immigrant workers. This includes a historic decision by the AFL-CIO Executive Council in 2000 to organize undocumented immigrants and to support demands for amnesty and an end to punitive legislation targeting workers and their employers.

---

[67] In 2000, after an arduous strike that included police beatings, janitors in Los Angeles won a contract that included a 25 percent wage increase, covering 8,500 workers. Thanks to this activism, which spanned almost a decade, 100,000 janitors across the United States were able to get increased wages, expanded health care benefits, and full-time jobs. The impact of their victory continues to reverberate. Similar fights for unionization and better working conditions include a successful effort by immigrant janitors, with support from students and faculty at the University of Miami and among immigrant women laundry workers in Washington, DC. The women fought for and won the right to unionize under the Union of Needletrades, Industrial and Textile Employees and Hotel Employees and Restaurant Employees. In 2004, they negotiated a favorable three-year labor agreement. Outside the service industry, there have also been successes. Seventy-five coal miners, most of whom were Mexican nationals, employed at C. W. Mining Company's Co-Op mine in Huntington, Utah, waged a successful two-and-a-half year struggle (beginning in 2003 and ending in 2006) for better working conditions.

The emergence of a mobilized and visible system of undocumented workers is especially significant, given the vulnerability of these laborers to immigration raids and other attacks.[68] Workplace raids are a longstanding component of U.S. immigration policy. They keep labor costs down and discourage workers from unionizing or participating in political activities. Thus, after the March 2006 immigrant rights demonstrations, few were surprised when federal agents raided several workplaces, particularly meatpacking plants.[69] Later in the year, raids at a plant in Greeley, Colorado, led the UFCW to publicly denounce ICE for violating workers' rights and for the brutal criminalization of these workers.

Where do undocumented students fit in this growing effort to respond strongly and positively to assaults on human dignity and human rights? During the spring 2006 marches, students acted as organizers as well as participants. They walked out of their classes and urged their peers to join them in pressing for equitable educational opportunities. Many of the students were undocumented high schoolers who are well aware that their immigration status limits their chances of gaining access to higher education. In most states, current education codes disqualify undocumented secondary school graduates from attending college, since the imposition of out-of-state or international fees on these students make costs prohibitively high (an average of three to six times higher than what other state residents are assessed). On the other hand, some of the older student participants and organizers were currently benefiting from the passage of laws in their home states that afforded them the opportunity to attend college paying the same in-state tuition as their documented peers.

---

[68] For example, during raids at Wal-Mart stores in October 2003, immigration agents arrested 245 nightshift janitors across 21 stores. Following the raids, 9 Mexican immigrant employees of a New Jersey store sued the company and the contractors who had hired them, citing among other things, the company's failure to pay overtime. Wal-Mart eventually agreed to pay $11 million to settle claims stemming from the raids (Associated Press, 2003).

[69] These actions were part of Operation Return to Sender. In Detroit, employers added their own harassment. At the Wolverine meatpacking plant, on the day after the march, bosses fired 21 workers who had attended the demonstration instead of reporting to work (Parsons and Ten Eyck, 2007).

Ten states now have laws that permit undocumented high school graduates to attend college. These legislative changes did not simply "happen." They are the product of advocacy, a process in which scores of undocumented students and their supporters within and beyond the country's immigrant communities have come together to push for the right to participate on equal terms in this society. In addition, the legislative victories indicate that the government and nativists have been unable to foment sufficient anti-immigrant sentiment, despite the intense and prolonged campaigns that began in the mid-1990s and escalated after September 11, 2001. Even with these unrelenting campaigns, there have been gains on the immigrant rights front. While far from sufficient or irreversible, these positive developments point to a deeper and broader historic sentiment of support for democratic rights and equal access to education, which immigrant rights supporters may be able to draw upon.

This multilayered context, in which strong social, historical, political, and economic forces vie with one another, is the backdrop against which the story of undocumented students' prolonged struggle to gain access to a college education unfolds. The subject of this book is the story of one of the various struggles led by immigrants, that of undocumented high school students who came to this country with their parents and found themselves deprived of access to higher education simply by virtue of their immigration status. This book offers two main contributions: First, it chronicles the history of in-state tuition legislation across the United States; second, it offers new arguments to advance the ongoing effort to ensure equal access to higher education. Much of the literature referenced in this book addresses aspects of educational access for immigrants. However, the analysis presented here makes an important, independent contribution by examining the crucial role of immigrant student advocacy in the passage of in-state tuition policies in various states. This book frames the problem of equal access to higher education as a question of human and civil rights rather than one of economics. As exemplified by the Apodaca case, undocumented students' attempts to participate more fully in society have spurred a nationwide discussion regarding their right to a genuinely equal opportunity to attend institutions of postsecondary education. This book argues that in-state tuition laws are necessary to remedy, in part, the disability imposed on already disadvantaged groups by unequal application of admissions criteria in higher education. As noted earlier, and as will be demonstrated throughout this book, opposition to these students' right to attend institutions of higher education has been mounted mainly on economic grounds. Equal access to education, it is argued, would be so costly as to drain state coffers. Those on the other side of this debate typically have based their position largely on the same economic framework, arguing that allowing these students to attend college is beneficial, as it will increase their tax contributions and will further strengthen the United States in its competition with economic rivals. This kind of response, which accepts the framework defined by the opposition, might be well intentioned, but it is misguided. Historically, arguments of economic efficiency have been shown to be ineffective in advancing the cause of freedom and equality.

Further, the arguments offered by some proponents of in-state tuition measures revolve around the disturbing premise that "it is cheaper to educate than to incarcerate." The portrayal of immigrant students as potential criminals, unless educated, is unfortunate and, ultimately, unacceptable, regardless of its alleged potential for swaying some legislators to support broader access to education.[70] Furthermore, as demonstrated by the immigrant rights marches in the spring 2006, immigrant students and their parents reject being portrayed as criminals.[71]

Replacing strategies that emphasize economics with arguments that focus on civil rights and human dignity could strengthen and advance undocumented students' fight. By identifying and analyzing some of the shortcomings of economistic ideas, this book does not aim to diminish the efforts of activists. On the contrary, it highlights advo-

---

[70] In 2007, several proposals were filed in the Texas legislature to overturn the in-state tuition law. Students and supporters crowded the room to offer their stories. In their testimony, members of the Texas Criminal Justice Coalition highlighted the importance of the law as a measure that would make immigrant students "20 percent less likely to commit crimes" (TCJC, 2007). Such a perspective is rejected by immigrants themselves. In an interview commemorating the 25th anniversary of the *Plyler v. Doe* decision, one of the original plaintiffs in the case stated: "we definitely would not have had what we have now. [But] I could not say that we would be here to steal" (Leal Unmuth, 2007).

[71] This was one of the loudest messages sent by participants in the spring 2006 activities. Many youths carried signs reading, "My father is not a criminal." Other signs asserted this population's place in U.S. society: "We are workers not criminals."

cacy by bringing into focus the critically important contributions of those who in their local and state struggles have positioned this issue as a question of civil rights. Framing the discussion this way will enrich the debate over how to better advance the cause of equal access to higher education.

The analysis begins, in Chapter Two, with historical background on immigration, public schools, and higher education. The chapter documents states' attempts to deal with the "immigration problem" by limiting access to public education. It examines the Texas law that eventually led to *Plyler* and discusses California's Proposition 187 and its assault on some of the basic precepts of the *Plyler* ruling. Chapter Two also explores some concurrent efforts at the state level to create higher education opportunities for immigrant students. Chapter Three introduces Texas as the state that first opened the doors of higher education to undocumented immigrants and highlights the students' activism. It begins by framing the issues faced by undocumented high school students seeking a higher education, and it addresses the impact of their immigration status on issues of academic access. The chapter then introduces House Bill 1403, the first in-state tuition law to pass in the United States, and explains the role that immigrant students, their supporters, and other advocates played in this initial victory.

Chapter Four addresses the laws in the other nine states that now have in-state tuition policies that include undocumented students. It provides a chronological overview of the twelve-year fight activists in California waged to secure immigrant students' access to higher education. It also refers to the advocacy in New York, which, like Texas and California, has a large share of the country's total undocumented population. The chapter closes with a brief review of salient aspects of the laws in some of the other states. Chapter Five turns to challenges that have been mounted against various in-state tuition policies across the United States. It gives specific attention to the defeat of a federal lawsuit in Kansas and discusses aspects of the defeat of similar attempts in California and Texas, brought in court by private organizations and in legislatures by politicians, to overturn these access laws.

Chapter Six shifts the focus to the federal level. It begins with a brief introduction of the proposed federal DREAM Act, which would allow undocumented students to normalize their status in the United States. The chapter concentrates on some of the work that immigrant students and their supporters have done to advocate on behalf of this measure. Chapter Seven, the book's concluding chapter, provides an overview of the new immigrant advocacy that gained momentum in the spring of 2006 and continues unabated, although smaller in size, despite government attempts to intimidate the immigrant population. It includes an analysis of the arguments that some advocates have put forward and a call to align such arguments with questions of civil rights rather than economic efficiency. It concludes by pointing to the similarities between the immigrant movement's message that "no human being is illegal" and the civil rights movement's affirmation of the humanity of Black women and men.

CHAPTER 2

Historical and Legal Context

The debate over undocumented students like Jesús Apodaca and their access to postsecondary education is relatively recent.[1] The question of immigrants' access to public education, however, is nearly as old as the history of U.S. public education itself.[2] This chapter provides background that links the current efforts of undocumented students to gain access to institutions of higher education to larger historical issues regarding immigrants, education, and the challenge of ensuring equality for all within U.S. society. It begins by sketching early attitudes toward the public education of immigrants and then moves to a more detailed review of a 1975 Texas statute that sought to limit immigrants' access to K-12 schooling by explicitly targeting their legal status.

The chapter also explores the concurrent efforts that led Mississippi, New York, and California (among other states) to address the more specific question of noncitizens' access to higher education. The discussion highlights the Leticia "A" case, California litigation initially filed in 1985. That case represents the first legal challenge to the barriers undocumented students faced as they attempted to qualify for in-state tuition rates at public colleges and universities. Keeping the focus on California, the chapter then turns to the 1994 voter-approved but court-blocked anti-immigrant initiative, Proposition 187. Among its other restrictions, that proposition sought to deny undocumented immi-

---

[1] The literature on this topic is large and continues to grow. For representative discussions, see Gonzales (2007); Erisman and Looney (2007); Olivas (1995, 2004); Stevenson (2004); Alfred (2003); Mehta and Ali (2003); Badger and Yale-Loehr (2000, 2002).

[2] See Spring (2001).

grants access to public education. The chapter concludes with an examination of Section 505 of the 1996 federal Illegal Immigration Reform and Immigrant Responsibility Act (IIRIRA), a provision that has been interpreted as preventing states from introducing legislation to allow undocumented students to attend college at in-state tuition rates.

IMMIGRATION AND EDUCATION: A HISTORICAL OVERVIEW

The U.S. government has instituted various immigration policies since the country's founding; many of these policies have reflected a strong nativist influence. Explicit bans on nonwhite immigration, for instance, began as early as 1790. The Naturalization Act, passed March 26, 1790, limited naturalized citizenship to free white persons only.[3] Thus, contemporary hostility toward immigrants' participation in higher education is best understood as another facet of a longstanding opposition, often codified into law, toward the presence of "foreigners." In colonial times, the fear that newcomers might succeed in transplanting their cultures to this country led to the development of charity schools whose primary purpose was to Anglicize German youth.[4] In some cities, neither German nor Polish immigrants were permitted to establish dual

---

[3] Johnson (2004). In 1870, the law was modified to include people of African nativity and descent. However, those unable to be categorized as white or Black continued to be excluded.

[4] This push for assimilation through schooling was a response to a perceived expansion of German culture in the United States (See Spring, 2001). Crawford (1996, p. 7) points out that "Benjamin Franklin became an outspoken critic of the Pennsylvania Germans, accusing them of resisting English and arrogantly preserving their own culture: 'Why should the Palatine Boors be suffered to swarm into our Settlements, and by herding together, establish their Language and Manners, to the Exclusion of ours? Why should Pennsylvania, founded by the English, become a Colony of Aliens, who will shortly be so numerous as to Germanize us instead of our Anglifying them?' (Read, 1937). Elsewhere Franklin (1753) warned that the colonial Assembly would soon have to employ translators 'to tell one half of our legislators what the other half say,' and he objected to bilingual advertising and street signs in Philadelphia." For additional commentary on Franklin's "Americanism" also see Portes and Rumbaut (2006) and K. Davis (2007).

language programs in the schools their children attended. The imposition of exclusionary language policies on immigrant children was a common characteristic of nineteenth-century public schools, as well. Not surprisingly, this approach generated friction between immigrant parents and their children, as the latter learned to consider anything that was not "American" as second rate.[5] The children of Irish immigrants who arrived after 1845, for example, came to view both their parents and their religion as inferior, as a result of the acculturating power of public schooling.[6]

Despite initial hostility, however, over time western and (most) southern and eastern European arrivals gained acceptance. Immigration policy itself played an important role in this process. From the passage of the Naturalization Act of 1790 until 1952, when Cold War conditions prompted changes, "the law prohibited most nonwhite immigrants from citizenship thereby forever relegating noncitizens of color to 'alien' status and effectively defining them as permanent outsiders to the national community."[7] The Immigration Restriction Act of 1924 (also known as the National Origins Act), the first federal legislation to use census counts to impose numerical quotas on immigration, institutionalized the image of a white America.[8] In this context, European

---

[5] That this view has not changed much is documented by contemporary research. See, for example, Olsen (1998) and C. Suarez-Orozco (2001).

[6] According to the historian of American education Carl Kaestle (1983, p. 164), "Poor Irish children in the public schools see their parents looked upon as an inferior race . . . and public schools taught children to feel ashamed of the creed of their forefathers, which is often assailed."

[7] Johnson (2004), p. 154. In the 1922 Supreme Court case *Takao Ozawa v. U.S.*, the Court ruled against a Japanese citizen who had been found ineligible for naturalized citizenship, although he had graduated from a California high school and had children who were U.S. citizens. In its decision, the Court asserted that the intention of the 1790 Act was to "confer the privilege of citizenship upon the class of persons whom the fathers knew as white, and to deny it to all who could not be so classified . . . The appellant, in the case now under consideration, however is not Caucasian and therefore belongs entirely outside the zone on the negative side . . . These decisions are sustained by numerous scientific authorities, which we do not deem it necessary to review. We think these decisions are right and so hold" (p. 198).

[8] Tienda (2002).

immigrants' white skin helped reduce their vulnerability and improve their chances of successful assimilation.[9]

By contrast, darker-skinned immigrants from Asia, Africa and Latin America were (and continue to be) the targets of harshly discriminatory immigration policies.[10] For instance, immigration from Mexico, which dates back to the signing of the Treaty of Guadalupe Hidalgo in 1848,[11] has prompted a wide array of policies designed, alternatively, to restrict (e.g., Operation Wetback) or to encourage (e.g., the Bracero Program) the flow of Mexicans, depending on how large a supply of cheap labor U.S. businesses demand.[12] The Chinese Exclusion Act, highly restrictive legislation passed in 1882, banned all immigration from China.[13] The Supreme Court upheld the act (which was

---

[9] Blauner (1987).

[10] Garcia (1995).

[11] Treaty terms forced Mexico to cede approximately half of its territory to the United States (Rodriguez, 1996; Rumbaut, 2006).

[12] "Operation Wetback" was the derogatory nickname of a government-sponsored quasi-military operation conducted between 1954 and 1955 "to reduce the number of undocumented crossings in the Southwest. A total of 1,075,168 Mexican immigrants were apprehended as a result" (Robledo, 1977). The deportation campaigns prompted by Operation Wetback also affected the U.S.-born Mexican American community, whose members were subject to expulsion if they could not prove U.S. citizenship (Johnson, 2004). For information about the Bracero program, see Chapter One and also Garcia (1995).

[13] Chinese immigration began climbing in the mid-nineteenth century, during the California Gold Rush. Soon after their arrival, Chinese miners were physically assaulted and driven from the foothills of the Sierra Nevada and elsewhere by white miners who claimed "California for Americans" (Pfaelzer, 2007). In 1862, California Governor Leland Stanford stated, "To my mind it is clear that the settlement among us of an inferior race is to be discouraged by every legitimate means. Asia, with her numberless millions, sends to our shores the dregs of her population" (quoted in See, 1996, p. 8). Eventually Stanford became president of the Central Pacific Railroad, which hired great numbers of Chinese laborers. Their numbers rose from 50 in 1865 to over 12,000 by 1868, making them the vast majority of the company's 14,000 workers. The railroad's owners found that "it was cheaper and faster to bring workers to San

renewed in 1892) on the basis of alleged "differences of race" and the view that "Chinese were a danger to American morals, institutions and the preservation of civilization."[14] The act was finally overturned on December 17, 1943, but it was replaced by a policy that imposed a "rigid quota system that worked out to [allowing entry to] 105 Chinese per year."[15]

After World War II, as the United States deepened its intervention in Asia, policies that disfavored nonwhite immigration became increasingly untenable. Thus, the Immigration and Nationality Act (INA) of 1952 repealed existing restrictions on eligibility for naturalized citizenship that had barred Indians, Filipinos, and Japanese. Although the INA was said to have ended the more than 160-year-old ban on nonwhite immigration, it retained the 1920 census as the basis for establishing quotas, thus maintaining an overall white national identity.[16] In addition, Congress used the Cold War atmosphere to add numerical ceilings for eastern European immigrants to the act.[17]

Francisco from Canton by boat than to recruit Caucasian laborers from east of the Mississippi" (ibid., p. 9).

[14] Smith (1985), p. 3. The U.S. Supreme Court upheld the application of the Chinese Exclusion Act to Chinese from Hong Kong—who were British subjects—because of these individuals' "race, language and color" (Pfaelzer (2007, p. 260).

[15] Pfaelzer (2007), p. 346.

[16] Tienda (2002). The INA was also known as the McCarran-Walter Act.

[17] Eastern Europeans had already been disadvantaged by the Immigration Act of 1924, as the quota system had reduced immigration from their countries. The INA reaffirmed the view that they were "racially inferior, poor and inclined towards anarchism, communism and other anti-American political ideologies" (Johnson, 2004, p. 9). As stated in the introduction, immigration law has been used as a method to control political ideology. Early laws, such as the Alien Enemy Act of 1798 and the Alien Act, empowered the president to deport noncitizens suspected of working against the U.S. government. Following this line, the Immigration Act of 1903 targeted anarchists and noncitizens in the labor movement, whose demands at the time included the eight-hour day. The Anarchist Act of 1918 and the Anarchist Law of 1920 reaffirmed and expanded "the ideological grounds on which noncitizens could be excluded and deported" (Johnson, 2004, p. 64). The passage of these laws took place at the same time as the Palmer Raids, a year-long campaign to arrest and deport immigrant

The impact of the civil rights movement and world events such as the Vietnam War brought further immigration changes. The abolishment of quotas through the passage of the Immigration Act of 1965 spurred the immigration of other groups, mainly from Asia and Africa. Increasing numbers of arrivals from Latin America were fueled by a shift "on the visa allocation preference system from labor market priorities to family reunification."[18] During this same year, the Higher Education Act of 1965 introduced federal financial aid for those pursuing postsecondary education, but the law was limited to citizens, permanent residents, refugees, and those granted asylum.

In 1973–1974, the United States experienced an energy crisis that destabilized the economy. Further turmoil occurred in 1974 as the Watergate scandal erupted and Richard Nixon was forced to resign the presidency. As in earlier eras, these economic and political crises prompted a backlash against foreigners. The rapid increase in the number of deportations attests to this. The number of undocumented workers apprehended rose from 30,000 in 1960 to 100,000 in 1965 and to 788,145 in 1974.[19] The increase in the number of apprehensions, along with the 1970 census figures reporting, for the Latino population alone, the presence of over 11 million Spanish-speaking people, fostered a perception of an "illegal alien invasion." This wave of newcomers provided a ready target to blame for the country's economic recession and rising unemployment.[20]

"radicals," suspected of planting a series of bombs on May 1, 1919. The terror campaign launched by then–Attorney General Mitchell Palmer has been equated with the similarly draconian response of the Bush administration to the September 11, 2001 events and its targeting of Arab and Muslim immigrants and citizens alike (Cohen, 2003; Johnson 2004).

[18] Tienda (2002, p. 591). Immigration from Latin America was controlled by imposing a ceiling of 120,000, thus satisfying those who feared an increase in number of arrivals from the rest of the Americas (Johnson, 2004). With the 1965 Act, the United States moved away from a quota system and imposed an across-the-board annual limit of immigrants per country that "although facially neutral, disparately impacts noncitizens of color from the developing nations" (Johnson, 2004, p. 26).

[19] See Robledo (1977).

[20] Ibid.

In the face of this alleged "invasion," individual states began to take the immigration issue as their own, passing policies either restricting the employment of undocumented immigrants (California) or banning the presence of undocumented children in public schools (Texas). A 1975 attempt by the Texas legislature to exclude undocumented immigrants from access to K-12 schooling is a good example of legislation targeting a select group of the school-age population, based on their race and national origin, while using the fig leaf of immigration status. The next section looks at that legislative effort, as well as others.

THE IMPOSITION OF LEGISLATIVE LIMITS ON ACCESS TO PUBLIC EDUCATION

In the post–World War II era, the first publicized attempts to limit undocumented students' access to education focused on the K-12 level. Texas took the lead in using access to public education as a means of responding to the perceived threat of the "alien invasion." The presence of immigrants in the state's public schools had sparked debate periodically, but prior to 1975, Texas law included few references to students' immigration status. Two key exceptions *affirmed* rather than challenged the legality of immigrant students' enrollment. These are a 1921 Texas Attorney General opinion holding that "[a]lien children have the same right to attend public free schools of the state as do the children of citizens of this state" and a 1940 opinion holding that "as the Legislature has not denied to the children of any race or nationality the right to enter our public schools, the question whether it might have done so does not arise in [the case in question]."[21]

---

[21] These excerpts from Opinion No. 2318 (1921) and from Opinion No. O-2318 (1940) are cited in Texas Attorney General Opinion No. H-586, 1975, p. 2. According to the State of Texas website, "An Attorney General Opinion is a written interpretation of existing law. The Attorney General writes opinions as part of his responsibility to act as legal counsel for the State of Texas. . . . Attorney General Opinions clarify the meaning of existing laws. They do not address matters of fact, and they are neither legislative nor judicial in nature. That is to say, they cannot create new provisions in the law or correct unintended, undesirable effects of the law. Opinions interpret legal issues that are ambiguous, obscure, or otherwise unclear. Attorney General Opinions do not reflect the AG's opinion in the ordinary sense of expressing his personal views.

In spite of these existing legal opinions, in 1975, the state legislature, alleging an economic burden in educating the growing immigrant population, amended the Texas Education Code (TEC) to exclude undocumented immigrants from K-12 public schools. The newly added Section 21.031 permitted school authorities to demand proof of citizenship and to deny admission to those who could not verify their legal immigration status.[22] The Texas law also prevented school districts from state reimbursement for undocumented children, thus placing the burden of payment on the students' families. Section 21.031 provoked a series of lawsuits, in both the state and federal court systems. The most renowned were those brought against the Tyler Independent School District (TISD) in 1977[23] and the subsequent legal actions against school districts within northern, western, and southern federal district courts during 1977 and 1978. The lawsuit against Tyler ISD was sparked by the district's decision, in 1977, to implement Section 21.031 and to make undocumented children's enrollment in the local public schools contingent on their paying tuition.[24] The lawsuit filed

---

Nor does he in any way "rule" on what the law should say." See http://www.oag.state.tx.us/opinopen/opinhome.shtml

[22] See Appendix A for the complete wording of Section 21.031.The law was passed during the 64th Texas legislative session.

[23] The case against Tyler ISD was filed on behalf of the children of four undocumented families: José and Lidia López, Humberto and Jacqueline Alvarez, José and Rosario Robles, and Felix Hernández. The families "had lived in Tyler for between three and 13 years, working in agriculture, meatpacking, foundries and the city's world famous rose industry. . . . All had at least one child who was a U.S. citizen" (Belejack, 2007). The plaintiff families would arrive at the courthouse in the early morning as a protective measure and to avoid publicity. While U.S. District Judge William Justice had "allowed the plaintiffs to be identified by pseudonyms—Doe, Roe, Boe and Loe—[he had] made it clear that he was obligated to release their identities if the Immigration and Naturalization Service asked him to do so" (ibid.). All the families decided to proceed with the case, even in the face of possible deportation. López's son recalled during an interview that "my parents knew we could be deported. We had everything we owned waiting in the car" (Leal Unmuth, 2007).

[24] Section 16.151, Chapter 34, of the Texas Education Code (1975) stated that the state's allocation per child was $90 per month. Some school districts de-

against TISD and its board of trustees was referred to initially as *Doe v. Plyler*[25]; the other ones were consolidated and became known as *In re: Alien Children Education Litigation.*[26] In both suits, the plaintiffs were children who could not enroll in grades K-12 under the state's new statute because they were undocumented.[27]

---

cided to charge tuition to students who were unable to show proof of immigration documentation, arguing that doing so would allow officials to recoup the expenses associated with these children's presence in the schools. In the case of Tyler ISD, beginning on July 21, 1977, the district sought to charge the families $1,000 for the students' education. "At the time, fewer than 60 students, out of a total enrollment of 16,000 were undocumented . . . [Judge] Justice issued a preliminary injunction directing Tyler schools to admit all children living in the district, regardless of their immigration status. He also ordered the Texas Education Agency to release funds to the Tyler school district for each undocumented child" (See Belejack, 2007). A report issued the following year, in 1976, by the Committee on Public Education of the Texas House of Representatives referred to the "alien enrollment as an urban problem" and identified "the definition of residency . . . as a major factor in the increased alien enrollment" (Texas House of Representatives, 1976, pp. 2–3). The Subcommittee on Alien Students issued four recommendations to deal with this issue. Two of the recommendations suggested that the State of Texas worked with the federal government to "assist all school districts adversely affected by the increasing immigrant/alien enrollment" (p. 3). An additional proposal suggested "state funds be set aside to assist school districts in providing educational housing for Mexican/immigrant alien students" (p. 3). More important, the committee recommended that "the law be amended to permit funding while the student is in the process of enrolling" (p. 4). This early interim report speaks to the challenges posed by the law during the first year after its passage.

[25] *Doe* refers to an anonymous party in a legal action (here, the plaintiff, undocumented children who, once the litigation began, had the legal burden of going forward with the evidence). When the Fifth Circuit Court ruled in favor of the plaintiffs, the burden shifted to the defendants and therefore the suit became known as *Plyler v. Doe* (1982).

[26] Seventeen lawsuits were consolidated into this statewide case and scheduled for trial for February 1980 in Houston. The case was to be heard by U.S. District Judge Woodrow Seals (see Belejack, 2007).

[27] *Doe v. Plyler* and *In Re: Alien Children Education Litigation* eventually became consolidated into one case. The earliest case that became part of *In Re:*

The two cases were eventually resolved in favor of the plaintiffs. In response, the state (along with the other named defendants, including the districts' superintendents, their boards of trustees, the Texas Education Agency, and local officials) appealed to the U.S. Court of Appeals for the Fifth Circuit, where the cases were consolidated. When that court upheld the previous rulings for the plaintiffs, the case went to the U.S. Supreme Court. In 1982, ruling in *Plyler v. Doe,* the High Court reaffirmed the right of undocumented children to a public education. Legal scholars have referred to the *Plyler* decision as the "apex of immigrants' rights"[28] and "a groundbreaking case."[29] It constitutes the first time that the Supreme Court applied the equal protection clause of the Fourteenth Amendment to matters affecting undocumented immigrants.[30] Specifically, Justice Brennan, writing for the majority, ruled,

---

Alien Children was filed soon after the law's passage in 1975, against the Houston Independent School District (see Robledo, 1977). In that case, the students were denied admission for the 1975-1976 school year, "except upon the payment of $90.00 per child per month tuition" (ibid., p. 131). In *Hernandez v. HISD,* the plaintiffs included undocumented students as well as those who were in the process of obtaining documentation from the Immigration and Naturalization Service. Since they could neither prove their status nor afford to pay the amount of tuition demanded by the school districts, the students remained unschooled for at least one full academic year (Robledo, 1977). Additionally, in the Hernandez case, some of the students were U.S. citizens but were unable to prove that and thus ended up paying tuition. In the Tyler school district case, the plaintiff children attempted to enroll in the 1977-1978 school year but were denied admission pending payment of a "full tuition fee" (*Plyler v. Doe,* p. 206).

[28] Olivas (1995), p. 1039.

[29] Pabón-López (2005), p. 1385.

[30] As detailed in Chapter One, in *Yick Wo v. Hopkins* (1886), the "Supreme Court had invoked the Fourteenth Amendment to stop California from banning Chinese laundries in wooden buildings" (Pfaelzer, 2007, p. 205). *Plyler,* however, constituted the first time that the High Court addressed the application of this constitutional protection to those not legally authorized to be in the country. The importance of the *Plyler* ruling has been recognized by both supporters and opponents of immigration. "The day the opinion was issued, a little-known Department of Justice lawyer co-wrote a memo chastising the U.S. solicitor

"that a person's initial entry into a State, or into the United States, was unlawful, and that he may for that reason be expelled, cannot negate the simple fact of his presence within the State's territorial perimeter".[31] In its defense, the State of Texas had maintained that Section 21.031 was a "financial measure designed to avoid a drain" on the state's limited resources.[32] The court majority also rejected this argument, finding no such drain.

The use of constitutional guarantees to reaffirm students' rights makes *Plyler* a key decision on behalf of immigrants' rights,[33] but the ruling did not address higher education. In fact, the Supreme Court has never "considered the constitutionality of denying higher education to

---

general for not filing a brief taking Texas' side" (Belejack, 2007). In direct contrast to the position taken by the Reagan administration and the Supreme Court majority in this case, the lawyer, now Supreme Court Chief Justice John Roberts, had supported the Texas law, which would have denied undocumented children a public education. The memo was read during the Roberts confirmation hearings in September 2005. The pertinent critique from Roberts reads, "As you will recall, the Solicitor General's Office had decided not to take a position before the Supreme Court on the Equal Protection issue in this case. The briefs for the State of Texas were quite poor. It is our belief that a brief filed by the Solicitor General's Office supporting the State of Texas and the values of judicial restraint could well have moved Justice Powell into the Chief Justice's camp and altered the outcome in the case. In sum, this is a case in which our supposed litigation program to encourage judicial restraint did not get off the ground, and should have" (Senate Judiciary Committee, 2005, pp. 403–404). When asked about this memo during the confirmation hearings, Roberts limited his answers to repeating portions of the majority decision in *Plyler*, stating that "I believe all children should be educated" (ibid., p. 426). He made clear that this was a personal, not a legal, opinion.

[31] *Plyler v. Doe*, 1982, p. 215.

[32] Ibid., p. 207. U.S. District Judge William Justice had already addressed such claims and had "chided the state for using the children to deal, in a backhanded way, with longstanding problems caused by a school finance system based on property taxes" (Belejack, 2007). He also explicitly noted that the state's policy "might have been influenced" by the fact that "little political uproar was likely to be raised" on behalf of undocumented children (ibid.).

[33] Olivas (1995); Pabón-López (2005).

undocumented immigrants."[34] Lower courts, on the other hand, had been wrestling with the question of noncitizens' access to higher education for nearly a decade before *Plyler v. Doe* reached the Supreme Court. Litigation on behalf of postsecondary students emerged in several states between 1975 and 1982, around the same time that various courts were addressing the K-12 case. The next section examines some examples of these cases.

INITIAL ATTEMPTS TO SECURE IN-STATE TUITION FOR NONCITIZENS

The mid-1970s mark both the beginning of state-level anti-immigration legislation in the area of education and the emergence of legal challenges to state statutes that prohibited noncitizens from being classified as residents for in-state tuition (and financial aid) purposes. This section, which is organized chronologically, begins by describing three early challenges: a 1974 suit in Mississippi, a 1975 case in California, and 1977 litigation in New York.[35] The common thread among these cases is that each challenges a discriminatory state statute limiting noncitizens' participation in college.

Unlike in *Plyler* and the other Texas-based cases involving undocumented immigrant minors, most of the mid-1970s' struggles over in-state tuition eligibility involved foreign-born complainants who were legal, permanent residents seeking a postsecondary education. They were precluded from achieving that goal because their status as noncitizens meant they were ineligible for the in-state tuition rates and aid packages that made college attendance financially feasible. Mississippi recorded the first legal challenge, in a case involving a 1974 statute that

---

[34] Yates (2004), p. 586.

[35] States that share a tradition of high immigration, such as Texas, California, and New York, typically also have similarly restrictive laws and policies regarding immigrants. However, tuition regulations have been no less discriminatory in states that traditionally have received few immigrants. Delaware's education code (1975), for instance, had a clause requiring one-year residence in the state, along with proof of voter registration for both the alien student and his or her parents (Maxwell, 1979). Given that the Constitution prohibits aliens from voting, this requirement effectively excluded noncitizens from qualifying for in-state tuition.

held that "all aliens are classified as nonresidents."[36] The suit, known as *Jagnandan v. Giles*,[37] was brought by a family from Guyana. Although the family members had been legal, permanent residents of the state between one and three years before deciding to enroll at Mississippi State University, they each were classified as nonresidents for tuition purposes. The family argued that the statute denied them residency and that it "violated the equal protection and due process clauses of the Fourteenth Amendment."[38]

In the deliberations that ensued, Mississippi was required to meet a newly increased burden of proof. In 1971, the Supreme Court had ruled, in *Graham v. Richardson*, that when a state makes a "classification based on alienage, it shoulders a heavy burden of justification."[39] The state's argument that its educational funds were limited and thus should be earmarked for U.S. citizens only was not compelling. Mississippi lost its appeal since it was unable to sufficiently justify the regulations it had enforced against noncitizens. Furthermore, the court found that the statute did violate the Fourteenth Amendment's equal protection clause.

In California, *Wong v. Board of Regents* (1975) challenged the limitations that the California Education Code (CEC) imposed on noncitizens' access to higher education. The CEC stated that "only permanent resident aliens [were] eligible to receive resident tuition benefits and even then, the alien must have held the permanent residency status for the previous year."[40] If the student was not an adult, the regulations also applied to his or her parents. The CEC contained an exception that allowed certain nonimmigrants (e.g., those holding G-4 visas that specifically allow permanent residence) "to be classified as residents if they had attended for at least three years and had graduated from a California *public* school."[41] The Wong case dealt with a student who

---

[36] Maxwell (1979), p. 519.

[37] *Jagnandan v. Giles*, 379 F. Supp. 117 (N.D. Miss. 1974).

[38] Maxwell (1979), p. 540.

[39] Ibid., p. 519.

[40] Ibid., p. 515.

[41] Ibid., pp. 519–520, emphasis in original. This provision, repealed January 1, 1978, became the core language of Assembly Bill (AB) 540, the in-state tuition law that the California state legislature passed in 2001. See Chapter Four for a discussion of this legislation.

was a bona fide resident of California. Ms. Wong, a Thai national, had entered the country on a student visa and had lived in the United States for eight years, including several in California. She subsequently adjusted her visa status to become a permanent resident. Five months before the beginning of the fall semester, she applied for admission at San Francisco State College. She was denied eligibility for in-state tuition fees because her formal documentation as a permanent resident of the state had not been in effect for a full year.

The law's residency requirement ignored the fact that regardless of their documentation status, some noncitizens, such as Wong, were bona fide residents of the state and therefore entitled to in-state tuition. She challenged "the additional burden the statute placed upon alien students" on the grounds that "citizen students were only required to live in California for one year to achieve residency status for tuition purposes."[42] As in the Mississippi case, Wong argued that the state had to justify its classification with compelling reasons. While the first court that heard the case agreed with her, declaring that the statute was unconstitutional and a violation of the equal protection clause, a state court of appeals reversed that decision. The California Supreme Court subsequently denied review of the case and it did not allow the lower court to publish its decision, thus rendering it ineffectual.[43] As a result, the statute remained in the CEC, providing for the continued exclusion of immigrants who had not been permanent residents of the state for at least one year. In 1977, State Assemblyman Joseph Montoya filed AB 459, which eventually passed, eliminating the one-year waiting period and allowing "lawfully admitted alien students" to be immediately counted as residents for tuition and apportionment purposes.[44]

The Mississippi and California cases were addressed at the state level. The first postsecondary tuition case to reach the U.S. Supreme Court, *Nyquist v. Mauclet* (1977), originated in New York in 1976. Two long-time state residents who were noncitizens challenged citizenship restrictions on eligibility for educational benefits, particularly stu-

---

[42] Ibid., p. 520.

[43] Ibid.

[44] See Black (2001). Apportionment refers to the reimbursements provided by the state based on the number of credit hours per student registered at a given institution.

dent loans. An applicant for financial assistance who was not a U.S. citizen had to sign a declaration of intent to become a citizen as soon as possible or had to be "a certain type of refugee."[45] One of the complainants was a French citizen who had applied for a state educational loan to cover his graduate studies at the State University of New York at Buffalo; the other was a Canadian national attending Brooklyn College who had qualified academically for a Regent's scholarship and "tuition assistance."[46] In both cases, the universities denied the applicants state-based financial aid because the men did not want to become U.S. citizens. Each then brought a suit in federal district court, arguing that the citizenship requirement was unconstitutional.

Both petitioners prevailed in district court, and the state appealed to the U.S. Supreme Court, which consolidated the cases as *Nyquist v. Mauclet* (1977). As in the Mississippi and California state courts, the Supreme Court ruled in favor of the noncitizens. Citing previous decisions "that classifications by a State that are based on alienage are 'inherently suspect and subject to close judicial scrutiny,'" the Court noted that "alienage classifications by a State that do not withstand this stringent examination cannot stand."[47] The state's main claims were that the statute was justified as a means of promoting naturalization and that the citizenship provisions were "tailored to the purpose of the assistance program, namely, the enhancement of the educational level of the

---

[45] Maxwell (1979) p. 521. As defined by the federal immigration agency, now the Bureau of Citizenship and Immigration Services (BCIS), a refugee is "any person who is outside his or her country of nationality who is unable or unwilling to return to that country because of persecution or a well-founded fear of persecution. Persecution or the fear thereof must be based on the alien's race, religion, nationality, membership in a particular social group, or political opinion. People with no nationality must generally be outside their country of last habitual residence to qualify as a refugee" (BCIS, 2007). The USCIS, which is under the authority of the Department of Homeland Security, officially replaced the Immigration and Naturalization Service as of March 1, 2003, as a result of provisions originally included in the Homeland Security Act of 2002. (The USCIS was briefly known as the Bureau of Citizenship and Immigration Services before being renamed.)

[46] *Nyquist v. Mauclet*, 432 U.S. 1 (1977).

[47] Ibid.

electorate."[48] In their defense, the plaintiffs pointed out that such political guidelines were not required of students who were U.S. citizens. In response to the state's argument that it "had a legitimate interest in limiting its funds to those aliens who make an affirmative political commitment to the United States," the justices concluded that the "state had gone beyond its permissible limits."[49] The Supreme Court determined that New York had not proven a compelling interest for excluding noncitizens and thus was in violation of the Fourteenth Amendment's equal protection clause. Additionally, Justice Blackmun, who wrote the majority opinion, pointed out that it was unfair to discriminate against permanent residents who paid taxes and supported the very financial aid programs that excluded them.

While the *Nyquist v. Mauclet* litigation was underway, a similar case emerged in Maryland. State policies there denied noncitizens who held G-4 visas the opportunity to attend college at in-state tuition rates.[50] The case was first brought to district court in 1976 and was adjudged by the Supreme Court in 1982, in *Toll v. Moreno,* only weeks after the Court's landmark decision in *Plyler v. Doe.* In *Nyquist v. Mauclet,* the Supreme Court had based its decision in favor of noncitizen students on the equal protection guarantee. Five years later, the Court "based its opinion on the premise that the federal government is preeminent in matters of immigration policy and states may not enact alienage classifications, except in limited cases of political and government functions."[51] Specifically, state statutes could not discriminate against nonimmigrants who had been authorized by the government to reside in the United States.

In 1983, following the *Toll v. Moreno* decision, the California legislature had modified the CEC "to eliminate the requirement that alien students seeking resident tuition rates prove that they have legal permanent resident status."[52] The changes enacted by the state legislature under AB 2015 (sponsored by Assemblyman Art Agnos) were short

---

[48] Ibid.

[49] Maxwell (1979), p. 550.

[50] G-4 visas are granted to international organization officers and employees, as well as to their immediate family members.

[51] Olivas (1995), p.1047.

[52] Yates (2004), p. 593. See also California Education Code section 68062(h).

lived.[53] A year later, at the request of the Chancellor of California State University, state Attorney General John Van De Kamp issued an opinion regarding the CEC's tuition provisions. He classified all undocumented students as nonresidents for tuition purposes, arguing that the changes brought by the legislature the previous year had been made to "conform to Toll and had not [been] intended to incorporate undocumented aliens."[54] In the wake of this legal opinion, five undocumented students filed suit against the University of California (UC) and the California State University (CSU) systems, "seeking a declaration that state law violated the equal protection clause of the U.S. Constitution."[55] The next section recounts the history and impact of this case.

THE LETICIA "A" CASE

Leticia "A" v. Board of Regents of the University of California, initially filed in 1985, became popularly known as the Leticia "A" litigation over the more than ten years in which it was argued. The five students who were parties to the suit had been admitted to the University of California for the 1984 fall term. Based on their interpretation of AB 2015, UC officials required payment of nonresident tuition and fees from each of the students.[56] Their classification as undocumented residents was made by default. The students' lack of U.S. citizenship or legal immigration status rendered them, in the eyes of the university, international students subject to international fees, regardless of the fact that they were long-time residents of California and had graduated from high schools in the state. Although the Supreme Court had asserted, in *Plyler*, that "illegal entry into the country would not, under traditional criteria, bar a person from obtaining domicile within the state," that same ruling did not guarantee such a person consideration for higher education.[57] In other words, the constitutional protections reaffirmed

---

[53] AB 2015 provided that, "[A]n alien, including an unmarried minor alien, may establish his or her residence, unless precluded by the Immigration and Nationality Act from establishing domicile in the United States" (Olivas, 1995, p. 1051). Also see Archie-Hudson (1993).

[54] Olivas (1986), p. 34.

[55] Archie-Hudson (1993).

[56] Olivas (1995), p. 1051.

[57] *Plyler v. Doe*, p. 219, fn 22.

under the *Plyler* decision did not extend to undocumented students wishing to attend college.

The California Superior Court rejected UC officials' interpretation of AB 2015, pointing to the fact that immigration laws on residence could not determine a noncitizen's ability to establish domicile and therefore qualify for in-state tuition. Additionally, the court held that the application of different criteria than the guidelines used to determine the residency of U.S. citizens was unconstitutional.[58] After all, many noncitizens had resided in the state as long as any U.S. citizen. In his 1985 opinion, the hearing judge stated, "The policies underlying the immigration laws and regulations are vastly different from those relating to residency for student fee purposes. The two systems are totally unrelated for purposes of administration, enforcement and legal analysis."[59] With this judgment, the court struck down the residency provision in the CEC. As in earlier rulings in other states, the judge recognized that undocumented immigrants living in California were bona fide residents of the state and subject to the equal protection clause of the California constitution. They could be considered residents for tuition purposes and also were eligible for state financial aid under the Cal Grant program.[60]

In 1990, five years after the judge's initial ruling in the Leticia "A" case, Donald Bradford, a University of California at Los Angeles (UCLA) registrar, challenged the ruling.[61] In *Bradford v. Board of Re-*

---

[58] Supinger (1999).

[59] Quoted in Olivas (1995), p. 1053.

[60] Olivas (1986), p. 42. This initial ruling in the Leticia "A" case preceded the passage of the federal Immigration Reform and Control Act (IRCA) of 1986, which authorized the legalization of undocumented immigrants who could prove they had resided in this country since 1982. The U.S. government clearly made residency a requirement to be eligible for the benefits established under IRCA. So, while state statutes were claiming that undocumented immigrants did not have a right to reside in a state and that they were not eligible for educational benefits afforded to other state residents, federal legislation was acknowledging their presence in the country and making their state residency part of the eligibility criteria for receiving immigration paperwork.

[61] A former official at the Office of the President of the UC system recalled that the issue decided in the Leticia "A" case had resurfaced when an undocu-

gents of the University of California (sometimes called "Bradford I"), the Los Angeles County Superior Court ruled in favor of Bradford, arguing that the 1983 CEC statute was constitutional because it precluded undocumented students from establishing residence. UC appealed the decision in *Regents of the University of California v. Los Angeles County Superior Court*.[62] When that court too ruled against UC, officials at all eight campuses began implementing (in fall 1991) the exclusionary policies dictated by *Bradford*. Undocumented students enrolled as of June 1991 were allowed "to keep their resident classification but . . . ..wly enrolled undocumented students [were required] to be classified as nonresidents."[63]

What followed *Bradford* was a stream of policies reversing the gains that undocumented students had achieved in the mid-eighties under the Leticia "A" decision. The California Student Aid Commission no longer awarded state financial aid grants to undocumented students. In addition, in 1992 the California Community Colleges (CCC) issued policies that interpreted *Bradford* as applying to its students as well and, like the UC system's revised rules, took the position that newly entering undocumented students would no longer be eligible for classification as residents for tuition purposes. *Bradford* created a dual-fee structure. Since the ruling did not apply to the California State University system, undocumented students enrolling at CSU campuses continued to be considered eligible for in-state tuition,[64] even though they could not acquire the same classification at any of the eight campuses of the UC system or at any of the 108 CCC campuses.[65] In addi-

---

mented student applied to UCLA. Bradford claimed that the university was coercing him to commit an illegal act by asking him to process the paperwork for an undocumented person (Ed Apodaca, personal communication, June 21, 2005).

[62] 225 Cal. App. 3d 972 (1990).

[63] Guillen (2002).

[64] A decade of legislation had resulted in a mismatch of the application of residency policies as they pertained to undocumented students (Olivas, 1995). In 1989–1991 in the UC system and 1986–1995 in the CSU system, students meeting state residency requirements were able to pay resident tuition and receive state financial aid (see also Barrera, 2002; Ortiz, 2002).

[65] The CCC system had originally faced the issue of undocumented students under *Gurfinkel v. Los Angeles Community College District*, 175 Cal. Rptr. 201

tion, despite being classified as residents by CSU, they could not receive state financial aid, since the Student Aid Commission considered them nonresidents.

These conflicting practices prompted a final lawsuit, filed to determine whether Leticia "A" or *Bradford* would prevail. The case, *American Association of Women (AAW) v. Board of Trustees of California State University*,[66] was brought by several anti-immigrant groups, the best known of which was the Federation for American Immigration Reform (FAIR).[67] The judge ruled in favor of the AAW and the other parties to the suit, affirming *Bradford* and prohibiting the CSU system from treating undocumented students as residents for tuition purposes. Although the ruling would likely affect an extremely small number of students (0.3 percent of the total number of students enrolled, system wide), no provisions for grandfathering continuing students were included.[68] The UC system was not affected, since *Bradford* had already made undocumented students wishing to attend UC campuses ineligible for in-state tuition.

Meanwhile, anti-immigrant forces put on the ballot a proposal to deny undocumented residents far more than access to in-state tuition rates. In 1994, 59 percent of those voting in California elections approved Proposition 187, which sought to prohibit "illegal aliens" from accessing public education at any grade level, seeking care at state hos-

---

(1981). The CCC "was considered to be bound by Bradford II, 225 Cal. App. 3d 972 (1990)" (Olivas, 1995, p. 1080). See also Wilson (1995). An estimated 13,625 undocumented students were expected to be adversely affected by that portion of the ruling (see Reid, 1995).

[66] 38 Cal. Rptr. 2d 15 (Ct. App. 1995).

[67] Formed in 1978, FAIR was founded by Sierra Club members based on a platform combining environmental concerns with a mission of restricting immigration. The Southern Poverty Law Center has identified this organization as a hate group (Beirich, 2007). Other anti-immigration parties to the suit, besides the American Association of Women and FAIR, included the California Coalition for Immigration Reform, and Valley Citizens for Fair Immigration. See Solis (2004, p. 11).

[68] The ruling was expected to affect an estimated 1,000 undocumented students out of a total enrollment of 320,000 students at the 21 campuses of the CSU system. See Wilson (1995).

pitals, or receiving other social and healthcare benefits. Although this was a state-specific measure, it set the stage for broader attacks against immigrants at a time when the federal government was also attempting to impose draconian measures against documented and undocumented immigrants alike. The next section briefly reviews Proposition 187's provisions, focusing on those which sought to overturn *Plyler v. Doe* and to tighten existing restrictions on access to higher education.

ENDING THE "ILLEGAL INVASION": CALIFORNIA'S PROPOSITION 187

At its core, Proposition 187 called for the denial of social services (public health and education) to the undocumented, as a means of discouraging immigration and thus saving the state money allegedly lost in providing services to this population. Nicknamed the Save Our State (SOS) initiative, the proposition was co-authored by Ron Prince, a self-employed accountant, and by former Immigration and Naturalization Commissioner Alan Nelson; it also had the strong backing of FAIR and other anti-immigrant groups, such as the California Coalition for Immigration Reform,[69] and it was supported by then-Governor Pete Wilson, who had taken an anti-immigrant stance in his reelection campaign. As the Texas legislature had attempted to do almost twenty years earlier, with the addition of Section 21.031 to the state Education Code, backers of Prop. 187 sought to "show the federal government that citizens were displeased with their efforts regarding illegal immigration and spur Washington to do more."[70]

Voter approval of the initiative generated an outpouring of opposition, including from several California school districts that sought injunctive relief.[71] Had Proposition 187 been enacted and enforced, it would have quashed, at the state level, the gains codified under the *Plyler v. Doe* ruling.[72] This certainty spurred thousands of high school

---

[69] Sifuentes (2004).

[70] Cooper (2004), p. 3.

[71] Carter (1997), p. 3.

[72] Proponents of Proposition 187, and in particular previous supporter Ron Prince, tried again in 2004 to get the same measure (Save our State) on the ballot (Sifuentes, 2004). While these efforts failed, in other states supporters of similar measures succeeded. The most renowned of these was Arizona's Propo-

students in Los Angeles and other California cities to march against the passage of Proposition 187. The questionable legality of the ballot measure also led the courts to intervene, issuing injunctions against enforcement a week after the measure had been approved by voters.[73] Despite never having been implemented, Prop. 187 is very important. Its passage and the challenges that followed show that while the issue of undocumented students' access to public education had been settled in the legal domain, its enforcement remains a subject of heated popular debate.[74] Indeed, on its twenty-fifth anniversary, *Plyler* continues to be attacked. In some areas, local governments have passed and are implementing anti-immigrant measures seeking to rid cities of undocu-

---

sition 200, approved by voters in 2004. As with Proposition 187, this initiative was funded by FAIR, under the banner of Protect Arizona Now. Carefully worded to avoid conflict with federal law, Proposition 200 "would require proof of immigration status when applying for child care, housing assistance and other benefits" but it would not "block federally mandated programs such as emergency healthcare [or] prohibit children from attending school" (Los Angeles Times, 2004). As in California, supporters of the measure hoped to pressure the federal government into increasing enforcement at the Arizona border, one of the busiest corridors for the entry of undocumented workers. As of 2007, Proposition 200 remains a valid state law.

[73] Johnson (1995).

[74] School districts, which were at the core of the *Plyler* litigation, continue to be key sites of debate. For example, in September 2002, twenty years after the Supreme Court's ruling, a New Jersey school superintendent denied admission to five undocumented children (Newman, 2002). The superintendent not only violated the students' rights by questioning their mothers about their immigration status but also threatened to turn them over to immigration authorities. This case involved a group of Canadian citizens of Salvadoran descent. Whether these children's right to a public education would have been denied had they not been Spanish-speaking Latin American immigrants can only be conjectured. The superintendent was ordered to retract his decision. His retraction is indicative of the hostility frequently encountered by immigrants in their dealings with school authorities: "While *diversity* [italics added] makes conflicts inevitable, these issues are related to governmental legalities and not to our commitment to all children, regardless of race and color, gender, ethnicity, or origin" (Perez and Llorente, 2002; Sutherland, 2003).

mented workers and their families. Those who follow this issue closely have identified these tactics as a "roundabout method of doing away with *Plyler*."[75]

There are striking similarities between California's 1994 ballot initiative and the Texas legislature's actions in 1975. In both states, anti-immigrant forces blamed immigrant students for the increasing cost of education.[76] And in both cases, the response, an attempt to deny educational services to undocumented students, targeted the Latino population. The allegations of fiscal burden caused by immigrants implicitly promoted anti-Latino attitudes.[77] This is a common strategy. Those

---

[75] Belejack (2007). On May 12, 2007, the north Texas suburban city of Farmers Branch passed Ordinance 2903, a local measure requiring landlords to verify the immigration status of their tenants, and imposing a misdemeanor fine of $500 per day on landlords who failed to comply (Weinstein and Clower, 2007). Not surprisingly, anti-immigrant forces such as the Federation for American Immigration Reform, which have long opposed *Plyler*, have applauded these measures: "We want to see a policy that convinces parents not to bring their kids here in the first place" (quoted in Leal Unmuth, 2007). The forces behind these measures have used the same arguments used in 1975 by the State of Texas, citing overburdened public schools as a chief motivation. Incredible demographic changes that have made the area 40 percent Latino, as well as a pronouncement by Tim O'Hare, the leading supporter of Ordinance 2903, seem to tell a different story: "The reason I got on the City Council was because I saw our property values declining or increasing at a level that was below the rate of inflation. When that happens, people move out of our neighborhoods, and what I would call *less desirable people* move into the neighborhoods, *people who don't value education*, people who don't value taking care of their properties." (Weinstein and Clower, 2007, p. 7, italics added). The Farmers Branch policy has affected nearby areas. In Irving, Texas, immigrant parents pulled nearly 100 children from the public schools as local police increased their deportation efforts. Meanwhile, Farmers Branch "city attorneys, on behalf of the City Council, have asked the local school district to supply them with the name and address of every child living in the city and enrolled in the public schools" (Treviño, 2007).

[76] Reich (1995); Seper (2004).

[77] Most commentators agree that Proposition 187 targeted the Latino population, especially Mexicans (e.g., see Garcia, 1995; Johnson, 1995; Olivas, 1995; Tamayo, 1995; Rush, 1998; Cooper, 2004). The politics of racial anxiety are

opposed to undocumented immigrants' access to a basic education use immigration status as a pretext, while targeting students on the basis of their race. While the exclusion of undocumented students from K-12 public education was at the core of Proposition 187, the initiative did not stop there. It also sought to prevent undocumented students from being admitted to institutions of postsecondary education by requiring that these public educational institutions verify the immigration status of all enrolling students every semester.[78] Section 8(a) of Proposition 187 prohibited public institutions of higher education from "admitting, enrolling or permitting the attendance of persons" who were not "authorized under federal law to be present in the United States."

Soon after Prop. 187 had passed, six undocumented students brought civil action in San Francisco Superior Court against the University of California.[79] These students had already applied to federal authorities to adjust their immigration status. Their civil action was directed against the possible implementation of Section 8(a). The suit claimed that Proposition 187 violated "the U.S. Civil Rights Act and a federal law requiring public education officials to keep students' records private."[80] The hearing judge issued an injunction preventing the enforcement of Section 8. However, a summary judgment issued in United States District Court of California in 1998[81] found that the section was preempted by federal legislation passed in 1996.[82] (This federal legislation is discussed in the final section of this chapter.)

---

best exemplified by Harvard University professor and former coordinator of security planning for the National Security Council in the late 1970s, Samuel Huntington. For a sample reading exposing his views see Huntington (2004).

[78] Alarcon (1994); Cooper (2004); Olivas (1995); Stevenson (2004); Yates (2004).

[79] Yates (2004). The action was filed February 9, 1995.

[80] Reid (1995), p. 17.

[81] This judgment was delivered in a rehearing of *League of United Latin American Citizens v. Wilson,* originally filed in 1995, challenging the constitutionality of Proposition 187. In the 1995 decision, the court had ruled that Prop. 187's denial of K-12 education was "impermissible" because it conflicted with the Supreme Court's ruling in *Plyler.* At the same time, the proposition's denial of postsecondary education was ruled as *not* in violation of federal law.

[82] Olivas (1995); Stevenson (2004).

The actions challenging Proposition 187's impact on higher education coincided with the end of litigation in the *Leticia "A"* and *Bradford* cases, with rulings that disallowed undocumented students from being considered state residents for tuition purposes at any of California's public colleges or universities. Thus, although the proposition was never implemented, its goal of barring undocumented students from college was achieved. By imposing the burden of nonresident tuition fees, these court decisions kept undocumented students from pursuing a postsecondary education.[83]

Proposition 187's supporters also achieved their goal of gaining the attention of the federal government. Referring to a proposal (discussed below) filed by U.S. Representative Elton Gallegly of California, then-Governor Wilson stated: "[D]espite the adverse ruling on Proposition 187, California taxpayers should know that Congress has heard our outrage and they are acting."[84] While President Clinton condemned Proposition 187 during his reelection campaign, he emulated it after the election, asserting that the federal government needed to do more to toughen immigration laws. The 1996 passage of both the Illegal Immigration Reform and Immigrant Responsibility Act (IIRIRA) and the Personal Responsibility and Work Opportunity Reconciliation Act (PRWORA)[85] delivered on that assertion—and went further than Proposition 187 supporters ever could have envisioned. Indeed, as Governor Gray Davis, Wilson's successor, put it, "'[T]he spirit of Proposition 187 lived on' in the federal legislation that supplanted it."[86] The final part of the chapter turns to this federal legislation, examining Section 505, a provision of the 1996 immigration law with serious consequences for undocumented students seeking a college education.

SECTION 505 OF THE ILLEGAL IMMIGRATION REFORM AND IMMIGRANT RESPONSIBILITY ACT

The 1996 Illegal Immigration Reform and Immigrant Responsibility Act was a sweeping attack on immigrants, both legal and undocu-

---

[83] Badger and Yale-Loehr (2002).

[84] Bolson (1995).

[85] IIRIRA was filed as HR 2022 in the House of Representatives and as S.1664 in the Senate; PRWORA was filed as H.R. 3734.

[86] Yates (2004), p. 595.

mented, that represented a new chapter in the nation's long history of a "politics of racial anxiety and xenophobia."[87] Section 505 of the act addresses postsecondary education benefits. The wording of this provision is especially important because immigration opponents argue that it prevents states from extending in-state tuition eligibility to immigrants.

The IIRIRA took form in the wake of Proposition 187-inspired hysteria. Whipped-up fear and resentment of "illegal aliens" fueled proposals for national-level legislation severely limiting all immigrants' access to public benefits and undocumented students' eligibility for in-state tuition fees based on their residence in a given state. While these measures were touted as ways to reduce the supposed incentives for the undocumented to seek social services and other public resources, supporters of these measures sought to eliminate immigrants' eligibility entirely.[88] Indeed, during the deliberations that led to the legislation that eventually became the IIRIRA, other restrictive proposals were considered but not approved. For example, one aimed to deny federal financial aid to noncitizen students who would otherwise qualify.[89] This would have quashed the gains of the 1965 Higher Education Act, which, as noted earlier, made federal financial aid available to permanent residents, refugees, and noncitizens with asylum status. Another effort, also unsuccessful, was H.R.1377, a proposal "To amend the Immigration and Nationality Act to authorize States to deny public education benefits to aliens not lawfully present in the United States," sponsored by Rep. Elton Gallegly in April, 1995. The Gallegly Amendment stated that "Congress declares it to be the policy of the United States that aliens who are not lawfully present in the United States not be entitled to public education benefits."[90] If included, this

---

[87] Alfred (2003), p. 631.

[88] One news report noted, "For many of the nation's 11 million *legal* [italics added] immigrants, there may be no more student loans. No Pell grants for college. No health care under the Medicaid program. No subsidized English classes, federal job training or Head Start programs for preschoolers . . . About 400,000 students receive Pell grants, a primary form of federal financial aid" (George, 1996).

[89] Reid (1995), p. 18.

[90] Carter (1997), n. 263.

amendment would have effectively overturned *Plyler v. Doe* and would have allowed states to deny access to public education to undocumented children.

Like the Gallegly Amendment, Section 505 of the IIRIRA sought to restrict access to education, but Section 505 addresses postsecondary levels—and unlike the Gallegly Amendment, it is part of legislation that did win Congressional approval and was signed into law by President Clinton. Although the IIRIRA does not overturn *Plyler,* some of its provisions have been interpreted as prohibitions on state-level laws that extend in-state tuition to undocumented students.[91] What Section 505 says is that a state cannot offer postsecondary education benefits to undocumented students on the basis of state residence *"unless* [emphasis added] a citizen or national of the United States is eligible for such benefit."[92] As originally crafted, this provision was aimed to prevent states from passing laws that would make undocumented residents in their jurisdictions eligible for in-state tuition. The underlying rationale was that by allowing undocumented residents of a given state to pay in-

---

[91] Section 505 is titled "Limitations on eligibility for preferential treatment of aliens not lawfully present on basis of residence of higher education benefits," and it reads as follows: "(a) IN GENERAL: Notwithstanding any other provision of law, an alien who is not lawfully present in the United States shall not be eligible on the basis of residence within a State (or a political subdivision) for any postsecondary education benefit unless a citizen or national of the United States is eligible for such a benefit (in no less an amount, duration and scope) without regard to whether the citizen or national is such a resident" (IIRIRA, Title V, 505(a)).

[92] In clarifying the meaning of this provision, Olivas (2004, p. 453) notes that this section "does not preclude any state from enacting undocumented student legislation due to the word 'unless.' A flat bar would not include such a modifier. The only way to read this convoluted language is: State A cannot give more consideration to an undocumented student than it can give to a nonresident student from State B. For example, California could not enact a plan to extend resident status to undocumented students after they had resided in the state for twelve months, and then accord the same status to U.S. citizens or permanent residents from Nevada or Oregon after eighteen months. No state plan does this; indeed, several of the plans require three years of residence for the undocumented, as well as state high school attendance–neither of which is required for citizen non-residents."

state tuition, the state was placing a higher bar on residents of another state, since these prospective students would be required to pay out-of-state tuition. The core purpose of this provision was to prevent institutions of postsecondary education from charging in-state tuition to undocumented aliens, because in doing so, the undocumented "would be treated more favorably than out of state residents who are citizens."[93] Beyond Section 505's provisions for making undocumented students ineligible for federal, state, and local benefits, the IIRIRA demanded additional immigration verification of legal permanent residents who requested financial aid.[94]

Despite the lack of guidelines for implementing this provision, Section 505 has discouraged states from determining their own educational policies. The mere presence of the statute at the federal level has been—mistakenly—interpreted by many states either as a prohibition or as a preemptive law that overrides state-level action regarding undocumented students' eligibility for in-state tuition.[95] Perhaps just as important, Section 505 by default has helped sustain a climate of antipathy and suspicion toward undocumented students and immigrants of color. Institutions avoid dealing with these students for fear of being

---

[93] Mulay Casey (1996), p. 2.

[94] Sections 506 and 507 also limit legal and undocumented immigrants' access to higher education. Section 506 demands from the Comptroller General a report to "determine the extent to which aliens who are not lawfully admitted for permanent residence are receiving postsecondary Federal student financial assistance" (Pub.L.104-208 IIRIRA of 1996). Section 507 requires that the state and institutions of higher education transmit to the Immigration and Naturalization Service (now the USCIS) copies of documents of those requesting financial aid assistance (Pub.L.104-208 IIRIRA of 1996). As with other immigration measures, such provisions are justified on the grounds that they apply only to undocumented immigrants, but as with all other immigration measures, in practice, they always cast a wider net.

[95] The in-state tuition laws that have been passed thus far (and that will be reviewed in the following chapters) allow undocumented students to be eligible on the basis of their high school attendance and graduation, not their state residence. This language further allows all high school graduates of a given state, whether they have established residence in the state or not, to qualify for in-state tuition.

penalized by the federal government or simply because accommodating such applicants requires additional paperwork.[96]

In the context of such harsh legislation, the issue of undocumented students' access to higher education appeared foreclosed. Pressure from anti-immigrant forces, which has mounted in the aftermath of the September 11, 2001 events, no doubt also has been an important factor discouraging many states from acting on behalf of undocumented youth. However, since 2001, some states have accurately interpreted IIRIRA and its clause pertaining to undocumented immigrant students' access to higher education. Indeed, ten states have implemented legislation offering postsecondary benefits to all eligible high school graduates, regardless of immigration status. The next chapter reviews the passage of Texas's in-state tuition policy, the first of its kind in the United States.

---

[96] Such attitudes toward undocumented immigrants are entrenched. A case in point was found by University of Houston professor Nestor Rodriguez while he was conducting interviews in the early nineties on the possible admission of undocumented students. He noted that "an admissions-office worker indicated that his response to applicants seeking admission varied by the characteristics of the applicants. The office worker simply directed applicants who 'look immigrant' or spoke with a marked accent to the admissions office for international students. Hispanics and Asians were usually the applicants sent by the office worker to the international-student admissions office" (Rodriguez, 1992, p. 48).

CHAPTER 3

Broadening Educational Access: How Texas Came to Craft and Implement HB 1403

In Texas before the mid-1990s, the story of undocumented students' quest for a college education was one of despair. Regardless of how high their level of academic achievement or how deep their interest in higher education, such students often faced closed doors.[1] Sometimes colleges or universities, unaware of these students' immigration status, would express interest but would then refuse admittance (or admit but refuse financial aid, effectively limiting enrollment) if a student's lack of legal documentation became apparent. One observer described this situation as the universities' "own version of the military's 'don't ask, don't tell policy.'"[2] From the students' perspective, this was a betrayal. They had put their trust in an "educational system that built their hopes up and then denied them higher education."[3]

As the preceding chapters have shown, the issue of higher education for undocumented students has long resonated within the immigrant community and among those who advocate for an expansion of democratic and civil rights for disenfranchised populations. The

---

[1] The early situation in Texas has been documented by Rodriguez (1992), who interviewed high school students about their college plans during a period when such aspirations were being met with restrictive state policy. Also see Treviño (2003).

[2] Mitchell (2001).

[3] Rodriguez (1992), p. 39.

changes in attitudes and policies that led the Texas legislature, in 2001, to approve House Bill 1403, the first law in the country allowing undocumented students access to college at in-state tuition rates, were not a matter of coincidence or luck. They occurred as a result of the organized efforts of immigrant students and their supporters, members of educational institutions (at the K-12 level and beyond), and some state legislators in particular State Representative Rick Noriega (Houston). This chapter traces the development of this advocacy work and its impact, beginning with the push for policies that opened the doors of community colleges to immigrant students in Texas, through the buildup of support for statewide legislation, to the crafting and implementation of HB 1403.

The discussion begins by focusing on successful campaigns within the Dallas County Community College District (DCCCD) and the Houston Community College System (HCCS) to offer in-district tuition to undocumented students. It then reviews initial efforts to press the Texas Higher Education Coordinating Board (THECB) to relax its restrictions on immigrant students' access to institutions of postsecondary education. Victories on these two fronts were important not only because they laid the groundwork that made possible the passage of HB 1403 but also because they confirmed the existence of strong interest and support for greater educational access for all high school graduates and others, regardless of their immigration status. The remainder of the chapter looks at the work of a broadly based group of pro-immigrant forces, especially in Houston, to collaborate with state legislators to amend the Texas Education Code (TEC) to make higher education a realistic goal for the state's undocumented students and then follows the progress of the bill from proposal through passage to final implementation. A final section reviews changes made to the law four years after its passage.

In Texas, as in California and other states, initial attempts to make noncitizens eligible for in-state tuition addressed students who had qualified for a change in their immigration status. A 1976 provision of the TEC, for instance, established that noncitizens who had filed a declaration of intent to become citizens qualified to become residents for tuition purposes.[4] In 1993, the legislature considered—but ultimately failed to pass—a bill that would have reduced the magnitude of the educational challenges facing students in the process of becoming permanent residents.[5] But the remainder, immigrant high school graduates who were living in Texas but who were not yet permanent residents and had not filed for citizenship, were caught in a Catch-22 situation. The TEC classified them as international students, which meant that they were ineligible to enroll in school paying in-state tuition fees and also unable to qualify for state financial aid. Thus, at the close of the twentieth century, much remained to be done to broaden access to higher education for all of the state's immigrant students.

POLICIES OF INCLUSION AT COMMUNITY COLLEGES

Examining the policy changes that administrators in the Dallas and Houston community college districts made over a period of several years reveals the importance of joint efforts undertaken at the institu-

---

[4] At the time, the Texas Education Code stated: "Aliens living in the United States under a visa permitting permanent residence, and aliens who are permitted by Congress to adopt the United States as their domicile while they are in this country and aliens who have filed with the proper federal immigration authority a declaration of intent to become a United States citizen have the same privilege of qualifying for Texas resident status for tuition purposes as do citizens of the United States" (TEC, Section 54.057). In reference to that section of the TEC, a letter from State Representative Rick Noriega to the chair of the Texas Higher Education Coordinating Board pointed out that "there is no declaration of intention to become a citizen which can be officially filed. Rather, there are applications for 'status' changes leading to permanent residency, then citizenship. There are considerable costs for, and specific timelines between each application for 'change of status' and the entire process can take many years" (Noriega, 2000b, p. 1).

[5] This was HB 2510, introduced on March 12, 1993 by Flores, during the 73rd Regular Session. Olivas (1995, p. 1034) describes this bill as targeting "intending permanent residents or persons permanently residing under color of law (PRUCOL)." The bill sought to amend Section 54.057 of the TEC by making any student who had "graduated from high school, who is waiting for final approval of a visa permitting residence and whose parents have a visa permitting residence" eligible to pay in-state tuition (Flores, 1993, p. 1).

tional and grassroots levels in bringing about developments that led to the 2001 passage of HB 1403.

Changes Within the Dallas County Community College District

The Dallas County Community College District was the first to allow undocumented students to register at in-district tuition fees. In the fall of 1997, DCCCD administrators began discussing how to meet undocumented students' interest in being admitted. The key question was whether undocumented immigrants qualified for enrollment at indistrict tuition rates. The prevailing policy linked tuition rates to federal immigration law. So, for purposes of tuition, noncitizen students were eligible for in-district tuition if they were permanent residents as defined by federal immigration law or if they held specific types of visas. Noncitizens who did not fit within either of these federal categories faced an onerous tuition burden, even if they met the district residency requirements (all students were required to show proof that they had lived in Dallas County for at least 12 months immediately prior to the semester in which they were enrolling in order to be considered eligible for resident tuition).

The initial impetus for a change in the DCCCD rules came when the college staff made the Board of Trustees aware that they had been turning undocumented students away due to their lack of documentation.[6] The story of one of these students, a recent valedictorian from a well-respected local public high school near Dallas who had been denied admission to a four-year state institution, included aspects common to all. Even if he had been admitted to a four-year institution, he could not have enrolled, because he would have been charged international tuition fees, which were generally three times higher than those paid by residents. To exacerbate the situation, this student's immigration status prevented him from receiving federal financial aid, and the DCCCD did not provide undocumented students with any state or local financial aid.

The valedictorian's story, combined with an awareness that many more students shared his predicament, helped persuade the DCCCD

---

[6] Biswas (2005). Board member Diana Flores, who was active in the community, was quite familiar with this issue from other sources. For a detailed discussion of the DCCCD's efforts, see Rodriguez (1998).

board to support a change in the in-district fee policy. DCCCD administrators hoped that the question of fees could be resolved by an opinion from the state attorney general regarding tuition classification for these students.[7] The DCCCD's legal counsel addressed a formal inquiry about this possibility to the Texas Higher Education Coordinating Board.[8] The THECB's legal counsel declined to request an AG opinion, arguing that existing law provided sufficient legal guidance. The THECB quoted section 54.051(m) of the Texas Education Code, which stated, "tuition for students who are citizens of any country other than the United States of America is the same as tuition required of other nonresident students."[9] On that basis, the board held that undocumented students would have to pay nonresident tuition. These students' basic right to enroll was not questioned, however.

Initially, the DCCCD capitulated, moving to "legally admit such students and charge them out-of-country tuition."[10] After conducting an additional review of their rules, however, the Dallas community college administrators concluded that undocumented students should be allowed to pay in-county tuition as long as they met the same county residency requirements expected of all other prospective students. As DCCCD Chancellor Wenrich argued, "It is patently unfair to require students without status and who are residents of Dallas County to pay

---

[7] In a letter to the THECB dated September 24, 1997, the general counsel of the Dallas County Community College District asked whether the THECB could require an opinion from the attorney general regarding the admissions of undocumented students (Rodriguez, 1998).

[8] According to its website, "The Texas Higher Education Coordinating Board was created by the Texas Legislature in 1965 to 'provide leadership and coordination for the Texas higher education system to achieve excellence for the college education of Texas students.' The coordinating board meets quarterly in Austin." The legislature is responsible for setting policy, but as its designated "planning body," THECB has autonomous powers, such as setting enrollment limits "at all institutions of higher education" in the state, developing funding formulas, and specifying "the role and mission" of all public colleges and universities. See Texas Higher Education Coordinating Board (1987).

[9] Rodriguez (1998).

[10] Wenrich (1999).

out-of-country tuition."[11] His position, which was supported by others on the board,[12] is best summarized as, "We are not operating for the *migra* and we should not be keepers; our function is to educate the people that let us operate."[13]

In January 1998, the DCCCD began implementing a district-wide policy to admit undocumented students and classify them as in-district students. The only stipulation was that these students, like all others, had to have lived in Dallas County during the previous twelve months. With this move, the college was recognizing the presence of undocumented students and their families within the county and extending to them the same benefits that accrued to other taxpayers in the district. The chancellor's memo explained the policy revision this way: "The policy of inclusion is based upon the fact that such students and/or their families have paid taxes either directly or indirectly to the support of this district."[14] The Board of Trustees and the Chancellor's Cabinet approved the revisions. This support, however, was not unanimous. Some college officials cited THECB rules and regulations and argued that the DCCCD was making a mistake that would jeopardize the district's share of state funds.[15] Despite these internal misgivings, the policy was implemented and became an inspiration to immigrant advocates in other areas of the state, including Houston.

Changes within the Houston Community College System

At the end of the 1990s, while administrators in the Dallas community college system were revising in-district tuition rules, the Houston Inde-

---

[11] Ibid.

[12] Board Trustee Diana Flores actively promoted the proposed revision in policy.

[13] Dr. William Wenrich (personal communication, October 10, 2002).

[14] Ibid.

[15] Ibid. Opponents' reference to funding alludes to state audits that, in the end, never took place. Under the DCCCD policy, the college did not submit the credit hours completed by undocumented students for state reimbursement (Biswas, 2005). A portion of that cost was covered with local funds from the college, which, in addition, opened one of its scholarships to undocumented students (ibid.). Public universities in Texas do not have that option because they do not have local funds like these.

pendent School District (HISD) was being touted as one of the premier school districts in the nation. Even so, HISD's achievement with respect to its college-oriented foreign-born students was dismal. Of the 210,000 students enrolled in HISD during the 2000 school year, 40,000 had been born outside the United States, and 55,000 were classified as English Language Learners (ELL). About 11,000 of the immigrant students lacked Social Security numbers.[16] This means that each year, a segment of undocumented students enrolled in the district's high schools faced the prospect of taking classes knowing that they would have no chance of continuing their education past the secondary level, while another segment remained unaware that their immigration status would foreclose their college opportunities. The former often chose to drop out before graduating, while the latter were left at graduation with little choice beyond joining the underground labor force.

During the fall of 1999, Rosendo Ticas, a young Salvadoran who had dropped out of the Houston high school he had been attending, brought the issue to wider attention. Ticas had obtained a General Equivalency Diploma (GED) and was doing odd jobs, though he aspired to become a pilot. His immediate goal was to enroll in a certification program for aviation mechanics sponsored by the Houston Community College System (HCCS).[17] Like many other immigrant students, Ticas was effectively prevented from enrolling in this or any other HCCS course, even though he had filed paperwork years earlier (when he was in middle school) to become a permanent resident. As had happened to other immigrant students who met the place and length of residency requirements, HCCS considered him ineligible for in-district tuition. The nonresident fees Ticas was assessed were beyond his means. He decided to take his case to Rick Noriega, a state legisla-

---

16 Over 130 countries were represented among HISD's student population at the beginning of the twenty-first century (Houston Independent School District, 2000). The Supreme Court's 1982 decision in *Plyler v. Doe* prohibits public school administrators from asking students to reveal their immigration status. However, students who do not provide a Social Security number upon registration are assigned a state identification number. Many, if not most, of the undocumented students in a given school or district have a state identification number (known as PEIMS in Texas), making them somewhat identifiable.

17 See Noriega (2000d).

tor representing the Houston area near where he had gone to school.[18] After hearing Ticas's story, Noriega, along with other community members, including David Johnston,[19] an HISD English as a Second Language high school teacher, and this author approached HCCS Chancellor Ruth Burgos-Sasscer and suggested that Houston system administrators consider the policy approach their counterparts in Dallas had devised. This request received a sympathetic response from the chancellor who was very interested in pursuing changes in the admission policies that would fulfill the *community* mission of the community college system. The next step was to bring the matter before a meeting of the HCCS Board of Trustees.

Noriega, Ticas, Johnston, and others prepared for the meeting, waging a letter-writing campaign that targeted each member of the Board of Trustees and the chancellor. In these letters, the group argued that the college should serve all students, including the area's growing immigrant population. At the meeting, Ticas pointed out that he had completed his secondary education in the United States and that he was a taxpayer. He posed two basic questions to the board: (1) Why should he be denied the educational opportunities available to other residents? and (2) why should he be required to prove citizenship status? Noriega, in his address to the board members, referred to a report issued by the governor's office, "Closing the Gaps by Moving Every Texan Forward," which proclaimed that the state sought to narrow the gap between the number of high school graduates and college applicants. Noriega used the document to argue in favor of a change in HCCS ad-

---

[18] Ticas had dropped out from Stephen F. Austin High School in Houston. After he received his GED, he tried for four years to enroll in the Houston Community College System. At one point, he *was* able to enroll, but he had to drop out mid-semester when he was asked by a college staff person for his country of origin (Ticas, personal communication, October 2002).

[19] Johnston's interest in the issue began in the mid-1990s, when he started teaching at Robert E. Lee High School in Houston, one of the district's most diverse schools. (The school has since been renamed Lee High School.) During that time, he worked with a group of immigrant students to create "Club de las Américas" (Club of the Americas), a student group for immigrant students that allowed them to become involved in extracurricular activities (Johnston, 1999b).

missions policy. Among the other supporters of immigrant students who attended the meeting, David Johnston was especially effective. He explained that the DCCCD already admitted undocumented students. The board did not reach any conclusion at the meeting, but in the interim, college administrators awarded Ticas a scholarship to HCCS. Although this was personally gratifying, the failure to bring about a change in policy meant that thousands of other students like Rosendo Ticas would continue to be denied admission to college.

Still, this initial inquiry did open the door to another group of students: those in the process of being granted immigration status with the Immigration and Naturalization Service (INS).[20] On February 24, 2000, the trustees recommended that HCCS allow a distinct category of noncitizens to register and pay in-district tuition fees. These were students who "reside in-district, have graduated from in-district high schools, have applied for permanent resident status, and have waited at least 12 months for a response [from the INS]."[21] Although this revision would likely affect only a small number of students, it did acknowledge the inequity of denying admission to individuals who had completed their secondary education in the college's taxing district and whose property taxes helped fund the very college system they were prevented from attending.[22]

While the college had partially opened its doors to those students who were in the immigration pipeline, the issue of access by undocumented students remained pending. After the meeting at which Ticas and others had made their appeal, the chancellor had contacted her DCCCD counterpart, William Wenrich, to explore the possibility of replicating changes regarding fees for undocumented students.[23] The initial recommendation Chancellor Burgos-Sasscer made to the board was to "adopt a policy allowing undocumented students who reside in

---

[20] The Immigration and Naturalization Service is now known as the U.S. Bureau of Citizenship and Immigration Services (BCIS) and is under the authority of the Department of Homeland Security.

[21] Houston Community College System (2000a), p.1.

[22] HCCS was not able to claim state funding for the few students who would enroll under this policy. The college considered absorbing this loss as part of its service to the community (HCCS, 2000a).

[23] Ruth Burgos-Sasscer (personal communication, October 4, 2002).

the HCCS service area to register and pay out-of-state tuition and fees."[24] This was the same approach the DCCCD initially had taken when confronted with the issue. This meant that while undocumented students were allowed to register, they still were not eligible for in-district tuition fees. Since few undocumented students could afford to pay out-of-district fees, this kind of revision would result in little help. In preparation for a vote on the issue at the board's May meeting, however, Dr. Burgos-Sasscer began providing the trustees with additional information, explaining the advantages of allowing undocumented students access to in-district fees and detailing the logistics that the change would require.

The initial appeals made by Ticas, Noriega, Johnston, and others, the supportive response of Chancellors Burgos-Sasscer and Wenrich, and the effectiveness of the students' arguments were crucial. They marked the beginning of what became a joint campaign on behalf of undocumented students seeking to attend college. The next section examines the evolution of what was a small and only loosely associated group of advocates into a formal coalition that acted as a powerful and articulate voice for change.

THE COALITION OF HIGHER EDUCATION FOR IMMIGRANT STUDENTS

David Johnston, the Houston high school teacher who accompanied Rosendo Ticas and Rick Noriega when they made their initial presentation to the HCCS Board of Trustees, had begun organizing a group called the New American Student Foundation in the late 1990s.[25] In letters to local community college administrators, Johnston shared his

---

[24] Houston Community College System (2000b), p. 1.

[25] Johnston envisioned this organization as "a foundation in the Gulfton area that would aid documented and undocumented high school students in Houston" (Johnston, 1999b, p. 2). Its goals were various, including the coordination of a "united front among community groups to assure that future legislation reverses the roadblocks that prohibit undocumented students who have graduated from Texas high schools from attending local colleges . . . and receiving in-state tuition" (ibid.). Although the New American Student Foundation never materialized, its goals became the core mission of the Coalition of Higher Education for Immigrant Students, co-led by David Johnston and this author.

own firsthand knowledge of the plight of immigrant students: Up to 40 percent of students in the school where he taught could not attend college because of their immigration status. Noting the obstacles created by the refusal of public and private colleges and universities to admit high school graduates who lacked student visas, he urged "local colleges [to] adapt their admission policies and financial aid structures to help ease the burden facing inner city high schools with high populations of undocumented students who drop out."[26]

Johnston's advocacy began to resonate with others who were similarly concerned about undocumented youths' access to education. In fall 1999, a committee composed of a handful of HISD employees, a university professor, a few immigrant students, and some members from community-based organizations was formed. The group became known as the Coalition of Higher Education for Immigrant Students (shortened here to the Houston Coalition). Eventually, the group incorporated various community organizations, city government officials, private businesses, students, and a wide array of university and school district representatives. This broadly based coalition worked alongside others to provide the grassroots support needed to propel the state legislature into passing its pioneering in-state tuition policy in 2001.

The Houston Coalition's main objective was to "change state residency laws that exclude graduating high school immigrants from higher education and educate the community about the serious educational problems and obstacles faced by immigrant students."[27] One such problem was these students' dismal graduation rates in districts like HISD. Another constituted the central concern of this coalition: that undocumented students generally were not accepted by the state's institutions of higher education and that if they were allowed to enroll, they were charged nonresident tuition.[28] The Houston Coalition soon began

---

[26] (Johnston, 1999a).

[27] Johnston (2000), p. 1. Initial meetings established a set of priorities: formally establishing the group as the Coalition of Higher Education for Immigrant Students, raising money to fund scholarships for immigrant students, conducting community outreach (mainly in the Latino community), and bringing about changes in policy that would broaden access to higher education.

[28] For example, the downtown campus of the University of Houston, an open admissions institution, required undocumented immigrant students to fill out an

working to bring about changes in policies regarding postsecondary education, beginning with the Houston Community College System. They targeted the May 2000 Board of Trustees meeting at which board members were scheduled to again consider the issue Ticas, Noriega, and others had previously brought to their attention.

Following the approach taken with the DCCCD trustees, Coalition members planned to personally address the board. In preparation, Johnston contacted DCCCD Chancellor Wenrich, who provided back-

---

"Undocumented Immigration Form" in which the applicant certified that she/he had graduated from a Texas high school, was undocumented, and was aware that this would mean that nonresident tuition fees would apply. In compliance with rules from the THECB regarding competitive scholarships, the university also offered an academic scholarship, open to all students regardless of their immigration status, which allowed the selected scholar to receive a waiver of out-of-state tuition. Other schools, such as the University of Houston-Central and Prairie View A&M University, also allowed these students to enroll, but classified them as out-of-state residents or international students (Houston Area Forum for Advisors to Internationals, 2001). The University of Houston did not report the students' immigration status; instead, they were designated as "X-1," a limbo category (Houston Forum, 2001). Prairie View A&M University coded them "XX." Commenting on similar procedures at other universities, Badger and Yale-Loehr (2002, p. 12) note, "there has probably been a deliberate (and probably wise) decision not to maintain records on undocumented students." Beyond undocumented youth, documented immigrants also faced limitations imposed on scholarship funds made available by private organizations. As an example, organizers of the annual Houston Livestock Show and Rodeo changed the eligibility of their scholarship, which had been open to permanent residents, to require proof of citizenship (Bryant, 1997). This restriction, effective in the fall of 1996, came in the midst of anti-immigrant sentiments associated with the passage of the IIRIRA in 1996. In clear violation of the Supreme Court mandate in *Plyler v. Doe,* the scholarship committee placed the burden of immigration verification on school officials. Thus in order to implement this initial change, the language in the application stated: "Applicant must be a citizen of the United States and a resident of the state of Texas. If place of birth of applicant as indicated on the application and/or transcript is other than the United States, proof of citizenship must be certified by high school counselor or other appropriate school personnel" (Zuniga, 1996, p. 1A).

ground information and supplied copies of the DCCCD application for admission, which included a category for undocumented students. In addition, the Coalition publicized the meeting, encouraged community representatives to attend, and distributed a petition to gather signatures in support of the policy changes. Students, parents, HISD employees, businessmen, and representatives of community organizations in the heavily immigrant area of Gulfton in southwest Houston all were present at the May board meeting.[29] With the encouragement of Chancellor Burgos-Sasscer and board member Abel Dávila, the board voted unanimously (9–0) to allow undocumented students to enroll at in-district tuition rates, as long as these students could demonstrate that they had resided within the taxing district for at least one year while attending a local middle school or high school.[30]

The policy also permitted undocumented students not meeting such requirements to enroll, but this group would be required to pay out-of-district tuition and fees. The chancellor noted that the newly adopted modifications represented a system policy and not a state law. This meant that the state would not reimburse HCCS for the students enrolled under these guidelines. Like her counterpart in DCCCD, the chancellor expressed her support for the policy as an economic investment and social contribution: "Just like other residents, these people [undocumented immigrants] pay state and local sales taxes and many of their families pay property taxes that help support our community college."[31] Given that the college was expecting to enroll 500 to 700 students under this policy, the board's decision was estimated to require only $150,000 to cover additional expenses for faculty and classes.[32] As Chancellor Burgos-Sasscer observed, "This is a small price to pay

---

[29] Testifying on behalf of undocumented students were community worker Gloria Barrera, teacher David Johnston, immigration attorney Elizabeth Mendoza Macias, student Juan Rene Rodríguez, and parent Josephina Gonzalez. Attending but not testifying were businessman Gasper Mir, Patricia Rojas, representing Congressman Ken Bentsen's office, and this author, formerly an HISD employee (Houston Community College System, 2000c).

[30] Herrera (2000).

[31] Houston Community College System (2000d).

[32] See Hegstrom (2000b).

to help this many young people become better educated, more productive members of society."[33]

Not surprisingly, the new policy had its opponents. There were those who seem always to oppose immigrants and who, in this case, questioned the policy as a measure that would "subsidize illegals." The other current of opposition came from international students attending HCCS colleges at fees that were four times higher than in-district tuition. These students argued that the revision was unfair because it penalized them for "playing by the rules," unlike undocumented immigrants. As advocates for undocumented students explained, those attending HCCS under international student visas did not meet the policy's requirement that the prospective student have attended an in-state middle or high school at least a year prior to enrollment.[34] The new policy prevailed over the opposition. In August 2000, after learning of the changes at HCCS, San Jacinto Community College (SJCC) in the Houston area followed suit, making use of the same language to implement a policy of admitting qualifying undocumented students in its taxing district.[35]

Around the time HCCS was implementing these changes, Adán Carranza, a valedictorian from Madison High School, a primarily Black school in South Houston, made the news.[36] He had achieved his cov-

---

[33] Ibid.

[34] HCCS administrators also responded to the international students, explaining that unlike undocumented students, international students are temporary visitors who have come to the United States explicitly to attend school. Sandra Mulay Casey (1996, p. 142) explains the legal basis of this distinction: "an F-1 student [i.e., an international student] in obtaining her visa declares that she will not abandon her homeland and thus cannot form the requisite intent to make a certain state her home, whereas an undocumented student does abandon her homeland and is capable of forming such intent."

[35] See San Jacinto Community College (2000), p. 9. During fall 2000, 35 undocumented students enrolled under this policy and were eligible to apply for the Texas Public Education Grant (TPEG) using the financial aid form known as Free Application for Federal Student Aid (FAFSA). See Houston Area Forum for Advisors to Internationals (2001).

[36] I interviewed Carranza during fall 1999, when he did not know yet that he would be the school's valedictorian but was certain that he would place among

eted academic status while overcoming the difficulties he faced as an undocumented Mexican immigrant.[37] His case was widely covered by the media. Unlike Ticas, Carranza was a high school graduate, but like Ticas, he could not attend college because he was not able to afford the cost imposed by the inequitable application of state residency requirements.[38] Although these two young men had had different experiences in the Houston public school system, their divergent stories illustrated the same problem: For undocumented immigrants, the door to postsecondary education was effectively closed. The media attention that focused on Ticas and Carranza and other immigrant students who were graduating in the top 10 percent of their classes but not going on to college underscored the need to change the rules that required certain high school graduates to pay international tuition and fees in order to attend state schools.[39] These real-life stories provided the vital "human

---

the top five graduating seniors (Rincón, 1999). As his May 2000 graduation approached, Carranza was featured in two *Houston Chronicle* articles (see Hegstrom, 2000a, 2000b).

[37] The following year, 2001, thanks to increasing efforts on behalf of this population, HISD began to notice and publicize the increasing number of immigrant, and undocumented, students who were achieving the high status of valedictorian. During the 2000–2001 school year, "six of the thirty-two HISD high school valedictorians are immigrant students. Thirteen out of thirty two valedictorians are former English Language Learners. Nine of the 13 students came to school speaking Spanish as a first language and were served in the district's Bilingual Education Programs. Three of the students speak languages other than Spanish and were served in ESL programs" (Alexander, 2001).

[38] Carranza had planned to attend Texas A&M University (TAMU) and eventually become a doctor but was not able to afford the $21,000 nonresident tuition that the university charged (Hegstrom, 2000a). After information about his case was disclosed to the media, he received calls from TAMU and University of Houston main campus officials to consider "possible full ride scholarships" (Hegstrom, 2000b).

[39] Also like Ticas, in the end, Carranza did attend college because he received financial aid—a full scholarship from Texas Southern University, a historically Black college and university in Houston. As long-time advocate for international and noncitizen students, Dr. Iris Perkins of TSU indicated, "He is the sort of student we want to attract" (Hegstrom, 2000b). Carranza was also ap-

element" needed to galvanize support for a campaign aimed at finally resolving this longstanding issue.[40]

For Rick Noriega and Houston Coalition supporters, the next step was to focus on bringing about change at the state level. To lay the groundwork for this legislative change, they turned their attention first to the Texas Higher Education Coordinating Board. As the next section shows, the tireless work the Houston Coalition and Rep. Noriega undertook with the THECB was critically important in paving the way for the legislature's eventual passage of the first in-state tuition law in the country.

POLICY CHANGES AT THE TEXAS HIGHER EDUCATION COORDINATING BOARD

In the summer of 2000, soon after the victory in the Houston Community College System and long before January 2001, when state legislators began gathering in Austin for the opening of the 77th session, Noriega and Houston Coalition members began actively pressing for changes within the THECB. Prior to that summer, the board had maintained that undocumented immigrants were not allowed to establish domicile in the United States and thus under the state residency laws were not allowed to establish residency in Texas for tuition purposes. In addition, according to the THECB's interpretation of the state's Education Code, U.S. citizens who were children of undocumented immigrants could not be classified as residents for tuition purposes because determination of their residency was based on their parents' legal status.[41] Thus, although there were no statues explicitly banning undocumented students from enrolling at institutions of higher education,

---

proached by the Fant Foundation, a small nonprofit seeking to help ten underprivileged students every year. Carranza, who mowed lawns after school to help supplement his family's income, was stunned by the multiple scholarship offers he received. Unfortunately while many students were in his predicament, few gained this kind of support and attention (Hegstrom, 2000b).

[40] Rick Noriega (personal communication, October 2002).

[41] Similar provisions were included in the California code, forcing U.S. citizen children of undocumented parents to be classified as nonresidents for tuition purposes and negatively affecting their eligibility for state financial aid (see Chapter Five).

their classification as nonresidents, and the cost associated with that, constituted a de facto ban.

Noriega's strategy involved an initial focus on those immigrants who had some kind of paperwork pending with immigration authorities. He wrote to the THECB, expressing concerns regarding the negative impact of Section 54.057 of the Texas Education Code, which stated that only "aliens who have filed with the proper immigration authorities a declaration of intention to become a citizen may be considered [as an] in-state resident student."[42] This requirement was an especially grave obstacle, given the backlog in INS processing, which could and often did last years. In the meantime, tens of thousands of potential students were denied the opportunity to attend college.[43] Noriega's letter deliberately called attention to the fact that immigrants who have submitted paperwork to the INS typically do so to initiate the process of becoming citizens. Thus, they should be allowed to attend college at in-state tuition rates while their applications for citizenship are being processed. Noriega also approached the Mexican American Legal Caucus, and he urged his fellow legislators to write letters to the THECB, pointing out that the board's language excluded immigrants who had formally signaled their intent to become citizens.

On July 13, 2000, Noriega, along with David Johnston and this author, attended a THECB meeting in order to personally address the members. He reiterated the problem facing undocumented students who could not afford to pay the steep fees required of those designated as international students in all but two Texas community college districts. THECB Commissioner Don Brown responded by describing DCCCD and HCCS as taking a risk by allowing undocumented students to pay

---

[42] Rick Noriega (2000a).

[43] The backlog at immigration services is longstanding because the number of applicants exceeds the visas available under the annual allocations disfavoring in particular immigrants from the Third World. For what the immigration service terms the fourth preference category (U.S. citizens petitioning their siblings), an immigration attorney observes: "This category has the most significant backlogs. Currently applicants from most countries have waited twelve years; however, for the Philippines the wait has been twice that amount" (Parsons, 2005). See also Hegstrom (2000d).

in-state tuition.[44] In his view, a person had to establish domicile in compliance with federal laws and state rules in order to receive in-state tuition privileges. Other board members argued that the THECB did not have the authority to make changes on behalf of undocumented students. This kind of policymaking, in their opinion, was the responsibility of the state legislature.

USING SPECIAL PROGRAMS TO EXPAND ACCESS TO HIGHER EDUCATION

Besides suggesting changes in the regulations for students in the process of becoming permanent residents, Noriega also inquired as to whether existing programs could be expanded to include the state's major metropolitan areas. Specifically, he suggested modifying a THECB special program that allowed the state to offer in-state tuition rates to certain nonresidents. This program has two components: (1) it allows universities on the Texas-Mexico border to enroll Mexican students at in-state tuition rates, and (2) it allows up to two Mexican students per 1,000 enrollment to qualify for in-state tuition fees at nonborder universities.[45] Using the University of Houston as an example,

---

[44] Commissioner Brown's remarks during the THECB regular quarterly meeting on July 13, 2000.

[45] This reciprocity program had been initiated, with the Texas' Legislature approval, in 1987 in response to the devaluation of the national currency in Mexico (peso). The program has a special subsection for Mexican citizens who live near the border and who can show proof of financial need. Mexican students who have applied for U.S. citizenship or permanent residency are not eligible for the program because its purpose is to benefit students who have maintained ties to their home country and intend to return to it. Program participants are eligible to receive an international student visa (F-1), although they are not required to have one. For universities located on the Texas-Mexico border, there is no limit to the number of students who can be enrolled under this policy. For schools that are not adjacent to the U.S.-Mexico border, the limit is 2 Mexican students per 1,000 in the general student body. At the University of Texas at El Paso (a border institution), this state initiative was implemented under the PASE program (Programa de Asistencia Estudiantil para Mexicanos—Program of Educational Assistance for Mexicans). At UTEP, the enrollment has increased from 223 students in 1987 to 1,150 in 1996, to 1,375

Noriega noted that expanding the program to that campus would yield an average of 66 Mexican students, given that university's enrollment of 33,000. In other words, according to this existing rule, state colleges and universities could admit more Mexican nationals, regardless of their immigration status, than was now occurring. He proposed that the THECB increase the number of enrollees allocated under this program, thus allowing more Mexican students in areas with high numbers of immigrants, such as Houston and Dallas, to attend college.

After further deliberations, the board left intact the special program granting in-state tuition to certain Mexican students. They did, though, agree to partially roll back the additional residency requirement, making individuals in the last stages of the permanent residency process eligible for in-state tuition.[46] Commissioner Brown's written explanation of the new policy specified that immigrants who were in the last stage of becoming permanent residents would qualify for in-state tuition fees as long as these applicants received approval from the immigration authorities. The Commissioner reaffirmed the THECB's position that anyone who had "initiated [only] the first step to be declared an immigrant [could not] be considered to have met the intent of the statute."[47] In other words, applicants who had filed with immigration authorities and had waited for years due to bureaucratic backlogs remained ineligible. Still, the revision in the rules seems to have been made at least in part in recognition of the inequitable conditions facing immigrant students. In explaining the new policy in a later communication to registrars, admissions officers, and chief fiscal officers in Texas, Commissioner Brown acknowledged that immigrants' long residence in Texas resulted in tax contributions and an overall benefit to the economy. He noted, as well, the dissonance between laws that allowed immigrant students to attend K-12 regardless of their immigration status

---

in 1999 (UTEP, 1997, 2000). In 2001, the program enrolled 1,366 students at UTEP; this increased to 1,817, 10% of the total university enrollment, in 2003 (Ramirez, 2004).

[46] Rojas (2000).

[47] Brown (2000a).

and state regulations that charged them nonresident fees at institutions of higher learning.[48]

In summary, the THECB's ruling in the summer of 2000, despite its importance, was beneficial only to those who had filed paperwork that had been formally acknowledged by immigration authorities. As it pertained to undocumented youth, the board continued to interpret state statutes narrowly, claiming that "undocumented students have to be considered nonresidents."[49] Undaunted by this slow progress, Noriega and Houston Coalition organizers began devising a strategy to move the issue to the state legislature. This phase of preparatory work is described in the next section.

THE GROUNDWORK FOR STATEWIDE LEGISLATION

The changes in admissions and tuition policies in the Dallas and Houston community college districts had grown from the frustrations of immigrant students, especially the undocumented. While some members of the educational community had organized to support the students in their fight for nondiscriminatory tuition fees, it was not until after the victory at the HCCS and the subsequent changes at the THECB level that the possibility of real improvement became evident. The Houston Coalition became the rallying organization for undocumented youth rights and Representative Noriega assumed a key leadership position in the campaign for new policies at the state level.

The Houston Coalition began outreach activities to lay the groundwork for a bill that would make college education affordable for undocumented students across Texas. The goal of the new legislation was to level the playing field for undocumented students by uncoupling state residency requirements from immigration status and instead requiring that students simply demonstrate high school attendance in the state as the basis for in-state tuition eligibility. The coalition began raising awareness about the need for legislation in educational conferences

---

[48] At that time, a credit hour for a student classified as resident cost $40, while a nonresident paid $255 (Caldwell, 2001). Thus, undocumented immigrant students would be required to pay as much as $6,000 per year more than their peers who were eligible for in-state tuition. This sum was simply too large for most to afford.

[49] Brown (2000b).

across the state and in monthly meetings that brought together diverse groups associated with school districts, community colleges, universities, businesses, and advocacy organizations.[50] In November 2000, after their victory before the THECB, the Coalition approached Noriega, who had already begun to investigate the possibility of introducing a state law, to discuss possible legislative alternatives.[51] Members also contacted state representatives in the Dallas and Houston areas and city officials, including Leonel Castillo, former INS Commissioner and then educational advisor for the city of Houston, in part to solicit their help in mapping out a statewide strategy and to widen the base of support for statewide legislation.

Meanwhile, Noriega was reaching out to organizations such as the National Association of Latino Elected Officials and the Mexican American Legislative Caucus. In December 2000, he held a preliminary meeting for people interested in lifting the additional residency burdens placed on undocumented students. Preparing the way for state legislation also included gathering persuasive data. During the THECB deliberations that led to initial policy changes, board members had expressed concerns about the number of students who would be affected by the changes. As plans for state legislation took shape, Noriega, together with the Houston Coalition, sought support from academics, entrusting them with the task of determining more information about the potential undocumented population who would benefit from a change in the law. In collaboration with the Houston Coalition, researchers at the University of Houston designed a questionnaire that was administered at HISD high schools with high immigrant populations. The purpose of the study was to "inform school administrators, legislators and other policy makers about the number and social characteristics of undocumented students and their aspirations for a college education."[52] The

---

[50] Participants included representatives from the Houston Community College System, Prairie View A&M University, University of Houston-Central, and University of Houston-Downtown. Educators from the Houston Independent School District were also represented. Community service providers included El Centro del Corazón, GANO-Carecen, and the Mexican Consulate, among many others (Johnston, 2000).

[51] Alanis (2004).

[52] Mindiola et al. (2002).

results of the survey were used to prepare a report that assessed the fiscal and social impact of barring undocumented students from attending college. This "white paper" provided legislators with research-based arguments on the need for an in-state tuition policy.[53]

THE EVOLUTION OF THE FIRST IN-STATE TUITION BILL

On January 24, 2001, Rep. Noriega introduced HB 901, an in-state tuition bill, into the Texas legislature. Domingo Garcia (Dallas) also introduced a bill (HB 158) with a similar intent.[54] Because their proposals addressed the same issue, the Higher Education Committee Chairwoman, Irma Rangel (Kingsville), negotiated an agreement between Noriega and Garcia to file their bills under the same number and with the same language.[55] This also meant that her committee would hold only one hearing for what became HB 1403. Republican Representatives Fred Hill (Richardson), Elvira Reyna (Mesquite), and Kino Flores (Mission) added their names to the list of co-sponsors.[56] State Senator

---

[53] A Harris County Tax Office paper titled "Undocumented Valedictorians" had been released the previous year. From a largely human capital perspective, the study interpreted changes in the laws as a way to allow undocumented students to acquire better jobs and contribute more to the economy. Many Houston Coalition members encouraged this perspective, supplying stories of undocumented valedictorians (Harris County Tax Office, 2000).

[54] Rep. Bailey also filed HB 528, a bill relating to the tuition charged to foreign students attending junior colleges. This proposal sought to waive out-of-state tuition for Mexican residents who demonstrated financial need. The bill's goal was addressed by Noriega's HB 901, as it pertained to all institutions of higher education and was not limited to nationals of specific countries.

[55] Garcia's bill also proposed classifying noncitizens as residents after high school completion in Texas and extended state financial aid eligibility to these students. A section of the bill sought to provide equal access to financial aid in the form of tuition waivers, student loans, scholarships or grants (Garcia, 2001a).

[56] Co-authors included Debra Danburg (Houston), Joe Deshotel (Port Arthur), Harryette Ehrhardt (Dallas), Scott Hochberg (Houston), Carl Isett (Lubbock), John Amos Longoria (San Antonio), Trey Martinez Fischer (San Antonio), Glen Maxey (Austin), Joe Moreno (Houston), Manny Najera (El Paso), Dora Olivo (Missouri City), Robert Puente (San Antonio), Arthur Reyna (Mesquite),

Leticia Van de Putte (San Antonio) introduced the Senate version of the bill (SB 1526) almost two months later.[57] The purpose of SB 1526, filed with identical language as a companion bill to the House version, was to uncouple immigration status from eligibility for in-state tuition fees.[58]

The initial version of HB 1403 proposed the following amendment to the Texas Education Code:

> . . . an individual shall be classified as a Texas resident until the individual establishes a residence outside this state if the individual resided with the individual's parent, guardian or conservator while attending public or private high school in this state and:
> (1) graduated from a public or private high school or received the equivalent of a high school diploma in this state; and
> (2) resided in this state for at least one year between the first day the person attended a public or private high school in this state and the day the person graduated from a public or private high school in this state or received the equivalent of a high school diploma.[59]

The bill also proposed to amend Section 54.057(a) of the TEC, by removing the requirement that a noncitizen be a permanent resident or have filed an intention to become a citizen in order to qualify for in-state tuition fees. Under the original language of HB 1403, those who had applied with immigration authorities, or who had a petition pending with "the Immigration and Naturalization Service to attain lawful status

---

Jim Solis (Harlingen), Carlos Uresti (San Antonio) and Mike Villarreal (San Antonio) (Keel, 2001a).

[57] Co-authoring the measure were Senators Mario Gallegos (Houston), David Sibley (Waco), and Tedd Staples (Dallas) (Keel, 2001b).

[58] Van de Putte (2001). The Senate bill also incorporated the University of Texas at San Antonio into the pilot program enrolling two Mexican nationals per 1,000 enrollments.

[59] Noriega (2001a).

under federal immigration law [would have] the same privilege of qualifying for resident status for tuition and fee purposes."[60]

Finally, HB 1403 maintained the provisions that permitted Mexican citizens to pay in-state tuition at border universities or at any of the schools in the Texas State Technical College System and sought to expand the program to any county with a population of over 100,000. The term "undocumented student" deliberately was not a part of the language of the bill, as the intent of the new law was to make immigration status irrelevant in the determination of residency for tuition purposes. Similarly, the bill did not offer preferential treatment to any group, as it required undocumented students to meet the same residency criteria as all other students. As a memorandum from Representative Garcia's office stated, the bill would allow undocumented students to establish "equal status with a U.S. citizen in meeting Texas' residency requirements for in-state tuition."[61]

THE CAMPAIGN IN SUPPORT OF HB 1403

One of the Houston Coalition's first initiatives involved participation in a city-wide event targeting Latinos in search of college opportunities. The event, held February 24, 2001 and organized by the Houston Hispanic Forum, provided coalition members with an opportunity to inform the community about the pending legislation. Noriega spoke at the event, and hundreds of signatures were collected in support of the bill. The Texas chapter of the National Association of Hispanic Nurses played a major role, gathering over 200 letters of support that were mailed to the Texas governor's office. Other organizations, such as the Society of Hispanic Professional Engineers, provided critical support by participating in the advocacy efforts as well as by reaching out to other organizations and promoting the Houston Coalition's efforts.[62]

Throughout this period, in various venues, supporters of HB 1403 noted that its passage would benefit the state by increasing the pool of students eligible for college. Nevertheless, some reservations were expressed. At a meeting of advisors to international students, for instance, a THECB representative commented, "The problem with this [House

---

[60] Ibid., p. 1.

[61] Garcia (2001b), p. 1.

[62] Hispanic Forum (2001).

Bill 1403] is that it will open the door for many people to apply and benefit . . ."[63] Opponents' concerns regarding costs and uncertainty over how the law would benefit the state led supporters to frame the bill's advantages mainly in economic terms. Using a fact sheet with 1986–1998 data (authored by the Intercultural Development Research Association), one Houston Coalition advocate pointed out that 1.2 million students had dropped out in 12 years, costing the state $319 billion dollars.[64] Similarly, based on figures from the THECB showing an initial enrollment of 3,154 immigrant students under the new policies, Harris County Tax Assessor Paul Bettencourt forecast a contribution ranging from $1.2 to $1.7 billion, resulting from the increased acquisition of higher degrees that would in turn lead to higher incomes and an increase in tax payments associated with the purchase of homes and related types of consumerism.[65] In addition to the financial argument, letters from advocates pointed out that since some community colleges were already accepting undocumented students, the focus would be on in-state tuition rates at four-year institutions of higher education. A related supporting argument was that the new law would relieve college admissions officers of the inappropriate responsibility of acting as immigration enforcement agents.

Additional support activities included a forum in February 2001 in which the Houston Coalition, in collaboration with the University of Houston, addressed admissions counselors and registrars from universities and colleges in the Houston area to help them prepare for students who would be registering in the fall under the new provisions, if the proposed bill passed. THECB representatives explained the previously

---

[63] Ibid.

[64] Johnston (2001d).

[65] The involvement of more conservative figures such as Paul Bettencourt exemplified the bipartisan support that the issue enjoyed, along with the diversity of the backers in the Houston area. Bettencourt had been approached initially by Marcelo Marini, director of programming for Telemundo, to help an undocumented student. After learning of the student's case, Bettencourt became convinced that the law needed to change. Besides conducting the study and sending his staff to share information with groups of immigrant advocates, Bettencourt volunteered to speak on conservative radio shows on behalf of the bill (Daniel Morales, personal communication, 2002).

adopted changes that allowed persons who had filed petitions with the INS to receive in-state tuition fees at district colleges and state universities. Rep. Noriega, who also participated in the forum, used the opportunity to explain the potential benefits of HB 1403. Some of the arguments made earlier in support of the bill reemerged. These included the creation of an educated workforce, higher tax revenues for the state, and lower high school attrition rates. The overall argument again posited that the bill would help make immigrant students productive members of Texas society. Research into advocacy efforts in other states, particularly California, as well as an awareness of the work underway in Texas, made it apparent that the state was poised to break new ground. Testimony at a hearing before the state legislature's Higher Education Committee, described in the next section, confirmed that the time was ripe for change.

HIGHER EDUCATION COMMITTEE HEARINGS

On March 13, 2001, dozens of undocumented immigrant high school students from all over the state converged at the Texas Capitol to tell their stories at a hearing before the Higher Education Committee.[66] The student who had initially brought the issue to Noriega, Rosendo Ticas from Houston, was first to speak, followed by high school students from Dallas, the Rio Grande valley, and El Paso. Students who had already graduated, and even those who had applications on file with the Immigration and Naturalization Service, overcame their fear of being deported and described their cases. The students, who represented the countries of El Salvador, Ethiopia, Mexico, and Peru, were clear proof that the concerns the bill addressed were not limited to Mexicans or Spanish-speaking immigrants. Other persons also testified before the Higher Education Committee in support of the bill. These included professors from various universities, chancellors' representatives, members of Latino civil rights organizations, and the lawyers who had provided legal counsel regarding the wording of the bill.[67]

---

[66] Berger (2001a).

[67] Students testifying included Lourdes Aguinaco, Maria Bautista, Olivia Bautista, Olga Lidia Cardoso, Edyael Casaperalta, Dulce Ibarra, Lissette Moreno, Alem Tewoldeberhan, and Rosendo Ticas. Other individuals who testified included Joseph Berra, immigration attorney with the Mexican Ameri-

Much of the discussion before the committee centered on whether the students' parents paid sales and property taxes and on the potential impact of the bill on the problem of school attrition.[68] A point reiterated by supporters, including MALDEF's general counsel, was that the bill did not grant preferential treatment to the new college population, as all students would now be meeting the same requirements. More important, supporters emphasized that there was no cost attached to the bill and therefore HB 1403 would require no additional funding appropriations. Better yet, freshmen entering within this category, who would not have otherwise attended a postsecondary institution, constituted a new source of revenue for the state's colleges and universities. At the end of the hearing, Chairwoman Rangel noted that the entire testimony favored the undocumented students. "You have made this a wonderful hearing," she told the students. "Every member of this committee is in favor of this bill. Take pride in the fact that no one testified against this bill."[69]

The bill was modified as it advanced through the legislature (some of the more significant modifications are discussed in the next section). Despite the changes, the initial intention of allowing immigrant students access to in-state tuition rates survived. A month after the hearing, students and their advocates, including the Texas Immigrant and Refugee Coalition, the Houston Coalition, and other groups, organized

---

can Legal Defense and Educational Fund (MALDEF), Francisco Perez with the San Francisco de Asis Episcopal Church, Felicia Escobar with the National Council of La Raza (NCLR), Felipe Reyes with the HCCS, Lico Reyes with LULAC District III, Civil Rights Division, Dr. Angela Valenzuela, University of Texas at Austin professor, and Dr. William Wenrich, chancellor of the DCCCD (Higher Education Committee, 2001). Present but not testifying were, among others, Terri Agüero with Houston ISD, Charles Galindo with the Society of Hispanic Professional Engineers, ESL teacher David Johnston, Lorenzo Cano and Rebecca Trevino with the Center for Mexican American Studies at the University of Houston (Central Campus), and this author.

[68] In a letter of support, David Johnston addressed the economic concern, noting the irony of the situation: "one must be documented to work [but] not having documents is never [an] excuse for not paying one's taxes" (Johnston, 2001c, p. 2).

[69] Rangel (2001).

a lobbying day in Austin to support passage of the bill.[70] The lobbying day also sought to alleviate some concerns raised by opponents of HB 1403, particularly the fear that expanding the program that allowed enrollment of Mexicans in nonborder universities would amount to subsidizing the tuition of nonresidents.

On May 7, 2001, the Senate's education committee held a hearing that addressed HB 1403. Committee Chair Senator Teel Bivens (Amarillo) objected to Rep. Noriega's preference for the original language of the bill, which specified only one year of high school attendance for residency. More significantly, Bivens sought to remove a critical provision that would allow undocumented students to be classified as residents for tuition purposes. In the final legislative phases, the bill was in danger of being stripped of its capacity to benefit the undocumented high school population, making it simply a positive measure for those who had started the adjustment process with the immigration service. A double compromise that allowed the bill's passage was reached. The residency time requirement was increased to three years;[71] and undocumented students who were to benefit under this bill would have to fill out an affidavit indicating that they intended to adjust their immigration status as soon as they were eligible to do so.[72] One month after

---

[70] Participants included students, administrators, and teachers from school districts and universities, members of immigrant advocacy groups, and representatives from unions such as the United Farm Workers. HISD participants included Johnston and Sherman Elementary School Principal Alma Lara, along with this author, who brought students from HISD schools and joined main organizer Adriana Cadena and Houston area supporter Ana Nuñez. The lobbying day also included a focus on the importance of supporting legislation that would allow undocumented immigrants to obtain driver's licenses.

[71] Berger (2001b).

[72] Testifying at the May Senate committee hearing were Daniel Morales from the Office of the Harris County Office of Tax Assessor/Collector, Paul Bettencourt and Vincent Ramos, executive director of Texas LULAC. Registering but not testifying were Jack Campbell for the Texas Association of Business and Chambers of Commerce; Bill Carpenter, assistant superintendent for governmental relations (Houston ISD); Richard Daly, executive director of Texas Catholic Conference; Anne Dunkelberg with the Center for Public Policy Priorities; Matthew Emal, assistant director of State Federal Relations for the City

the last changes were made, Governor Rick Perry signed HB 1403 into law. On June 16, 2001, it became Texas Education Code 54.052.[73] The door of higher education was now partially open to those immigrant students who met the requirements of the new law.

CONFLICT OVER THE INTERPRETATION OF TEC SECTION 54.052

The passage of HB 1403 was an important event in the fight to secure immigrant students equal access to higher education. Implementation of its provisions, however, almost immediately proved challenging. Since the bill's passage, the THECB has chosen to interpret Section 54.052 narrowly, limiting the number of students eligible under its provisions. The THECB's approach, which places additional hurdles in the way of potentially eligible undocumented students, the vast majority of whom are of Latino descent, appears to contradict the board's own stated concern over this group's lagging educational achievement.[74] These restrictions are in keeping with the history of the state's educational institutions' resistance to increasing access for underrepresented students. Institutional disruption of desegregation plans, busing, and bilingual education are a few examples of this historic disregard among Texas educational entities in fulfilling their stated institutional mission.[75]

---

of Houston; William Harrell, counsel for the American Civil Liberties Union; Rene Lara, legislative liaison with the Texas Federation of Teachers; Joe Sanchez with MALDEF, Lauren Smith with the Association of Texas Professional Educators, Michael White, attorney with the Greater Houston Partnership, and Barbara Hines, lecturer and immigration attorney with the University of Texas Law School.

[73] While the governor's endorsement might seem to have been supportive of immigrant rights, it was a concession given his veto of a driver's license bill that would have benefited a larger number of undocumented immigrants, workers and students alike.

[74] The THECB has proclaimed in its Closing the Gaps campaign that it seeks to narrow the differences in college attainment for minority populations, especially Latinos. As a group, Latinos show the lowest proportional participation in Texas's institutions of higher education.

[75] Texas, like most other states, has a long history of undermining efforts to expand public education, including higher education, to include minority and

Supporters of the original initiative identified three areas of particular concern regarding HB 1403. Two of them involve the interpretation of the law adopted by the THECB. The first involved the new Section 54.052(j)'s specification that high school students must have lived in Texas with parents, guardians, or conservators in order to be considered state residents. This requirement, demanded by opponents of the bill, was intended to differentiate between immigrant students who came because of their parents' decisions and those who arrived independently. During meetings with the THECB to discuss implementation of this new section of the Texas Education Code, immigrant advocates explained that many immigrant students live with relatives such as grandparents, aunts and uncles, older siblings, and cousins.[76] These relatives often are themselves undocumented, which would make it unlikely that they would be willing to go before a court of law to obtain legal guardianship of another undocumented person. Despite being

---

disenfranchised populations. The scope of issues is wide and includes matters related to school finance, bilingual education, and affirmative action, among many others. As an example, during the 1970s, school districts in Texas, and specifically HISD, attempted to thwart desegregation efforts mandated by the *Brown* decision two decades earlier (see San Miguel, 2001). And, in 1981, a federal district court found that Texas denied equal educational opportunity to Mexican American students, who were discriminated against on the basis of their national origin and language—see *United States v. Texas*, 506 F. Supp. 405 (E.D. Tex. 1981). See also Chapter Two, for a discussion of the state's efforts to deny public education to undocumented children and how this eventually launched the case of *Plyler v. Doe*.

[76] Regarding the THECB interpretation to require legal guardianship of eligible immigrant students, an e-mail communication sent from State Representative Noriega's chief of staff clarified the intent of the law: "the THECB states that they believe this was legislative intent and it has been made abundantly clear to them that it was not" (Noriega, 2001c). A subsequent letter from Noriega to Commissioner Don Brown stated, "Low income and minority children are more likely than their affluent peers to reside with relatives other than a parent, are less likely to afford or have access to legal remedies; therefore they are more likely to be affected by the new rule. [Further] a court order has not been required previously to establish residency" (Noriega to Brown, August 28, 2001).

made aware of the informal guardianship issue, the THECB decided to deny access to this significant subset of the potentially eligible immigrant population.[77] Denying students estranged from their parents and placed in the care of relatives access to postsecondary education only aggravates their already onerous circumstances.[78]

---

[77] Advocates for the Mexican and Central American immigrant community in Houston sent a joint letter requesting clarification of specific aspects of HB 1403, in particular the requirement of legal guardianship for the student: "Given the different family situations in our immigrant community, we know that many immigrant students live with family members who are not their parents. It would be very difficult and a lengthy process for these relatives to obtain Legal Custody dictated by a court in order to prove their value as Guardians" (Aguiluz and Reyes, 2001). Their position was supported by Project Grad, a large national nonprofit with sites in many Houston high schools. In a letter to Noriega's office they wondered, given the interpretation of the THECB, whether the original legislation made reference to a "legal guardian." Referring to the intent of the law, they stated, "Many arguments we heard in testimony reflected the fact that children do not have a say as to their immigration status. Likewise, in some of these families and extended families, *children do not choose under whose roof they live in* [bold and italics in original]" (Morris, 2001). In a July 10, 2001 meeting called by Representative Noriega's office, the THECB's general counsel argued that if undocumented students really wanted to attend college, they would seek legal guardianship from their relatives because this was a "simple process." This argument presupposes that immigrants come to the U.S. in order to avail themselves of benefits like a college education. On the contrary, and as amply demonstrated by research cited in Chapter One, immigrants come mainly in search of jobs. They generally reject anything that appears to threaten their livelihood, such as going to a court of law. In the end, though, the THECB General Counsel's narrow interpretation prevailed.

[78] In Texas, students are eligible to receive a public education until they turn twenty-one, but many school districts deny admission to students who are over eighteen, the compulsory age. The Texas Education Code states that "(a) A student is entitled to the benefits of the Foundation School Program if the student is 5 years of age or older and under 21 years of age on September 1 of the school year and has not graduated from high school" (Texas Education Code, 1995). In many instances, recent immigrants in this age bracket (over eighteen)

A second challenge involves provisions in Section 54.052(j), sub-sections (1) and (3). The first ties residency to completion of three years of high school in Texas. The three-year provision encompasses students from countries that have a long history of immigration to the United States, such as Mexico. But students who have a more recent history of immigration and those who have completed only one or two years of high school in the state are automatically disqualified, significantly lessening the law's potential impact—and thus also lowering the chances that these students will be motivated to graduate from high school or even aspire to attend college. Subsection (j)(3) adds another restriction. It specifically provides that students who attended college before the fall of 2001, when the bill became law, were not to be grand-fathered and therefore could not benefit from in-state tuition fees. Poli-cymakers justified their decision to exclude students who had overcome obstacles imposed on them by their immigration status, had started col-lege before the fall of 2001, and were paying international fees, by ar-guing that the bill could not cover everyone and that if those who were already attending college were allowed to pay in-state tuition and fees, the universities would lose money.[79]

The argument that grandfathering previously enrolled students would decrease a university's revenue is flawed. First, the number of undocumented high school graduates attending college at international tuition rates prior to the passage of the law was negligible. Therefore, a loss of revenue from this source could not be significant and certainly would be offset by the newly admitted students who would be paying in-state tuition.[80] Furthermore, before passage of HB 1403, most un-

---

are denied admission to high school on the grounds that they will not be able to complete enough high school credits in the remaining time and thus will be-come discouraged and drop out. The inclusion of GED recipients in HB 1403 was an important victory for students in this predicament as that route remains their only option.

[79] Some of the supportive legislators and their staffers felt that by striking this small group out, the bill would be able to pass the House Committee on Educa-tion because it would have a "zero fiscal note." In other words, the bill's sup-porters could claim that the new law would not require any additional funding.

[80] The Texas Legislative Budget Board calculated that "resident tuition paid by new students who would not have otherwise attended universities is estimated

documented students did not attend universities due to the cost, and the few who did, and paid international tuition and fees, soon dropped out.[81] The original intent of the law to broaden educational opportunities was thus diminished by the decision not to grandfather previously enrolled students, since the continuing high cost of their education would eventually lead undocumented students who were not grandfathered to drop out, or prevent them from ever applying for admission in the first place.[82]

The THECB's interpretation of HB 1403's limitations, particularly Section 54.052(j)(3), widens the restrictions still more, gratuitously excluding students the bill was in fact meant to cover. The board determined that "high school students taking dual-enrollment classes prior to fall 2001 as well as high school graduates or GED students who have taken summer 2001 classes" were not eligible under the provisions of subsection (j)(3), and thus would have to pay international tuition and fees if they enrolled in college.[83] In a letter to Commissioner Brown, Rep. Noriega explained that during the legislature's discussion of HB 1403, it was clear that the language referring to currently attending students "was meant to include only those who were enrolled as full time students prior to the fall 2001 semester."[84] Moreover, Noriega stressed, "It simply was never considered that such language could be interpreted to include 2001 high school graduates, just because they qualified for advance courses in high school."[85] The board acknowledged that their interpretation of the law "penalize[d] students who showed initiative" by taking college courses before high school graduation. Nevertheless, it maintained the narrow interpretation of the provision,

---

to be $811,340 in fiscal year 2002 and $1,378,600 in fiscal year 2003. . . . The additional General Revenue formula costs for new students at both universities and community colleges is estimated to be $14,462,676 in fiscal year and $16,730,478 in fiscal year 2005" (Keel, 2001a).

[81] Rodriguez (1992); Mladinich (1995).

[82] De los Santos (2004).

[83] "Under dual enrollment programs, bright, achievement-oriented high school students can take college courses while they are still in high school" (THECB, 2001, p. 8). This statement, however, did not apply to undocumented students.

[84] Noriega (2001c).

[85] Ibid.

arguing that someone with prior college credit technically was not an "entering student" and thus could not qualify for possible classification as eligible for in-state tuition rates. The board's exclusionary view prevailed, despite objections from Noriega and other supporters of HB 1403.[86]

A final provision of the new policy also merits comment. The law states that to qualify for in-state tuition fees, undocumented students must file an affidavit declaring that they intend to apply for permanent residence as soon as that is a viable option. This requirement was added when discussions leading to the passage of HB 1403 showed that at least one member of the legislature would withhold support unless there were assurances that students would not leave the country and cause the state to forfeit the investment in their education.[87] It is a widely accepted fact that undocumented persons typically seek to legalize their immigration status without any additional prodding from the government. After all, doing so is in their best interests. Requiring that students formally reveal their undocumented status, on the other hand, seriously burdens these young people, since such a public declaration

---

[86] A related problem was faced by future HB 1403 students who could not qualify for dual credit and concurrent enrollment at the local community colleges because they had not "graduated" and thus technically were not covered by the bill. In Austin, education advocates were able to have the Austin Community College (ACC) "waive tuition and fees for this group" (Kinslow, 2004). This meant that the college would not get a reimbursement from the state for the total hours in which these students enrolled under the Early College Start program. In its letter to the AISD Superintendent, the ACC interim president [urged AISD to "work with its community advocates to encourage local legislators to address this issue in the future so that the funding issue for community colleges will be *treated the same* [italics added] for both documented and undocumented students participating in Early College Start opportunities while still in high school" (Kinslow, 2004).

[87] This demand that immigrants affirm their intention to legalize their status is almost identical to the one imposed on noncitizens in New York and challenged in *Nyquist v. Mauclet* (1974) (see Chapter Two). The affidavit also resembles a form required of undocumented students enrolling at the University of Houston-Downtown (UHD) under pre-HB 1403 provisions which allowed them to register as nonresident students.

of their status would make them immediately subject to deportation. At the same time, this provision exposes a central paradox that haunts much of the in-state tuition legislation—namely, that a group of people barred by federal law from even being in the country are required by state law to affirm their intention of staying here.

IMPLEMENTATION OF HB 1403

By spring 2007, almost six years since the passage of HB 1403, a total of 11,139 immigrant students in Texas had at one point registered and begun attending the state's colleges and universities at the same tuition rates paid by fellow high school graduates and other eligible students.[88] As this section explains, this number would be much higher if the state's K-12 public education system better fulfilled its role as a disseminator of information—to teaching and administrative staff, as well as to students and parents. This gap points to the fact that counselors and other school personnel do not effectively inform the thousands of potentially eligible high school students about the law's provisions or about changes made to the state's education code in 2005 (described below), in part because they themselves lack the necessary knowledge and training to do so. Many eligible students report encountering disinterest or even outright hostility among counselors, registrars, and other school administrators in their quest to enter higher education.[89] At the postsecondary level, improvement is also necessary. The THECB has yet to take an active, positive role in promoting all students' access to postsecondary education.[90]

---

[88] Castillo (2007).

[89] The barriers immigrant students and their parents face in secondary schools are documented by Ruiz-de-Velasco, Fix and Chu Clewell (2000). In their research on immigrant students in U.S. secondary schools, they address issues of postsecondary access faced by these students given their lack of knowledge about the high school to college transition and the fact that "counselors, too, are gatekeepers of every student's course assignments" (ibid., p. 57). School tracking and its impact on issues of educational equity have been masterly documented by Oakes (2005).

[90] The total number of undocumented students in institutions of higher education represents less than 1 percent of the total state enrollment. Specifically, in 2005, the number of students matriculated under the provisions of HB 1403

Since the passage of HB 1403, the media have continued to report widespread ignorance of the law among public school counselors. Indeed, the accounts of students described in newspaper articles and echoed at Houston Coalition meetings indicate that counselors sometimes fail to inform students of the course requirements for gaining admission to colleges and universities.[91]

Few school districts have taken a proactive role and instituted college-related programs to address the specific needs of the immigrant student population. For instance, in HISD, one of the nation's largest school districts (with over 30 high schools), the main efforts to provide services to these students come from advocacy work conducted by David Johnston at the College Center located at Lee High School. While Johnston provides updated information to various HISD units, including the department of Student Support Services, individual attention to immigrant students is largely unavailable in other HISD high schools, so many of these students go underserved. In the Austin Independent School District (AISD), which is considerably smaller than the HISD, the Bilingual/ESL Education Department has established the

---

totaled 8,940, which amounted to 0.75 percent of the total state enrollment (1,190,000). The low enrollment under HB 1403 affects the THECB campaign Closing the Gaps, begun in October 2000, with the aim of adding 500,000 more postsecondary students by 2015 (Texas Higher Education Coordinating Board, 2000c). The THECB acknowledges that minority enrollment is particularly low in a state where Blacks and Hispanics represent roughly 55 percent of Texas' 15-to-34 population, but approximately 36 percent of the students in Texas higher education system (Texas Higher Education Coordinating Board, 2006).

[91] See De los Santos (2004); Fischer (2004); McGee (2004); Treviño (2002). During my tenure with two Texas school districts, I witnessed many of the challenges undocumented students faced in attaining a higher education. On one occasion a registrar provided the student with an incomplete diploma that did not indicate the pupil had completed the Recommended High School Program (RHSP), curriculum that qualifies students for state financial aid. When questioned about this failure, the registrar argued that the student did not need the RHSP seal because she "knew" the pupil in question was not a U.S. citizen and thus could not go to college, making it clear that this had not been an oversight. Despite these obstacles, the student persevered and graduated with a four-year degree.

College Program for Immigrant Students. Its aim is to "increase the number of AISD's immigrant students graduating and enrolling in higher education [and] to identify, inform and assist students who are eligible under House Bill 1403, including those immigrant students who are not U.S. citizens or permanent residents."[92] As in HISD, the ongoing challenge is to reach *all* students.[93]

In addition to the lack of information provided by public high schools, there have also been reports of registrars at the higher education level who openly oppose the state law and therefore fail to inform students of its provisions.[94] Advocates have tried to counter these and other problems by distributing information and holding public meetings about the new policy. For example, even before HB 1403 had been formally signed into law, the Houston Coalition had begun addressing the lack of information at the postsecondary level, aiming its initial

---

[92] Orozco (2005), p. 1.

[93] In 2007, 2,000 AISD students "were never evaluated to see whether they needed bilingual education or English as a second language services" (Humphrey, 2007, May 16). This issue is one of the claims included in a 2006 lawsuit filed in a U.S. District Court in Texas by MALDEF and META (Multicultural Education, Training, and Advocacy Inc.). The plaintiffs, the American GI FORUM and LULAC, "urge the Court for supplemental relief to require that the State of Texas, et al., Defendants, monitor, enforce and supervise programs for limited-English proficient students in the Texas public schools so as to ensure that those students receive appropriate educational programs and equal educational opportunities" (Civil Action No. 6:71-CV-5281, 2006, p. 1). The ruling in this case, issued in 2007 by Judge Wayne Justice (who had sided with undocumented children during the *Plyler* case), was in favor of Texas. Judge Justice concluded, "There is evidence that the [bilingual and ESL] program succeeds, statewide, in assisting elementary students in mastering basic English skills. Encouragingly these students continue to succeed" (Texas Education Today, 2007, p. 14). Educational statistics contradict this statement as it pertains to ELLs in secondary schools, a fact acknowledged in the ruling. Thus, the pattern of either not providing or providing only limited mandated educational services to this population continues, no doubt affecting initiatives, such as the ones described in this book, that seek to expand higher educational opportunity to this growing population.

[94] Eldridge (2005).

outreach efforts at community colleges to inform potential beneficiaries about the new law and to encourage them to enroll under its provisions. The coalition also put together informational materials to provide others with current information about the changes in the law.[95] As the fall of 2001 approached, members proposed a workshop with representatives from all Texas universities to inform them about the law's provisions as they prepared for registration.[96] Soon after, the coalition conducted additional events at other Houston-area universities, including Historically Black Colleges and Universities, and outreach to the immigrant community has taken place at different venues statewide.[97]

Although the implementation of House Bill 1403 has been impaired by the limited dispersal of information about its benefits among the potential beneficiaries, the THECB's decision to hew to a narrow interpretation of the law has created even greater obstacles. Students the bill's backers had included under its provisions have been deemed ineligible. In fall 2004, the THECB issued a memo to state their interpretation pertaining to GED students. As previously noted, HB 1403 states that an eligible student must have "(1) graduated from a public or private high school or received the equivalent of a high school diploma in this state." The legislative intent here was to include students who earn a GED, since this is an important option for many who are forced to drop out of high school but still seek to complete their secondary

---

[95] Johnston (2000).

[96] The program was organized by this author on behalf of the Houston Coalition in conjunction with the THECB and was sponsored jointly by HISD (the state's largest school district) and the University of Houston-Downtown (the city's largest open admissions university).

[97] Some of the colleges where public meetings have taken place include Lamar Institute of Technology, Midwestern State University, Stephen F. Austin State University, University of Texas at Arlington, University of Houston-Downtown, and University of Houston main campus. In addition, most of the major Texas universities participate in a panel that the Houston Coalition has organized every year, since February 2000, as part of the Houston Hispanic Forum. Beginning in 2007, the coalition created an additional "follow up session" where immigrant students and their parents can receive individualized attention (from higher education personnel and students who have gone through the process) and answers to their college-related questions.

education. In a November memo, however, the THECB reinterpreted the law's eligibility requirements to conclude: "The student who did not attend high school, but rather only pursued and acquired a GED, could not meet this requirement."[98] This change continued the THECB practice of excluding originally eligible students.

Overall, the board's failure to provide the state's colleges and universities with strong, centralized leadership with regard to the state's new education policy has left its enforcement up to the institutions themselves, often to the detriment of the students. For instance, it took the THECB three years from the bill's passage to provide a generic version of the affidavit required of undocumented students and incorporate it into the state's electronic application for admission (Texas Common Application). As a result, undocumented students applying to more than one university had to fill out different affidavits, which varied in both language and requirements. Even individuals who are well informed often describe the process of first sorting out which students qualify and then passing along the necessary information as an exercise in frustration.[99] The lack of dispersal of information about the opportunities created by the law, along with the exclusionary interpretations by the THECB, represents a long institutional history of impeding underrepresented students' access to higher education.[100]

---

[98] The memo claimed that the original interpretation including all eligible GED students was an "error" that had been brought to the attention of the THECB through "the help of some *astute* university registrars and admissions officers [italics added]." See Paredes (2004), p. 1.

[99] Alanis (2004); Yachnin (2001).

[100] An open attempt to subvert the purpose of the bill at the El Paso Community College (EPCC) illustrates this problem. At the beginning of the 2002 school year, the college denied admission to a handicapped undocumented student. Contrary to the requirements of HB 1403, the admissions director requested an interpretation from the INS, and when he was told that unauthorized entrants did not have the right to be in the United States, he refused to enroll the student (Hendry, personal communication, August 2002). Noriega's office sent a letter to THECB Commissioner Brown to request that a memo of clarification on the issue be released, stressing that "regional or local INS officer(s) do not make policy on college admissions" (Noriega, personal communication, August 7, 2002). Following this communication, Brown forwarded to all Texas

Recent Modifications to HB 1403: The Passage of Senate Bill 1528

In 2005, four years after the passage of HB 1403, Texas state legislators modified the law, through provisions of Senate Bill 1528, passed during the 79th session of the legislature.[101] SB 1528 continues the eligibility of undocumented students to qualify as residents if they have lived in Texas for the 36 months prior to high school graduation or are the recipients of a GED. The main change, and this is a positive feature, is that the new law expands the criteria for establishing residency to other high school graduates too (regardless of parents' residency in the state).[102] Also positive is the fact that SB 1528 deletes the requirement that students not have earned any credit hours prior to fall 2001 and that it removes the interpretation of the THECB that students must have lived with a parent or guardian while attending high school. This change not only clarifies the original legislative intent, it also affirms that the THECB's original interpretation had been arbitrary.

Unfortunately, one change in the law is not positive. SB 1528 deems ineligible some students intentionally included under HB 1403's original provisions, namely those who do not meet the high school eligibility criteria but who have begun the immigration paperwork process. Under HB 1403, these students were able to qualify as long as they could prove that they had filed with the immigration service. Now, these same students must prove that their application has been *approved* by the immigration service. This imposes an onerous burden on this population, since they are at the mercy of the immigration service and its extended application backlog. The rationale for this change was that some international students (who come to the United States under a student visa and thus are charged international fees) were taking advan-

---

higher educational institutions a letter from Noriega's office reiterating that "the U.S. constitution . . . reserves to the states the authority to legislate for the general health, *education*, and welfare of the people [italics added]" (Noriega, 2002).

[101] See Zaffirini (2005). SB 1528 is codified into the Texas Education Code as TEC 54.052(a)(3).

[102] "A student born and raised in Texas whose parents move out of state while he/she was in high school will not lose his/her claim to residency if the student remains in Texas for the required 36 months and graduates or acquires the GED" (Texas Higher Education Coordinating Board, 2005a, p. 1).

tage of HB 1403 (presumably because while attending school here they had filed paperwork to become permanent residents). The fiscal note for SB 1528 indicated that this would be the only group "on which the bill will have a significant impact."[103] Once again, the THECB interpreted the law in a way that differs from the legislative intent.[104] The board's interpretation punishes those students who have started the adjustment process with immigration services and other low-income immigrants as well, in order to make sure that (presumably wealthier) international students do not receive a tuition break.[105] The ongoing efforts to limit the number of students enrolled in the Texas higher education system seems to run counter to the alleged goals of the

---

[103] See O'Brien (2005), p. 2.

[104] During meetings held in August 2005, the THECB general counsel justified their interpretation by arguing that it had never been Noriega's intention to extend in-state tuition benefits. This is factually incorrect. A letter (dated June 29, 2000) from Noriega to the Mexican American Legislative Caucus argued for the need to change THECB policies that disparately affected students who were in the process of filing with immigration. Even before HB 1403, initial outreach to the THECB had been aimed at explaining that immigrants who have filed with the INS do so because they intend to become U.S. citizens and thus should be allowed to attend college at in-state tuition rates while their paperwork is pending.

[105] Education advocates pointed out that if one of the intents of SB 1528 was to limit the ability of international students to qualify for in-state tuition, then the final rules must reflect specifically that intent. Students with paperwork in process with the immigration service do not have the same financial ability that international students have (because the latter are required to show proof of a certain income level in order to receive a student visa to come to the United States). Thus the THECB interpretation robbed the former group of the opportunity to start their college education promptly. The analysis from the Legislative Budget Board estimated fiscal savings since some students will have no recourse but to drop out of school: "it is estimated that some students, rather than pay the nonresident tuition rate while their BCIS paperwork is pending, will choose not to attend college in Texas . . . Those who drop out of school because they will no longer be paying the resident rate will represent saved formula funding for the state . . ." (O'Brien, 2005, p. 2).

THECB's Closing the Gaps by Moving Every Texas Forward campaign.[106]

Positive Contributions: The HB 1403 Taskforce

During this same period, a more positive development, one aimed at informing and assisting immigrant students with regard to their newly acquired educational rights, took place. In July 2005, under the auspices of the Texas Guaranteed Student Loan Corporation (TGSLC), various universities and education-related organizations came together as the HB 1403 Taskforce.[107] This group recognized the need for a single document and a set of common practices across the Texas higher educational system that would reduce the complexity of applying for financial aid, especially for immigrant students. They worked together to create the Texas Application for Student Financial Aid (TASFA). Prior to the creation of this application form, immigrant students, their families, and those assisting them had to learn each of the different procedures used by community colleges and public universities to determine economic need and award state financial aid. In addition, students had previously been forced to complete the form known as the Free Application for Federal Student Aid (FAFSA), which invariably

---

[106] The law became effective during fall 2006. Comparing the number of students who had originally benefited under these provisions with those enrolling in fall 2006 shows a decline of over 200 students at the community college level (Texas Higher Education Coordinating Board, 2007).

[107] The TGSLC is known informally as TG. "Created by the Texas Legislature in 1979, TG is a public, nonprofit Corporation that administers the Federal Family Education Loan Program (FFELP) (The FFELP was formerly known as the Guaranteed Student Loan Program)." For a more detailed description, see http://www.tgslc.org/abouttg/overview/index.cfm. Maria Luna-Torres from the TG spearheaded this effort, with support from staff members Jacob Freire and Richard Sapp. They brought together representatives from the DCCCD, Prairie View A&M University, Texas A&M Kingsville, Texas A&M University, Texas State University, University of Houston main campus, University of Houston-Downtown, and University of Texas at Austin, as well as representatives from the THECB. David Johnston and this author were invited by the Taskforce to represent the student perspective.

increased their fear of deportation. The new approach aimed to increase students' sense of security.[108]

The overall goal of the HB 1403 Taskforce, as one member explained, was to develop a process that would result in a "less obstructionist" approach to applying for financial aid. All of the members identified limited state grant funding as a major obstacle for immigrant students, and they took advantage of their joint effort on the taskforce to remind the THECB that its determination to exclude otherwise eligible undocumented students from the state loan program was unfair.[109] The group also addressed several other important issues affecting immigrant students' applications for state financial aid. These included how to determine the Estimated Family Contribution (EFC); questions related to selective service verification (males, including those who are undocumented, are required to register for selective service if requesting state financial aid); documentation to prove income; high school diploma requirements (many financial aid offices were not processing immigrant students' applications for aid until they had received copies of their high school diplomas, a procedure not applied to other high school senior applicants); and affidavits and the process for securing the signature of the adult providing economic support to the student (parent, guardian or other).[110] After one year of work, the new, more streamlined application was ready. The TAFSA form saw its first use during the 2006–2007 academic year.[111] Ongoing training remains the

---

[108] FAFSA requires applicants to provide their Social Security number, which is checked against the records of the immigration service to determine eligibility for federal financial aid.

[109] The state's Be On Time Loan, which forgives the debt for students completing their degree plan, requires the student to be eligible for federal financial aid—a provision that effectively excludes undocumented applicants.

[110] Aware that some families and students lack proof of income or even visible means of support, the taskforce also sought to humanize the application by allowing third-party documentation and even a narrative from the student, parent, or counselor.

[111] The TASFA application (also available in Spanish) can be found at http://www.collegefortexans.com/residency/TASFA.doc. While there is still inconsistency in the processing of immigrant students' financial aid applica-

highest priority, both to ensure awareness of the form and to ensure equal treatment of immigrant students during the financial aid application process.

Despite the state's mixed record in informing potential beneficiaries of the new laws, the increase in numbers of undocumented students attending college in Texas has had an impact across the United States. The news of positive change in Texas has spread to other states, influencing the passage of similar legislation. To date, nine more states have passed in-state tuition policies: California, Illinois, Kansas, Nebraska, New Mexico, New York, Oklahoma, Utah, and Washington. The next chapter describes these legislative initiatives, focusing mainly on California and New York, and reviews the extent to which they have opened the door of higher education to undocumented immigrant students.

---

tions, as of January 2007, at least 60 colleges and universities were using the TASFA form (Luna-Torres, 2007).

CHAPTER 4

In-State Tuition Policies Gain Momentum

Over the period 2001–2006, nine states—California, Illinois, Kansas, Nebraska, New Mexico, New York, Oklahoma, Utah, and Washington—joined Texas in passing in-state tuition policies, opening the door to higher education for undocumented students. This chapter reviews the changes legislated in these states and, where possible, compares and contrasts them with the policy passed in Texas. The chapter's main focus, however, is on developments in California and New York, since these two states, together with Texas, are home to almost half of the nation's undocumented residents.[1] Proponents of higher education for undocumented students have been active in California and New York since the 1980s, but passage of in-state tuition policies did not occur until the start of the twenty-first century (2001 in California, and 2002 in New York). In both states, as this chapter will show, it was sustained advocacy on the part of many groups and individuals, and the students themselves, that brought the new policies into being.

---

[1] Of the nation's total undocumented population, estimated at 11.1 million in March 2005, California is calculated to have up to 2.7 million and New York, over half a million. Texas stands in the middle, with up to 1.6 million of the total (Pew Hispanic Center, 2006a).

CALIFORNIA: DECADES OF ADVOCACY

In California, as in other states, minors make up a significant percentage of the undocumented population. One source estimates that "California has about 40 percent of the estimated number of undocumented students (all grades and levels)" in the nation.[2] The issue of equal access to higher education is therefore of special concern, and the question has been the subject of litigation in California since the mid-1970s. Important victories emerged in the mid-1980s, such as the initial ruling in *Leticia "A" v. Regents of the University of California*, which found the students eligible for in-state tuition rates and state financial aid (Cal Grants).[3] This section reviews advocacy efforts on behalf of California's undocumented students that led to the eventual passage of an in-state tuition law in 2001, after fifteen years of intense legal and legislative battles.[4] It highlights the pioneering work of the Leticia "A" Network, in particular.

The Leticia "A" Network (hereafter, the Network) emerged in 1985 as an advocacy group named after the student who had first challenged the tuition and fee structure applied to undocumented students at campuses of the University of California system. The group's original composition was similar to that of the Houston Coalition[5]: high school teachers and counselors, representatives of institutions of higher education, immigrant students and parents, and community and civil rights organizations such as the Mexican American Legal Defense and Educational Fund (MALDEF), which successfully argued the Leticia "A" case in court.[6] Eventually the group also included the Coalition for

---

[2] Passel (2003), p. 2.

[3] See Chapter Two for details. Also, in the early eighties, a community college district in Los Angeles decided to allow undocumented students to enroll as residents for tuition purposes (Olivas, 1995). Such decisions mirror ones in Texas, where policy changes took place at the local level (community colleges) before being implemented by the state. See Chapter Three for details.

[4] See Yñiguez (2006).

[5] See Chapter Three for information regarding the Houston Coalition.

[6] Guillen (2002). "This effort was led by counselors such as Arnulfo Casillas of Glendale College; Hilda Solis, now a state senator; Alfredo Figueroa of the University of California Riverside; Alfred Herrera of UCLA; and Ramon Muñiz of CSUN" (Acuña, 1996, p. 126). Other founding members included Irma

Humane Immigrant Rights of Los Angeles (CHIRLA).[7] The Network advocated on behalf of undocumented students who gained admission to California's institutions of higher education, making sure that the provisions of the 1985 Leticia "A" ruling were understood and enforced.

Unfortunately, that court victory was reversed in 1990 with the ruling in *Regents of the University of California v. Los Angeles County Superior Court* (known as *Bradford*) and all access was foreclosed five years later, with the ruling in *American Association of Women (AAW) v. Board of Trustees of California State University*, which deemed undocumented students previously eligible to attend college under the Leticia "A" case ineligible for in-state tuition rates (see Chapter Two). This setback did not, however, deter the Network from continuing with its advocacy efforts. Members' ongoing actions helped bring about the successful passage of California's in-state tuition law, Assembly Bill (AB) 540, in October 12, 2001.

Between the initial Leticia "A" ruling (1985) and the final AAW ruling (1995), a number of attempts were made to implement in-state tuition bills that would have settled the issue. One proposal, AB 592, was filed by Assemblyman Richard Polanco (Los Angeles) in 1991.[8]

Archuleta (then with Compton Community College) and Dennis Lopez (then with the University of California at Irvine). Their work was also aided by Ed Apodaca who oversaw Admissions and Registration for the University of California system. Their college outreach work during the eighties, prior and after the 1982 Supreme Court decision in *Plyler,* had brought to light the issues faced by undocumented students graduating from high school. A decade and a half after its formation, the coalition retained some of its original members, with Alfred Herrera from UCLA and Irma Archuleta of Santa Ana College as chairpersons (De Cardenas, 2001; Loya, 2002; Nicholson, 2003). Others founding members who remain associated with the Network include Dennis Lopez and Betsy Regalado, both of whom played a key role in the MALDEF litigation lead by Counsel Linda Wong.

[7] CHIRLA was formed in Los Angeles in 1986 soon after the passage of the Immigration Reform and Control Act of 1986, to defend immigrant rights on various fronts.

[8] This was just one year after University of California, Los Angeles registrar Donald Bradford filed his taxpayer suit challenging the admission of undocu-

AB 592 proposed to restore undocumented students' ability to establish residency for tuition and financial aid purposes. The Leticia "A" Network engaged in a grassroots informational campaign that resulted in the passage of AB 592 in the California State Assembly and Senate. Governor Pete Wilson vetoed the bill but, undeterred, Polanco filed it again in 1992.[9] This time, the bill, AB 3525, sought to return to the campuses the authority to establish residency, and therefore eligibility requirements for the Cal Grant, for undocumented students. The governor vetoed this bill as well.

Assemblywoman Hilda Solis (San Gabriel Valley) filed the next proposal, AB 2114, in 1993.[10] Her bill would have allowed undocumented students to be classified as residents for in-state tuition fees. It contained language that has now became the norm for most of the in-state tuition bills across the nation. AB 2114 required students to meet the following criteria: (1) be a graduate of a California high school; (2) provide proof of having entered the country as a minor and of having attended high school in the state for at least three years; and (3) show evidence of having filed an application with the INS to adjust their immigration status.[11] Assemblywoman Solis's proposal passed the As-

---

mented students at in-state tuition rates at the University of California. See Chapter Two.

[9] In his veto message, after the bill had passed both Houses, Governor Wilson argued that since "the federal law classified undocumented students as illegals . . . [it] would be inconsistent to 'confer upon them a benefit that is based upon legal residence.' He added that the state "has a legitimate interest in not subsidizing the education of those who may be deported" (Acuña, 1996, p. 126). Given Wilson's role two years later in promoting the anti-immigrant Proposition 187, which would have resulted in massive deportations if implemented, it is not hard to guess what he envisioned for these students.

[10] The bill was introduced March 5, 1993.

[11] A bill analysis by California Assembly Committee on Higher Education stated that AB 2114 was intended to prevent those who were holding nonimmigrant visas, as well as undocumented students—that is, those who did not have a "reasonable likelihood of remaining"—from attending college at in-state tuition fees. To demonstrate their intent to remain in the country, immigrants had to have met the above requirements in addition to attending a California institution of postsecondary education (Archie-Hudson, 1993).

sembly Committee on Higher Education, but it did not make it to the governor's desk.[12]

BACKLASH

In 1994, as anti-immigrant forces in California were preparing to launch Proposition 187, several anti-immigrant initiatives were introduced into the state legislature, aimed at preventing immigrant students, documented and not, from enrolling in college. SB 1652 (filed by state senator Marianne Johannessen) invoked the Immigration and Nationality Act (INA) to achieve that purpose.[13] Assemblyman Mickey Conroy (Orange) filed the draconian ABX 70, which "would make it a *felony* [emphasis added] for any student who cannot show proof of citizenship or legal status to enroll in any public postsecondary institution."[14] Conroy also filed AB 3380, another restrictive proposal that prohibited "any person from establishing residence in California for the purpose of paying in-state tuition unless he or she is a citizen of the United States."[15] This citizenship requirement was expected to exclude more than 265,000 students who had full, legal permission to be in the country, such as "permanent and temporary immigrant residents, nonimmigrant residents with visas, students in the federal amnesty program and refugees."[16] In addition, the bill proposed to verify the citizenship

---

[12] For more information, see Cabaldon (2001).

[13] Kersten (1994). Johannessen's proposal would have exempted students whose parents were granted legal status under the Immigration Control and Reform Act (IRCA) of 1986.

[14] Conroy's AB 3380 was opposed by the Board of Governors California Community Colleges (Cabaldon, 2001, p. 8). Two additional and identical proposals, AB 2228 (Mountjoy) and AB 1801 (Conroy), also sought to prohibit undocumented students from attending public institutions of higher education. Both failed. See Archie-Hudson (1994).

[15] In 1994, when this bill was filed, the California State University system was still allowing undocumented students to be classified as residents for tuition purposes (Archie-Hudson, 1994; Olivas, 1995).

[16] See Archie-Hudson (1994), p. 4. This estimate did not include international or undocumented students. As if preventing noncitizens from establishing residency were not enough, Conroy also proposed a constitutional amendment (Assembly Constitutional Amendment 44) that specifically targeted undocu-

status of every student and estimated a "potential savings of $550 million from decreased enrollment (assuming 80 percent attrition) and a net revenue increase of $200 million from assessment of nonresident tuition."[17] The additional revenue in nonresident tuition would have been gained through tuition increases to be applied to noncitizens, ranging from 300 percent for students at the University of California and 550 percent for those at California State University, to 825 percent for students at the California Community Colleges.[18] It was estimated that as many as 200,000 students would drop out due to these astronomically high tuition increases. In short, AB 3380 aimed to preclude noncitizens (including undocumented) from college both by statutory provisions and by raising tuition to impossibly high levels.

In the end, the Board of Governors, which oversees the operations of the community colleges in California, opposed Conroy's restrictive measure. The bill analysis conducted by the Assembly Committee on Higher Education made a valid point, but one that is seldom used in arguments against proposals that seek to limit noncitizens' access to higher education—namely, that such legislation is unconstitutional because it discriminates against immigrants based on the fact that they are not citizens. Citing several court rulings, the Committee concluded that "the state cannot place limitations [on] the full participation of noncitizens without offending the Equal Protection and Supremacy clauses of the Constitution."[19] Further, the analysis noted that the constitutionality of applying nonresident tuition rates to undocumented students remained an open question. Although Conroy's proposal was defeated, in 1995, when the Los Angeles appellate court made its final pronouncement regarding litigation that had spanned a decade since the Leticia "A" case, it ruled that all systems of higher education in California must require students to show proof of U.S. residency and must impose out-of-state tuition on undocumented residents.

During this anti-immigrant period in California, typified by the adverse rulings against immigrant students and voter approval of the na-

---

mented students and aimed to ban them from attending institutions of higher education. For more information, see Archie-Hudson (1994).

[17] Archie-Hudson (1994), p. 1.

[18] Ibid.

[19] For more information, see Archie-Hudson (1994).

tivist Proposition 187 (see Chapter Two), one of the most important contributions of the Leticia "A" Network was to repeatedly remind school counselors and other personnel in contact with undocumented students that they were "not obligated to report students or families who do not have U.S. documents."[20] Indeed, much of the Network's advocacy efforts during the late 1980s through the mid-1990s consisted of "fighting off legislative proposals to preclude legal immigrants from establishing state residency, prohibiting enrollment of undocumented immigrants or requiring citizenship verification procedures."[21] Throughout this period, Network members also continued to pursue the issue of immigrants' access to college, but mainly by reaching out to those who had been able to file paperwork to change their immigration status.[22] In presentations conducted across the state and the country, the Network informed students of their rights and explained that while they could enroll in college, they would have to do so at international rates and without the benefit of federal or state financial aid.[23] Network members suggested undocumented students try alternative strategies to lessen the financial burden, such as applying to private schools, since these institutions are allowed to provide funding at their discretion.[24] In their tips for high school and college counselors, members of the Network emphasized the importance of communicating to the families of ninth graders that they need to "start the immigration process early [stressing that] the senior year is too late to start the process."[25]

---

[20] For more information, see Caine et al. (1999).

[21] Guillen (2002), p. 2.

[22] Cabaldon (2001).

[23] Leticia "A" Network (1999).

[24] Johnston, R. (2000).

[25] Caine et al. (1999), p. 20. This advice, commonly offered by educators, gives the impression that families' immigration status is a matter under their control. In fact, given the immigration backlog, there is no guarantee that an application for residency will be ready in time for the student's enrollment in college, regardless of when the process was initiated. Moreover, as noted in Chapter One and elsewhere in this book, immigration law severely limits undocumented residents' opportunities to apply for legalization. The possibility of deportation and prohibitions on re-entry ranging from three to ten years haunt

RENEWED LEGISLATIVE EFFORTS

In 1999, the Network rallied behind a legislative proposal, AB 1197, which sought to overturn the ban placed by the 1990 *Bradford* ruling (see Chapter Two) on granting in-state tuition to undocumented immigrants. Filed by Assemblyman Marco Antonio Firebaugh (South Gate), the bill came in the aftermath of Proposition 187.[26] The purpose of the bill was to provide access to in-state tuition to students who met the following requirements: "(1) attended a California high school for at least three years, (2) graduated from high school and (3) is admitted to a CSU or a CCC campus. The University of California is not included in the provisions of this measure."[27] The core of the proposal was to allow high school graduates to be assessed only mandatory fees, estimated at about $1,506 in the 1999 school year, and not out-of-state tuition, calculated at about $9,253 for the same period. An estimated 750–1,500 students would have benefited from this provision of the proposed law.[28]

The bill's exemption of the University of California system may have been warranted, since UC was where the initial battle (the Leticia "A" case) was fought. The Senate Committee on Education, in voting to recommend implementation of the bill, stated that if the bill were to become law, adoption of its provisions would be left to the discretion of

---

all individuals who entered without a visa and have been living in the country without documentation (Poole, 2006).

[26] Marco Firebaugh's work on this issue spans a decade. In the early 1990s, he began working for state Senator Richard Polanco who, as noted earlier, was the sponsor of the earliest measure on behalf of undocumented immigrant students (Rojas, 2003).

[27] See Firebaugh (1999). As initially filed, the purpose of the bill was twofold: (1) to provide certain exemptions to the assessment of nonresident tuition at community colleges for up to 10 percent of enrolled foreign citizens who could demonstrate financial need; and (2) to waive the entire cost of tuition for undergraduate students of exceptional academic ability attending a California State University (CSU).

[28] Using U.S. Census figures, the number of potential beneficiaries was considerably higher—an estimated 9,000 to 10,000 students. See R. Johnston (2000) and Rojas (2003).

the UC Board of Regents. Upon further deliberation, the legislature requested that the Regents take action on the matter.

The bill analysis prepared by the legislature noted that the "educational rights of undocumented students is a long standing issue that has been debated within legislative and judicial arenas for years."[29] Given this history of controversy, AB 1197, did not seek to change the definition of a California resident. Instead, it proposed to allow certain students to pay resident tuition fees on the basis of their high school attendance and graduation. Subsequent changes to Firebaugh's bill in the Senate added a requirement that students have an application pending with the INS in order to be exempt from nonresident tuition.[30]

Although the bill passed with no opposition in its initial stages, the argument that many of the students would eventually become U.S. citizens did not resonate with then-Governor Gray Davis. He eventually vetoed the measure, citing conflict with federal immigration law.[31] Davis argued that offering in-state tuition to undocumented students "would require that all out-of-state legal residents be eligible for the same benefits," resulting in a "revenue loss of over $63.7 million to the State."[32] The governor's interpretation of Section 505 of the federal Illegal Immigration Reform and Immigrant Responsibility Act (see Chapter Two) assumed that all students then classified as nonresidents would be offered in-state tuition fees and ignored the fact that the new group of eligible students would constitute a source of additional revenue. His veto message also noted that "the State's priorities and funding must focus on higher education attainment for California *legal* residents."[33]

---

[29] For more information, see Supinger (1999), pp. 1–2.

[30] Firebaugh (2000).

[31] Assemblyman Firebaugh had pointed out that many of the parents of the students in question were already in the process of adjusting their status with the immigration service (Supinger, 1999). Indeed, while the children were undocumented, many of the parents were beneficiaries of the 1986 amnesty program (Plotkin, 1999).

[32] See Davis (2000).

[33] Ibid., emphasis added.

THE PASSAGE OF AB 540

It was not until 2001 that the Network's advocacy activities finally resulted in the passage of California's in-state tuition law. This law, which was originally introduced as AB 540 by Assemblyman Firebaugh, took effect January 1, 2002, with the initial implementation limited to the CCC and CSU systems. In contrast to Texas, the law did not automatically apply to all public institutions. The UC system was not bound by AB 540 because, according to the California constitution, the UC system is governed by the policies adopted by its own Board of Regents.[34] Seeking uniformity, the bill included a request that the UC Regents adopt and implement the policy. It took a special vote of the Board of Regents to do so and required a legislature-approved amendment that limits the financial liability of the UC, the CSU, and the CCC, in case of lawsuits brought by U.S. citizens classified as out-of-state residents for tuition purposes.[35] The amendment makes no reference to state residency in order "to steer clear of a conflict with the federal law, which specifically prohibits benefits awarded on the basis of residence."[36]

---

[34] UCLA campus officials nonetheless voiced their support for the measure and were entered in the legislative record as supporters of AB 540 (Boloorian and Anton, 2001).

[35] This provision reflects the UC system's experience a decade earlier in the *Bradford* litigation (see Chapter Two). The administration agreed to adopt the policy put forth in AB 540 if the legislature provided protection "limiting the relief state courts would be authorized to award in any suit [thus] eliminat[ing] or reduc[ing] the potential financial exposure to an acceptable level" (University of California Office of the President, 2002).

[36] University of California Office of the President (2002), p. 2. The amendment was filed as AB 1543. It reads: "This bill would authorize a state court, if it finds that the above provision, or any similar provision adopted by the Regents of the University of California, is unlawful, to order that the administering entity that is the subject of the lawsuit terminate any waiver awarded under that statute or action, as equitable relief, and would prohibit the award of money damages, tuition refund or waiver, or other retroactive relief. The bill would provide that the California Community Colleges, the California State University, and the University of California are immune from the imposition of any

Prior to the Regents' vote, advocates increased their efforts on behalf of undocumented students. Understanding that the stakes were high, supporters organized a forum at the UCLA campus a week before the Board of Regents meeting on the adoption of AB 540. [37] The forum aimed to teach the history of the struggle of undocumented students, to update participants on the campaign to have AB 540 implemented across the UC system, and to press the Board of Regents to adopt AB 540. A follow-up rally was held the day of the meeting to demand that the university open its doors to all students regardless of immigration status, and a petition was presented to the Regents.[38] The Board adopted AB 540 by a vote of 17–5.[39] The regulations did not take effect until June 2, 2002.

As initially filed, AB 540 had sought to classify eligible students as also meeting the residency requirements. This would have qualified them for California student aid programs such as the Cal Grant, which provides funds to cover tuition costs at both UC and CSU campuses.[40] However, last-minute negotiations removed provisions that would have allowed undocumented students access to state financial aid.[41] Undocumented students now qualified under the law if they met all of the

---

award of money damages, tuition refund or waiver, or other retroactive relief in a lawsuit" (Firebaugh, 2002c, p. 94). For more information, see Hebel (2001).

[37] Cesar E. Chavez Center, University of California at Los Angeles (2002).

[38] UCLA (2002).

[39] Conservative regents such as Ward Connerly were part of the opposing minority (Barrera, 2002; Connerly, 2002). Connerly lead the 1996 anti-affirmative action proposition dubbed the California Civil Rights Initiative and eventually founded the American Civil Rights Institute an organization dedicated to the reversal of affirmative action policies across the United States.

[40] "Cal Grant A awards (equivalent to CSU tuition) are $1,428 and require a 3.00 GPA. Cal Grant B awards (access for subsistence) are $1,551 and require a 2.00 GPA. For the purposes of estimating a fiscal impact, it is assumed 90 percent of eligible students would be from lower-income families and would qualify for a Cal Grant B award and 10 percent of the students would qualify for a Cal Grant A award for additional eligibility costs of $769,350 in the first year" (Franzoia, 2001, p. 2).

[41] For more information, see California Immigrant Welfare Collaborative (2001).

following four requirements: (1) had attended a California high school for three or more years; (2) had graduated from a California high school or received a GED; (3) were registered or enrolled at an accredited institution of higher education in California; and (4) had filed or would file an affidavit as required by individual institutions, stating that they would apply for legal residency as soon as possible.[42] The affidavit was merely an expression of intent, as there were no provisions in AB 540 requiring students to prove that they had been able to start the immigration process.[43]

The arguments on behalf of AB 540 paralleled the ones in support of HB 1403 in Texas. Section 1(a) of AB 540 declares that the legislature acknowledges the long-time presence of undocumented students in the state and also recognizes the limited opportunities faced by these students in their quest for higher education. The recommendation for a fair tuition policy was grounded in an awareness that such students had demonstrated their academic ability by being accepted into California's universities and that by providing access to them the state increased its "collective productivity and economic growth."[44] Another argument was that undocumented students' families paid taxes and therefore family members should have access to educational benefits. Additional arguments came from Mexican President Vicente Fox during his 2001 address before a joint session of the California Legislature, where he spoke in favor of AB 540 as a way to recognize immigrants' contributions to the state's economic prosperity.[45]

With the passage of AB 540, California joined Texas as one of the two states in the nation that provided undocumented students with equal access to higher education. Although HB 1403 and AB 540 achieve essentially the same end, the two bills differ in a number of ways, providing other states with two distinct models of in-state tuition policies. The next section examines the most important aspects of the two approaches.

---

[42] For more information, see Firebaugh et. al. (2001b).

[43] For more information, see P. Mitchell (2001).

[44] Firebaugh and Maldonado (2001), p. 2.

[45] Smith and Bustillo (2001).

Residency versus Waiver of Nonresident Fees

The California provisions, unlike the Texas statute, do not classify students eligible under the law as residents for tuition purposes. Instead, they are eligible for an exemption from nonresident tuition fees. California regulations pertaining to resident students, which are codified under Title V of the California Code of Regulations, are thus not affected by the passage of AB 540.[46]

This way of classifying undocumented students has profound implications for financial aid. The law noted that while undocumented students were exempt from paying nonresident tuition, they were still classified as nonresidents. This made them ineligible for any state financial aid, including the Educational Opportunity Program (EOP), California Community College Board of Governors (BOG) Fee Waiver, California Grant, and/or the Governor's Merit Scholar Program.[47] For the community colleges especially, this way of classifying undocumented students was economically beneficial, since they reported them as full-time equivalent students (FTES) for apportionment purposes.[48] The students, however, were left with a tuition that, al-

---

[46] With respect to students who have started the immigration process, Title V states that an alien's classification as a resident cannot be made until that person has "taken appropriate steps to obtain a change of status from the Immigration and Naturalization Service" (Black, 2001).

[47] For more information, see Montemayor et al. (2003). At the University of California, EOP/Academic Advancement Programs is not a financial aid–based program, so it can provide services to undocumented students (Herrera, 2007).

[48] Before AB 540 was passed, undocumented students could not be claimed for apportionment purposes, as it was considered that doing so would constitute a subsidy to their education. In a letter from the Chancellor's Office of the California Community Colleges, the general counsel further explained the policy: "this does not mean that districts may not admit undocumented aliens to their noncredit courses. It meant only that if a district admitted an undocumented alien to a noncredit course, it had to absorb the cost of serving that student and could not claim him or her for apportionment purposes" (Black, 2001, p. 4). Also see Young and Noldon (2002). This situation resembled the financial impact of the measures taken by two community colleges in Texas that decided to open their doors to undocumented students and enroll them at in-district tuition fees prior to the passage of HB 1403 in 2001. See Chapter Three.

though significantly reduced, was still out of the reach of many.[49] On the other hand, students who showed that they had started the permanent residency process with immigration authorities and had resided in California for over a year were classified as in-state residents for tuition purposes, in particular by the community colleges, which then awarded them BOG fee waivers and/or book grants.[50]

The lack of state financial aid for the majority of AB 540–eligible students left only scholarship monies, which were never sufficient and often required proof of valid immigration status, as their only recourse for financial assistance. To alleviate that problem, and in anticipation of increased enrollments for the fall 2002 semester, the Leticia "A" Network organized a scholarship drive, with the goal of raising enough money to award 12 students scholarships of $2,500 each. The funds were collected through donations from employees of the Los Angeles Unified School District and corporate donors and were funneled through the Hispanic Scholarship Fund (HSF). Although the HSF did not provide any additional monies, the Network used this organization as an intermediary to guarantee that the funds went directly to the students.[51] As a Network chairperson explained, giving the scholarship money to a California college or university would turn the donation into state funds, which could not be released to undocumented students. The fact that over 200 scholarship applications were received and only 12 awards could be funded underscored the need for policy change at various levels.[52]

To address the problem, legislation to provide undocumented students access to state financial aid was filed not long after the passage of AB 540. Network chairpersons Alfred Herrera and Irma Archuleta met

---

[49] Guillen (2002). The impact of tuition costs, even at in-state levels, on these students and their families was noted in the legislative analysis of Firebaugh's first in-state tuition proposal (AB 1197), which Governor Davis vetoed (Firebaugh, 1999).

[50] See Loya (2002).

[51] HSF stated that it did not have support from its corporate donors to fund undocumented students (Loya, 2002).

[52] See Loya (2002). For stories on the challenges faced by students who are prevented by their immigration status from qualifying for financial aid, see Abrego (2002).

with Assemblyman Firebaugh to develop a strategy for securing Cal Grants as well as other state funds for undocumented students.[53] SB 328, a draft bill addressing this issue, was introduced during the 2003–2004 regular legislative session by Senator Martha Escutia (Norwalk); the Assembly version of the bill was co-authored by Assemblymen Firebaugh and Thomas Calderón (Montebello). This legislation sought to provide state financial aid (in the form of BOG fee waivers) to community college students eligible for in-state tuition under AB 540.[54] The language of the bill was modified several times and advocates had to fight off efforts to gut the proposal.[55] Although the measure passed both houses, Governor Davis vetoed it, arguing that the economy did not permit the state to provide financial aid to its undocumented residents.[56]

Undeterred, advocates for undocumented students have continued to push for legislation that would allow AB 540 beneficiaries to receive state financial aid. During the 2005–2006 legislative session, Senator Gilbert Cedillo (Los Angeles) introduced the California DREAM Act (filed as SB 160), with the aim of establishing "procedures and forms that enable persons who are exempt from paying nonresident tuition (under AB 540). . . to apply for, and participate in, all student aid programs administered by these segments to the full extent permitted by federal law."[57] Despite of the bill's having passed the Assembly and the Senate, Governor Schwarzenegger vetoed it, arguing that the measure "would penalize students here legally by reducing the financial aid they rely on to allow them to go to college and pursue their dreams."[58]

---

[53] For more information, see Loya (2002) and Nicholson (2003).

[54] The new bill also required the CSU and CCC to implement an internal procedure to determine the financial need of undocumented enrollees, since these students are unable to fill out the Free Application for Federal Student Aid (FAFSA).

[55] One such amendment sought to make AB 540 inapplicable to the CSU system. This seemed inconsistent with the main purpose of the bill, which was to make undocumented students eligible for in-state tuition aid (Office of Senate Floor Analyses, 2003).

[56] See Davis (2003).

[57] Legislative Counsel's Digest (2006).

[58] See Schwarzenegger (2006).

During the 2006–2007 legislative session, Senator Cedillo refiled the California DREAM Act (now numbered as SB 1).[59] The governor again vetoed the bill, on the grounds that during a period of increasing tuition costs, California could not afford to strain state funds.[60] As with previous versions, the bill enjoyed wide support throughout the student, advocacy, and educational communities. For instance, UCLA's Center for Labor Research and Education organized a conference on undocumented students to press for passage of both the federal Dream Act and the state's version. The event, which took place on May 19, 2007, brought together many organizations with interests in this issue, such as IDEAS at UCLA, the California DREAM Act Network, the Office of Senator Cedillo, CHIRLA, the Koreatown Immigrant Workers Alliance, the Korean Resource Center, MALDEF, and Movimiento Estudiantil Chicano de Aztlán, among others.

Implementation of AB 540

As in Texas, California lacked a funded, statewide campaign to inform undocumented students of their newly acquired eligibility for in-state tuition.[61] Immigration advocates in the Network have repeatedly observed a lack of knowledge about the law among university and community college administrative staff.[62] As a result, undocumented stu-

---

[59] The bill would have provided "eligibility for Cal Grant Entitlement awards, California Community College Transfer Entitlement awards, Cal Grant C awards, Assumption Program of Loans for Education awards, State Nursing Assumption Program of Loans for Education awards, Child Development grants, Law Enforcement Personnel Dependents grants, and the California Community College Board of Governors (BOG) fee waiver." (Office of the Senate Floor Analyses, 2007).

[60] In light of the governor's previous veto citing limited state funding for financial aid programs, SB 1 did not make undocumented students eligible for the "Competitive Cal Grant A or B awards, for which over 112,000 eligible applicants were denied in 2005–06" (Office of the Senate Floor Analyses, 2007).

[61] For more information, see Rojas (2003).

[62] During the May 19, 2007 conference at UCLA, long-time advocate Alfred Herrera noted many challenges facing supporters of AB 540. He mentioned the need to provide information and training to increase secondary school counsel-

dents have often been charged out-of-state fees.[63] Since the passage of AB 540, Network members, such as MALDEF representatives, have requested students to notify them of any colleges not implementing the law properly.[64]

While a statewide informational campaign has been lacking, the work of the AB 540 College Access Network[65] has helped increase dissemination of information and has influenced implementation and enforcement of the law. In fall 2006, the Network, together with the University of Southern California Center for Higher Education Policy Analysis, published "The College and Financial Aid Guide for: AB 540 Undocumented Immigrant Students." This guide, which is modeled after an earlier publication distributed by Assemblyman Firebaugh's office, provides a variety of resources, including information about federal laws as well as California's policies, links to websites, answers to frequently asked questions about AB 540 and undocumented students' rights, suggestions for how to apply to and succeed in college, list of available scholarships for undocumented students, and so on.[66] The publication of informational fliers and questionnaires from the

---

ors' familiarity with the law, to provide assistance to secondary school administrators to help them understand and execute their responsibilities, and to promote greater knowledge of the provisions of AB 540 within postsecondary admissions offices. See also Olivérez (2006).

[63] For more information, see Loya (2002).

[64] The fund has been notified by community college enrollees of instances where their identification as "AB 540" students resulted in the assessment of penalty fees. For this and other challenges with the implementation of the law see Olivérez (2006).

[65] This is a new, larger group that includes some of the same participants who have been affiliated with the historical work conducted by the Leticia "A" Network.

[66] Assemblyman Firebaugh's office produced and distributed *AB 540 Assisting Immigrant Students to Pursue Higher Education.* That manual aimed to improve public knowledge about AB 540. It included information in English and Spanish about the content of the law, its requirements, the cost of college tuition, a sample affidavit, and many other useful resources, such as an explanation of the process to adjust one's immigration status, a list of immigrant assistance organizations, etc. See Firebaugh (2002a).

California Community College Chancellor's Office also has aided in the dissemination of information regarding the law and its benefits.[67]

Only a couple of years after the passage of AB 540, anti-immigrant forces sought to overturn it, blaming undocumented students for enrollment cutbacks at state colleges and universities.[68] Assemblymen Tom McClintock (Thousand Oaks) and Bill Emmerson (Rancho Cucamonga) proposed legislation in 2005 designed to recapture slots anti-immigrant groups believed were occupied by "illegal immigrants."[69] This belief was unfounded. During the academic year 2002–2003, system wide the UC campuses reported only 719 students as qualifying under AB 540, 93 of whom were thought to be undocumented.[70] None of the proposals to weaken AB 540 filed in 2005 passed the Senate Education Committee. Later that year, anti-immigrant forces filed a class action lawsuit on behalf of out-of-state

---

[67] See Young and Noldon (2002) and Gill, Regalado, and Riegel (2002).

[68] During the 2003–2004 school year, an estimated 7,500 qualified applicants to the UC system were turned down because of enrollment cutbacks.

[69] McClintock filed SB 349 (2005) and Emmerson filled SB 589 (2005). For more information, see Hiltzik (2004).

[70] Since AB 540, like the other in-state tuition bills, allows high school graduates (irrespective of immigration status or parents' residence) the opportunity to pay in-state tuition fees, it benefits more than the undocumented population (Rojas, 2006). In addition, SB 160, in the version presented in the Senate Education Committee, proposed to expand "the group of students eligible to be exempt from paying nonresident tuition to include students who have attended an adult school" (Anton, 2007, p. 1). Although the law did not pass, a new policy from the Los Angeles Community College District (LACCD) would help some of the students who would have benefited from SB 160—namely, those who attended adult schools (and who currently do not qualify under AB 540). Beginning January 1, 2008 the LACCD would allow students who do not qualify under AB 540 to receive a waiver of nonresident tuition if they enroll part-time (six units or less). As approved in October 2007, the measure will be evaluated on annual basis to determine its financial impact, if any (see Los Angeles Community College District, 2007).

students, challenging AB 540.[71] The case was eventually dismissed in state court.[72]

From 2001, when California passed its in-state tuition policy, to 2006, when the law was affirmed in state court, eight more states passed in-state tuition policies. In the next section, the discussion focuses on advocacy in New York; subsequent sections provide a brief overview of the history of the emergence of similar policies in the other seven states.

NEW YORK: A POLICY OF INCLUSION LOST AND REGAINED

The New York legislature's 2002 decision to permit undocumented students to attend college at in-state tuition rates marked the successful outcome of repeated efforts by the state's immigrant communities and their advocates to establish their right to attend college on equal terms with U.S. citizens. Historically, New York has been a receiving state for immigrants and is one of the most demographically diverse states in the country. Although overall the state has fewer undocumented residents than either California or Texas, an estimated 20 percent of the population of New York state is foreign born.[73]

Policies put in place in the 1980s at New York's two largest systems of higher education, the City University of New York (CUNY) and the State University of New York (SUNY), allowed undocumented students to pay in-state tuition. This access to college was cut off, however, with the passage of the IIRIRA in 1996, and further highly restrictive measures were put in place following the September 11, 2001 events.

Until the passage of the IIRIRA, "undocumented students could qualify for in-state tuition, although many SUNY campuses did not

---

[71] *Martinez v. Regents of the University of California,* No. CV-05-2064 (Yolo County Super. Ct., filed Dec. 14, 2005).

[72] For more information on this litigation, see next chapter.

[73] This estimate is based on figures from the 2000 Census. It should be noted that the percentage of foreign born is higher for New York City—it is calculated at 36 percent (New York State Education Department, 2005).

permit it."[74] This apparent contradiction was due to the fact that some university officials believed that federal law (specifically, Section 505 of the IIRIRA) prohibited colleges from offering in-state tuition rates to the undocumented. This interpretation of the law led SUNY administrators in June 1998 to bar these students from access to an affordable education.[75] The revised policy regarding immigrant students stated that "students who are unable to present valid documentation of their alien status are not eligible for in-state tuition rates."[76]

The situation at CUNY was more complex. This system had a long history of providing a tuition-free higher education to all qualified applicants. This approach changed in 1976, when the university began charging tuition and established a distinction between residents and nonresidents. Undocumented students began being charged nonresident tuition at this time.[77] The policy was modified in 1989 to allow undocumented students to enroll at in-state tuition rates.[78] The inclusive policy even survived the 1996 federal-level immigrant legislation. Following the passage of the IIRIRA, the university had received legal advice that it did not have to abandon its inclusive policy, given that Congress had not implemented regulations or sanctions that pertained to Section 505 and its apparent ban on undocumented students' access to higher education.

---

[74] Badger and Yale-Loehr (2000), p. 415. These authors also provide additional historical information regarding the policies in the CUNY and SUNY systems.

[75] Harvard Law Review Association (2002).

[76] Badger and Yale-Loehr (2000), p. 415.

[77] See Yates (2004), p. 598.

[78] "Since 1989, undocumented immigrant who could prove they were a New York resident or who had attended a state high school for the previous two semesters was charged the in-state tuition rate. The policy was an outgrowth of an executive order issued by Mayor Koch in August of 1989 that stated, 'any service provided by a City agency shall be made available to all aliens who are otherwise eligible for such service unless such agency is required by law to deny eligibility for such service to aliens.' This order was reaffirmed by both Mayor Dinkins and Mayor Giuliani, making CUNY one of the only institutions of higher education in the country that treated undocumented immigrants as state residents" (Wong, n.d., p. 1).

The policy of inclusion did not, however, survive the anti-immigrant hysteria that followed the events of September 11, 2001. Several politicians fanned these fears by making immigrants the scapegoat for the attacks on the Twin Towers. For example, State Senator Frank Padavan, representing Queens, with its high immigrant population, decried CUNY's inclusive policy, calling it "a national security issue and an insult to every citizen and legal immigrant seeking higher education."[79] Soon after Padavan made this remark, CUNY adopted a policy that required undocumented students to pay out-of-state tuition rates. The passage of the restrictive policy also coincided with proposals to increase the cost of tuition and cuts in financial aid programs, including the Peter Vallone scholarships and the state Tuition Assistance Program (TAP).[80]

More September 11–prompted changes occurred over time. CUNY Chancellor Matthew Goldstein, along with general counsel Frederick P. Schaffer, ended the in-state tuition rates for undocumented New York residents, effective in spring 2002.[81] Approximately 2,000 undocumented students were expected to be affected by this curtailment of CUNY's twelve-year-old policy. These students constituted only 1 per-

---

[79] Quoted in Paget-Clarke (2002), p. 2.

[80] According to the New York Public Interest Research Group, "the Mayor's Preliminary Budget cuts $6.5 million from the Peter F. Vallone Merit Scholarship program at the senior college level and $500,000 at the community college level. These cuts terminate the award at CUNY" (NYPIRG, 2002). A briefing paper presented by the Human Services Division before the City Council Committee of Higher Education noted that at CUNY, "approximately 70 percent of their full-time degree students receive financial aid [and] the University's data reveals that each year approximately 110,000 CUNY students receive federal Pell Grants, New York State TAP grants and federal Work-Study grants" (Van Ooyen, 2005, p. 1).

[81] Despite this decision, Chancellor Matthew Goldstein testified in favor of the in-state tuition bill, participated in advocacy activities pressing for changes in the law, and attended the signing ceremony where advocates celebrated the passage of the policy (Professional Staff Congress, 2002). For additional information, see Yates (2004), p. 598.

cent of the total 200,000 enrolled in degree programs.[82] Although the number of beneficiaries was negligible, many reportedly dropped out because of their inability to pay out-of-state fees.[83]

The policy changes in the CUNY system, particularly those targeting undocumented students, generated an outcry from the students. They organized as the Mexican American Student Alliance (MASA) and filed an Article 78 petition, with the intention of nullifying the chancellor's decision.[84] The petitioners argued that the IIRIRA's Section 505 was "so vague as to be unenforceable."[85] They also charged that the reclassification of undocumented immigrants as nonresidents constituted an anti-immigrant act. Despite this spirited challenge, the judge reviewing the case concluded that "the Chancellor's efforts to comply with federal law were not arbitrary or capricious."[86] Meanwhile, CUNY faculty and students responded to the policy change by organizing under the "CUNY Is Our Future" banner. Both this group and MASA aimed to raise awareness of educational issues pertaining to undocumented students, but MASA students also sought to support international students with visas who had come under attack after September 11.[87]

Other supporters of in-state tuition for undocumented students included civil rights organizations such as the Puerto Rican Legal De-

---

[82] Some estimates cited a likely 3,000 students affected, most of whom (2,800) were attending CUNY (Barnard News Center, 2002). See also Szelenyi and Chang (2002).

[83] Paget-Clarke (2002).

[84] Article 78 petitions are filed by New York residents to appeal decisions of state agencies in cases where the filer feels the "state action is without sound basis in reason, is arbitrary or capricious, or is illegal as a matter of law" (Yates, 2004, p. 599).

[85] Ibid.

[86] Ibid.

[87] Following the September 11 events, Senator Orrin Hatch (Utah) co-sponsored Senate Bill 1627 with Texas Senator Kay Bailey Hutchinson to establish a database to screen and identify inadmissible or deportable aliens. The measure had been introduced originally by U.S. Senator Dianne Feinstein (Calif.) and included several provisions requiring educational institutions to report data on foreign students.

fense and Education Fund, the Hispanic Federation, the National Korean American Service & Education Consortium, the New York Immigration Coalition, the Citizenship and Immigration Project, Youth Empowerment Activists, and unions such as the Professional Staff Congress, Jobs with Justice, the Mexican-American Workers Association; and the New York Public Interest Research Group.[88]

Assemblymen Peter Rivera (Bronx) and Adriano Espaillat (Manhattan) entered the fray, offering in-state tuition proposals, and State Senator Pedro Espada introduced a similar bill.[89] Advocates for legislation that would allow these students to be classified as residents for tuition purposes at CUNY and SUNY testified before the New York City Council, organized marches to City Hall, and rallied at the steps of City Hall. The basic proposal, which eventually became law, classifies as residents all those students who (1) attended an approved New York state high school for more than two years and applied to a state institution of higher education within five years of high school graduation or (2) received a GED certificate and applied for admission to a state institution of higher education within five years of earning the GED; and (3) filed an affidavit indicating their intention to submit an immigration application as soon as they were eligible to do so.[90] The bill also allowed for the retroactive charge of in-state tuition to immigrant students attending SUNY or CUNY during the 2001–2002 academic year.[91] The retroactive application of the law effectively grandfathered students who had been paying resident tuition rates prior to CUNY's reversal of its long-time policy and whose likelihood of completing their programs of study would be severely affected by the increase in tuition rates.

The bill was signed on August 9, 2002, making New York the fourth state to pass such legislation (see Appendix B). The signing

---

[88] Youth Empowerment Activists is a youth program of the Latin American Integration Center (Ponce de León, 2003).

[89] Rivera is the chairman of the state Assembly's Puerto Rican/Hispanic Task Force (Somos El Futuro, 2005).

[90] Rivera and Espaillat's proposal was filed as AB 9612 (2002). The companion legislation was Senate Bill 7784 (2002).

[91] While the legislation was pending, students were allowed to defer payment on their nonresident fees (Hebel, 2002).

ceremony was a testament to New York's diversity and the fact that the new in-state tuition law was for all immigrants and not just Latinos, as some had portrayed it.[92] The organizations that had advocated for the changes, MASA in particular, issued statements exhorting both CUNY and SUNY to guarantee the confidentiality of the students' immigration status and to provide legal counseling for those filling out the affidavit regarding their immigration status.

The in-state tuition measure made SUNY and CUNY more afford-able, but financial aid programs continued to be limited, forcing many undocumented students to combine work with school or to enroll on a part-time basis.[93] Qualifying criteria for most of the state's financial aid programs include a twelve-month residency period in the state prior to college enrollment, possession of a high school or GED diploma, acceptable academic standing, and financial need. However, the inclu-sion of immigration-related requirements disqualifies otherwise eligible and needy undocumented students.[94] Yet, even with the burden im-

---

[92] An undocumented African student attending City College addressed the crowd during the signing of the bill, and other immigrant students participated in the ceremony. Soon after the measure was signed, Senator Olga Mendez also drew attention to this diversity, commenting, "Once more, Governor Pataki has shown caring for all Spanish speaking communities in New York State" (Office of the Governor, 2002, p. 1).

[93] Students who lack financial aid are inevitably forced to seek employment, given their overall poverty. A CUNY study found that 48 percent of registered undocumented students had a mixed pattern of attendance ranging from full to part time. Financial need also affected their academic performance, as only 31 percent had a grade point average of 3.0 or higher (Dozier, 2001).

[94] This is particularly true of the TAP program, which provides financial aid to a large segment of eligible students attending CUNY. "CUNY has a few schol-arships available for undocumented students. If you graduated from a New York City High School, public or private, with a B average, you may qualify for a New York City Council-Vallone Academic Scholarship. To get a Vallone Scholarship, you must enroll in a CUNY college within two semesters of your high school graduation. To keep the scholarship you must maintain a B average in college. The full tuition grants of the CUNY Honors College are also avail-able to undocumented students. The Honors College is available to only the most outstanding students" (Wernick, 2004, p. 20).

posed by a lack of financial aid, the foreign-born population of New York's higher education systems remains large. According to CUNY's Office of Institutional Research and Assessment, half (49.5 percent) of that system's undergraduates are immigrants, with 20 percent of them lacking U.S. citizenship or permanent residency, and 2.7 percent attending under student visas.[95] This confirms CUNY's place and role as an immigrant-educating institution.[96]

The principle of equal access to education for all affirmed in New York is being weighed by state educational institutions and legislative bodies across the country, as the immigrant influx prompts reconsideration of tuition policies. Besides Texas, California, and New York, other states have now passed inclusive policies that extend the benefits of in-state tuition to undocumented immigrants. The next section examines some of the similarities in these states' experiences and in the laws they passed.

COMMONALITIES ACROSS IN-STATE TUITION POLICIES

The passage of in-state tuition measures in Utah (2002), Washington (2003), Illinois (2003), Oklahoma (2003), Kansas (2004), New Mexico (2005), and Nebraska (2006) occurred over a five-year period and followed patterns broadly comparable to those in Texas, California, and New York. So, for example, as in the three pioneering states, in some of the remaining seven, educators undertook advocacy; community organizations and other advocacy groups launched broadly based campaigns of support that were sustained by a network of advocates; the immigrant population that would benefit under the new law was diverse; and the administrative hurdles included sorting out complex residency classification issues, waivers of nonresident tuition, and financial aid eligibility criteria. And, despite the precedent set by Texas, California, and New York, at least one state's efforts were temporarily derailed by controversy over the exact meaning of federal law, particularly Section 505 of the IIRIRA.

---

[95] Torres and Van Ooyen (2004). In addition, a study of academic performance at CUNY found that 76 percent of the undocumented had completed their high school education in the United States and were long-time state residents (Dozier, 2001).

[96] Bailey and Weininger (2002).

All of the states to pass new, more inclusive higher education policies have experienced new immigrant flows.[97] Moreover, it was common for the issue of undocumented students' access to higher education to have surfaced before the passage of the in-state tuition bills. In Illinois, one of the six largest immigration-receiving states, prior to the passage of HB 60 two of the state's nine public universities allowed undocumented students to enroll at in-state tuition rates.[98] Even in states with much smaller foreign-born populations, the question of undocumented students' equal access to higher education often emerged before the issue reached the state legislature. Nowhere was this pattern more evident than in New Mexico.

On several occasions before the New Mexico state legislature approved an in-state tuition law, advocates for undocumented students requested an opinion regarding eligibility from the state Attorney General (AG). In 1983, the AG issued an opinion stating that "an illegal alien who has resided in New Mexico for the past ten years and graduated from a New Mexico high school cannot be denied resident classification at the New Mexico State University."[99] This opinion applied specifically to New Mexico State University; whether it was applicable to the state's other postsecondary institutions was not clear. Indeed, in 1991 the Mexican Consulate contacted University of New Mexico officials to voice concern regarding the number of undocumented students attending Albuquerque high schools who had good grades but had no options after graduation.[100] During the years that followed the consulate's expression of concern, the issue appeared to lose prominence. In September 2001, perhaps in response to the in-state tuition victory in Texas, supporters of undocumented students again turned to the AG, requesting advice regarding these students' opportunities to attend New Mexico colleges and universities.[101] By that time, polls conducted by

---

[97] Nebraska, which passed the most recent law in 2006 allowing undocumented high school students' access to in-state tuition, has experienced a growth of the immigrant population chiefly due to the demand for labor within the meatpacking industry (Institute of Agriculture and Natural Resources, 2006).

[98] Illinois Government News Network (2003).

[99] Legislative Education Study Committee (2001), p. 10.

[100] Ibid.

[101] Ibid.

the Legislative Education Study Committee (LESC) and the Commission of Higher Education (CHE) indicated that at least two institutions (University of New Mexico and New Mexico State University) allowed in-state tuition for undocumented immigrants.[102] However, the lack of uniformity and consistency on the issue across institutions had resulted in a great deal of confusion. The executive director of CHE therefore requested the AG's opinion, in 2003, regarding the eligibility of undocumented immigrants for post-secondary educational benefits at public colleges and universities.[103] The AG concluded that

> (1) undocumented immigrants are not prohibited from attending public colleges and universities in New Mexico; (2) an attempt by state colleges and universities to refuse admission to undocumented immigrants would likely be challenged as preempted by federal law and in violation of constitutional equal protection principles; (3) absent a state law expressly making them eligible, undocumented immigrants may not participate in the lottery tuition scholarship program; and (4) although open to challenge, the CHE arguably has sufficient legislative authority to promulgate regulations making undocumented immigrants eligible for in-state tuition.[104]

The CHE did not change the regulations, despite the AG's opinion that it had the latitude to make revisions. A year later, however, the commission reported that there "was institutional support for modifying

---

[102] Further, when the inquiry was made, Texas had already changed its policy, and certainly New Mexico recruiters had used it as an example. The University of Texas at El Paso was accepting undocumented students from New Mexico because under reciprocity agreements, Texas institutions bordering with other states are allowed to accept eligible students from those jurisdictions and offer them the benefit of in-state tuition. Section 21.735 of the Texas Higher Education Coordinating Board Rules, titled Waiver Programs for Certain Nonresident Persons, reads: "(ii) Persons residing in New Mexico and Oklahoma may pay a lowered nonresident tuition when they attend a public technical college located within 100 miles of the border of their home state" (THECB, 2005a).

[103] See Attorney General Opinion at Glenn (2003, p. 1).

[104] Ibid.

the Commission's rule to remove language that prohibits the treatment of undocumented students as residents."[105] Meanwhile, concerns over legal challenges had prompted institutions of higher education in the state to express support for changes explicitly approved by the CHE. All parties recognized that "explicit statutory authority to treat undocumented students as residents would alleviate these concerns."[106]

Thus, after two decades of inquiries from advocates, a true awareness of the plight of undocumented students seemed to have reached public officials and others. In spring 2005, the state legislature passed an in-state tuition law, making New Mexico the ninth state to offer in-state tuition to undocumented high school graduates and the third state, along with Texas and Oklahoma, to extend the possibility of state financial aid to these students. Across the policies of all ten states, New Mexico's measure is by far the most comprehensive. It requires only one year of high school attendance in state (as opposed to the three years required by most) and makes undocumented students eligible for financial help, including loans and scholarships funded by the state lottery.[107] In addition, a New Mexico reciprocal agreement extends the in-state tuition benefit to eligible students in Colorado, where current state law prohibits state universities from offering in-state tuition to high school graduates who are undocumented.[108]

The success achieved in New Mexico, as well in some other states, was possible largely because of the advocacy work of teachers, and especially language instructors, who often are the first people outside the immigrant community to establish meaningful contact with undocumented students. In Utah, for example, Gerry Maak, a Spanish language teacher at Park City High School (a public school whose student body has one of the highest percentages of Latinos in the state) pressed State Representative David Ure to address the issue.[109] In Kansas, Spanish language teacher Jerry Toledo, who sponsors the Hispanic Club at Topeka's Highland Park High School, used his knowledge of

---

[105] Commission on Higher Education (2004), p. 4.

[106] Ibid.

[107] See Massey (2005) and Russell (2007).

[108] For the fall 2007 term, seven Colorado students reportedly took advantage of this program. See Horwedel (2007).

[109] See Park Record (2002); Reade (2002).

the challenges faced by this population to advocate for equal laws.[110] And, like Maak in Utah, English as a Second Language (ESL) teacher David Johnston in Texas has been recognized as one of the forces behind the movement that resulted in HB 1403.[111] Johnston, along with this author, also an educator, founded the Coalition of Higher Education for Immigrant Students, which was one of the key organizations that galvanized the support necessary for bringing about the Texas legislation.

In other states, it was a broad coalition of supporters that assured passage of in-state tuition laws. For instance, in Washington, advocacy efforts were led by the Latino/a Educational Achievement Project (LEAP), which worked closely with the state representatives who filed HB 1079, Phyllis Gutierrez-Kenney (Seattle)[112] and Don Cox (Colfax).[113] This coalition resembled ones in Texas, California, and New York. The members came from school districts, colleges, and universities, and also included 17 school boards, as well as church, civic, community, and labor organizations.[114]

---

[110] See Adamson (2005).

[111] See Chapter Three for additional evidence of Johnston's efforts, and coverage in Alanis (2004), Axtman (2002), and Fischer (2004).

[112] Born to a family of migrant workers, Gutierrez-Kenney is co-founder of the Washington State Migrant Child Care centers, is founder of the Educational Institute for Rural Families, and helped establish the Farm Workers Clinics in Washington.

[113] Ricardo Sanchez, chair, LEAP Board of Directors provided much of the ground support for the legislative proposal. LEAP's central mission is to improve the academic achievement of Latino/a students in Washington state. LEAP's network includes partners in K-12 (nine educational associations, including groups in the Yakima valley, an area with a high migrant population) and in higher education (four community colleges and three state universities). For more information on the Washington in-state tuition bill, and on the coalition of advocates and legislators who worked to bring about on the bill's passage, see LEAP Educator (2003).

[114] Undocumented students' advocates typically secure explicit backing from public school boards, as this is an effective way to strengthen the network of support beyond the student community. In Kansas, for instance, the in-state tuition bill (filed as HB 2145) was endorsed by the State Board of Regents and

Another, similar example is the advocacy work conducted by the Illinois Coalition for Immigrant and Refugee Rights, a statewide coalition that included over 100 organizations from the Chicago metropolitan area.[115] Notably, like the Houston Coalition's work with researchers from the University of Houston, this group collaborated with the Center for Urban Economic Development and the University of Illinois at Chicago to develop and administer a survey that would determine the potential impact of an in-state tuition bill.[116] Those organizing in support of Illinois's HB 60 were successful in portraying the in-state tuition bill as a measure that would benefit a diverse population of immigrants. Immigrant activists provided statistics on the breakdown of the immigrant population in the city of Chicago alone, where Europeans of Polish descent were found to make up almost 20 percent of the total undocumented residents, Latin Americans nearly 70 percent, and Asians of Korean descent a small portion of the total unauthorized population.[117] As figures such as these demonstrate, in-state tuition policies are not created simply to advance the interests of the Latino population.

---

the school districts in Wichita, Shawnee Mission, and Olathe. However, not all of those tasked with the job of ensuring public education for all children agree. Connie Morris, a Kansas State School Board member, proposed during her 2002 campaign for this public post to bar undocumented children from public schools, "saying the cost of educating them is draining away state tax dollars" (Associated Press, 2002). Like other immigration restrictionists, Morris opposes in-state tuition for undocumented immigrants on the flawed grounds that this population does not pay taxes (see Adamson, 2005). For an accurate portrayal of undocumented immigrants' tax contributions, see Lipman (2006).

[115] Mehta and Ali (2003).

[116] See Chapter Three and Mindiola et al. (2002) for more information about the study conducted by the Center for Mexican American Studies at the University of Houston.

[117] Among Latin Americans, the overwhelming majority were Mexicans (60 percent), while another 10 percent were from Central and South America (Mehta and Ali, 2003). Notably, in Chicago, over 60 percent of the undocumented student population lived in households that earned less than $20,000 a year (Mehta and Ali, 2003).

Illinois advocates, like their counterparts in other states, presented the idea of in-state tuition as a measure that would benefit all undocumented immigrant students. Also, although the bulk of the state's undocumented population was of Latino descent, advocates often included non-Latino students in their activities. While the New York and Texas advocates included African students in the hearing and bill-signing ceremonies, in at least one reported instance, advocates in Utah secured the support of Asian students of Indian descent.[118] Advocates also engaged in other efforts that promoted the idea of diversity within the immigrant population. In New Mexico, for instance, proponents of the in-state tuition bill helped repeal legislation that would have excluded undocumented immigrants from nations deemed "terrorist" by the State Department.[119]

In spite of the efforts to secure inclusive bills benefiting a diverse array of immigrant students, most of the states reviewed have registered low enrollment figures under the new inclusive policies. For example, in Utah the number of students taking advantage of the in-state tuition policy has climbed slowly, with 87 in the 2003–04 academic year, 116 in 2004–05, and 182 in 2005–06. Given that the total enrollment in the Utah system of higher education hovers around 100,200, the percentage of immigrant students enrolling is insignificantly small.[120] Washington State faces a similar situation. According to one researcher, even the in-state tuition rates are beyond the means of the parents and guardians of undocumented students, many of whom are impoverished migrant

---

[118] For stories on the bill-signing ceremonies in New York, see NYPIRG (2002); for those in Utah, see Ghandi et al. (2002). In California, a spring 2007 activity at UCLA supported the passage of SB 1 (2007), which would have provided financial aid included students from Bangladesh, Pakistan, Mexico, the Philippines, Romania and one student of Vietnamese descent who was born in Germany (Amaya et. al., 2007).

[119] See Massey (2005). A similar attempt (also unsuccessful) to gut the bill took place in Washington State, where an amendment was introduced to exclude children of undocumented migrant workers from eligibility (Washington State School Directors' Association, 2003).

[120] Robinson, 2007, p.5.

workers.[121] Nebraska, the state to most recently pass an in-state tuition law, is experiencing the same problem. When queried in spring 2007, one semester after the bill took effect, officials at the University of Nebraska-Lincoln and the Nebraska University system indicated that thus far they had no reports of undocumented immigrant students having enrolled. A University of Nebraska regent commented that based on experiences in the other states, he "was not expecting an immediate or large enrollment increase of undocumented immigrants at Nebraska schools."[122]

The classification of undocumented students as residents of the state for tuition purposes is one of the key differences among the various in-state tuition laws and is perhaps one of the "best lessons" learned thus far. States must aim to pass policies that either explicitly grant undocumented students state financial aid or classify them as residents for tuition purposes, based on their high school graduation, thus making them eligible for the pool of state financial aid. As explained previously, in states like California and Nebraska, where the laws do not classify undocumented students as state residents, they are then not eligible for state-funded financial aid. Thus, the costs of higher education remain too high to be affordable for many undocumented students, and they either do not ever begin or cannot finish their college education. New Mexico, Oklahoma, and Texas are the only states that make the students eligible for various grants under their state financial aid programs; these states therefore are more likely to have a higher num-

---

[121] See Sullinger (2004a). During the first semester of implementation, there were fewer than 10 undocumented students taking advantage of the new opportunity. See Iwasaki (2003).

[122] Chapman (2007). LB 239, filed by Dianna Schimek, has an interesting legislative history. It had been defeated during the 2005 legislative session. The following year, she refiled it. The bill then made it all the way to the governor's desk, but the governor decided to veto it. Advocates worked against the clock to gather the necessary votes for a legislative override. The bill became law on April 13, 2006. Following its passage, Nebraska University's president recommended a university policy in compliance with the law. Two months after the bill was passed, the Nebraska Board of Regents passed the policy (Chapman, 2007).

ber of students benefiting under their policies.[123] In other states where these students are considered residents for tuition purposes, financial assistance is limited to certain programs. For instance, in Washington (under HB 1079), undocumented students are not eligible to apply for state financial aid under the Future Teachers Conditional Scholarship and Loan Repayment Program.[124] In addition, scholarship monies are limited to those interested in careers in education and must be repaid with interest if the student fails to pursue teaching. This policy presents a problem for undocumented students. They cannot know in advance whether their immigration status will have been adjusted by the time they graduate from college, and without legal documentation, they may not be able to secure employment. Even with a college degree and a teaching credential, they cannot be certain of gaining a job as a teacher. Similarly, advocates, especially those in California and Texas, have pointed out that undocumented college students who pursue majors that prepare them for careers such as nursing and teaching, where background checks may be required, face the possibility of being unemployable, despite their training and degrees.[125] Provisions in the

---

[123] In Oklahoma, undocumented students eligible under the in-state tuition bill also qualify to receive the Oklahoma Tuition Grant.

[124] The Latino/a Education Achievement Project reports that a bill to address financial aid for undocumented students was presented during the 2007 legislative session but not acted on. "Representative Zack Hudgins (Renton) sponsored HB 2157 [which] would extend State Need Grant financial aid to undocumented students. Co-sponsors of HB 2157 were Phyllis Gutierrez-Kenney and Bob Hasegawa" (LEAP Educator, 2007, p. 6). See also earlier discussion on financial aid impact provided in LEAP Educator (2004).

[125] Advocates in California have already noted that undocumented students pursuing careers in education have been denied their teaching credentials. See Yñiguez (2006). In Texas, this problem came to light as early as 2004. A story published in the *Dallas Morning News* recounted the story of two students from the University of Texas at Arlington who could not comply with the requirement to do an internship at a local school. Their lack of a Social Security number precluded a background check, which is required for any person working in a school district. In order to be able to finish their studies, the students had to change their degrees (González, 2004). Advocates in other states are beginning

DREAM Act (proposed federal legislation discussed in Chapter Six) could resolve this predicament, which will only grow worse as more and more of the undocumented student population now in college begins graduating.

The victories for the principle of equal access to education for all represented by the in-state tuition laws now in effect in ten states are cause for celebration. Still, it is important to stress that the issue of undocumented immigrants' access to higher education continues to be challenged, as anti-immigrant groups file court cases claiming that these policies violate federal immigration law. Restrictionists formulaically cite Section 505 of the IIRIRA to buttress their claim that states are barred from providing undocumented immigrants postsecondary education benefits on the basis of their residence in a given state. This claim has led all states with in-state tuition policies to craft their legislation in ways that link eligibility to high school attendance, not state residence. Even so, the possibility of litigation based on the preemptive power of federal law has caused some states to avoid passing any tuition relief for undocumented students and has prompted others to implement their in-state policies more slowly. In Utah, for example, the in-state tuition bill was delayed in its implementation for a significant portion of 2002, pending Congressional passage of a similar federal measure, namely the DREAM Act, filed by Utah's Senator Orrin Hatch.[126] If the federal bill had passed, it would have allowed undocumented immigrants to adjust their immigration status for employment after college graduation.

---

to see the same situation arise, as exemplified by concerns raised by administrators at a Washington college campus (Nerini, 2006).

[126] Utah's in-state tuition bill was to become effective in July 2002, but it was not given a green light until November of that year, when the AG opined that Utah could remove state restrictions without the federal government's lead (Evans, 2006). After signing the bill into law, Governor Leavitt stated: "I don't understand why the federal government has the right to dictate to the state Board of Regents who it can give in-state tuition to and who it can't. This is a state prerogative, not a federal one" (House, 2002). Noting that Utah's higher education law allows in-state tuition for out-of-state students after they have earned 60 credit hours, he said: "It's a matter of equal protection" (ibid.).

Although the laws in Texas, California, and New York did not face such implementation obstacles, other states have deferred to restrictive interpretations of federal regulations. In that respect, the 1996 IIRIRA has achieved its purpose of creating a climate that excluded undocumented immigrants from being considered for in-state tuition eligibility. By imposing immigration regulations on state educational policy, the federal government has undermined a significant power reserved to the states by the U.S. Constitution—namely, the right of the states to determine their own educational policies. The next chapter reviews some of the legal challenges, particularly those mounted by the nativist organization FAIR, that have appeared since the passage of in-state tuition policies. These cases are designed to have effects that go beyond the targeted states— deterring other jurisdictions from implementing nondiscriminatory tuition policies on behalf of the growing undocumented high school population in this country.

CHAPTER 5

Challenges to In-State Tuition Laws

As all ten states that have passed an in-state tuition policy to provide more equal access to higher education for undocumented immigrants have discovered, creating such a policy is only the first step. Implementing it requires even more effort and commitment. This chapter addresses several obstacles to implementation these states have faced, including legal challenges from anti-immigrant groups; existing federal immigration law that precludes the legalization of undocumented immigrants, even if they have attended school in the United States; and restrictive provisions such as Section 505 of the IIRIRA, which has been used by anti-immigrant forces to argue against in-state tuition policies.

The discussion begins by focusing on the impediments devised by anti-immigrant forces. These groups have waged more than a decade-and-a-half-long campaign to maintain the status quo by preventing immigrant students' participation in institutions of higher education. An early attempt occurred in California, when anti-immigrant forces rallied behind UCLA registrar Donald Bradford's challenge to the gains made under the Leticia "A" decision.[1] Since then, FAIR has led the charge

---

[1] The Citizens Protection Fund (CPF) of the American Association of Women (AAW) provided support for what they term the "historic 1991 *Bradford v. UC Regents* decision regarding tuition fees and residency policy for undocumented students." For a brief note on what the AAW terms "accomplishments," see http://www.americanassociationofwomen.org/AAW_Accomplishments.html.

against these policies.[2] Their efforts and those of similarly inclined anti-immigrant forces have coalesced around three main strategies: (1) bringing class-action lawsuits in federal and state courts against the implementation of in-state tuition laws; (2) filing formal complaints regarding these laws with agencies of the federal government; and (3) working within state legislatures to overturn in-state tuition measures or to pass restrictive legislation impeding undocumented students' access. The next section examines examples of the first strategy, highlighting cases brought against the laws in Kansas (2004) and California (2005).

FAIR'S LAWSUITS IN KANSAS AND CALIFORNIA

On May 20, 2004, Kansas became the eighth state to open the door of higher education to undocumented immigrants, with passage of a state law making these students eligible for in-state tuition rates at public colleges and state universities.[3] The requirements specified by the bill align with those in states with similar policies: (1) attendance at a state high school for at least three years; (2) graduation from high school or receipt of a GED; and (3) a filed affidavit stating the student's intention to adjust his or her immigration status as soon as eligible to do so. The law was to take effect on July 1, 2004, and it was expected to benefit 370 incoming freshmen (or 0.22 percent of the 165,000 students enrolled in the state's system of higher education).[4]

On July 19, 2004, FAIR filed a lawsuit in federal court against the state, the University of Kansas, Kansas State University, and Emporia State University.[5] This lawsuit was the first legal challenge of in-state tuition laws since Texas passed HB 1403. Representing FAIR was Chris Kobach, a professor at the University of Missouri.[6] The plaintiffs

---

2 For FAIR involvement against in-state tuition in California, see Chapter Two.

3 Representative Sue Storm (Overland Park) filed the Kansas in-state tuition proposal, House Bill 2145.

4 Anti-immigrant groups had predicted 2,000 new enrollees, 1.2 percent of the total (Hendricks, 2004; Sullinger, 2004a).

5 Complaint for Injunctive and Declaratory Relief, *Day v. Sebelius* (D. Kan. filed July 19, 2004) (No. 04-4085).

6 Kobach was the chief advisor to the U.S. Department of Justice on immigration and homeland security from 2001 to 2003 (Federation for American Immigration Reform, 2004a; Sullinger, 2005a). While filing the lawsuit, Kobach was

were 24 U.S. citizens who had been classified as nonresidents for tuition purposes. They responded to advertisements placed by FAIR in the campus newspapers of the University of Kansas and Kansas State University in Manhattan.[7] Intervening in the case as defendants were the Kansas League of United Latin American Citizens (KLULAC) and the Hispanic American Leadership Organization (HALO).[8]

---

seeking the Republican nomination for one of Kansas's seats in the U.S. House of Representatives (Hebel, 2004). His campaign in the 3rd district against incumbent Democratic Congressman Dennis Moore was unsuccessful (Hendricks, 2004; Sullinger, 2005a).

[7] Similar strategies have been used by other anti-immigrant groups. On its website, the Friends of Immigration Law Enforcement (FILE) invite students classified as out-of-state residents in Washington State, California, New York, Illinois, Oklahoma, Texas, Utah, and some schools in Georgia to provide details of their experiences, with the lure that they "may be entitled to a refund" (FILE, 2004). In the Kansas suit, one of the plaintiffs from Wisconsin acknowledged that he had not been following the in-state tuition bill and had simply responded to an advertisement (see Adamson and Moon, 2004). For more information on the strategy used in Kansas, see Sullinger (2004b); Visalaw (2004).

[8] Three anonymous undocumented immigrants were also among the interveners. In an effort to intimidate them, the plaintiffs insisted that undocumented immigrants be required to disclose their identities if they were to have standing as interveners. The undocumented students were subsequently removed from the lawsuit because they did not disclose their names. The plaintiffs also tried to prevent KLULAC and HALO from being accepted as interveners, on the grounds that they lacked "associational standing." The court ruled in favor of the interveners and concurred with other courts that "have determined that interveners need not make a show of standing" (*Day v. Sebelius*, p. 13).

The suit sought both injunctive and declaratory relief.[9] Injunctive relief was to be achieved by preventing the law from taking effect and by preventing the defendants from applying it. Also, injunctive relief was sought to prevent the defendants from "discriminating between students who had been classified as legal residents of Kansas and them [plaintiffs]."[10] Given its history and mission, it is doubtful that FAIR would have been satisfied had the court met the group's own demand that "the state of Kansas [be required] to extend the in-state tuition benefits to *everyone* [italics added] attending a public university in the state,"[11] since this would have included undocumented immigrant students. In their request for declaratory relief, the plaintiffs asked the court to declare the in-state tuition law both unconstitutional and a violation of federal law.[12]

The 24 student plaintiffs, backed by FAIR, alleged that they were harmed by the denial of the same educational benefits that Kansas was offering to undocumented immigrants. In the words of FAIR's executive director, "Under the guise of compassion, Gov. Sebelius and the

---

[9] Injunctive relief is defined as follows: "A situation in which a court grants an order, called an injunction, telling a party to refrain from doing something—or in the case of a mandatory injunction, to carry out a particular action. Usually injunctive relief is granted only after a hearing at which both sides have an opportunity to present testimony and legal arguments" (www.nolo.com). Declaratory relief involves "a judge's determination (called a 'declaratory judgment') of the parties' rights under a contract or a statute" (http://legaldictionary.thefreedictionary.com). A declaratory judgment is "A court decision in a civil case that tells the parties what their rights and responsibilities are, without awarding damages or ordering them to do anything. Unlike most court cases, where the plaintiff asks for damages or other court orders, the plaintiff in a declaratory judgment case simply wants the court to resolve an uncertainty so that it can avoid serious legal trouble in the future" (www.nolo.com).

[10] Complaint for Injunctive and Declarative Relief, *Day v. Sebelius*, p. 2.

[11] For more information, see Federation for American Immigration Reform (2004a).

[12] In response to the filing of the lawsuit, the Kansas Board of Regents, which oversees the state's public colleges and universities, explained that the statute did not violate "federal law because it is based on where students attend school, rather than where they live" (Adamson and Moon, 2004).

[Republican dominated] Kansas Legislature are denying educational opportunities and financial assistance[13] to hard-working, law abiding Kansans and Americans from other states."[14] Soon after the lawsuit was filed, anti-immigrant forces received a boost from Kansas Attorney General Phill Kline, who refused to "defend the Governor and the Board of Regents [by] delegating the task to the Civil Litigation Commission of his office," arguing that Kansas tuition law "rewards illegal activity while placing our institutions of higher learning in legal jeopardy for actions inconsistent with federal law."[15] The lawsuit claimed that the Kansas in-state tuition law violated federal immigration law, as well as regulations concerning alien students. The other claims further alleged that the in-state tuition law was preempted by federal law, created a residency status contrary to federal law, infringed on exclusive federal powers, and violated the equal protection clause of the U.S. Constitution. Because these or similar claims are repeatedly raised by opponents of in-state tuition policies, a closer look at each is warranted.

The first count alleged a violation of federal immigration law, specifically, the Personal Responsibility and Work Opportunity Reconciliation Act (PRWORA), Section 1621. The plaintiffs claimed that this provision prohibits states from offering any state or local benefit to undocumented immigrants. However, Section 1621 (d) entitled "State authority to provide for eligibility of illegal aliens for State and local public benefits" states the following:

---

[13] While there is no available information on the Kansas plaintiffs' eligibility for financial aid, students who decide to attend a college outside of their state do so with the understanding that tuition will be significantly higher than in their home state. In the Kansas case, the parents of one of the plaintiffs from California had bought a house for him which was later used as a reason that should qualify them for in-state tuition. As stated by the representative who filed the bill: "Students from other states are eligible for resident tuition in their home states. Illegal immigrant students don't have that option" (Adamson and Moon, 2004).

[14] See Howard Price (2004).

[15] Federation for American Immigration Reform (2004b), p. 1.

A state may provide that an alien who is not lawfully present
in the United States is eligible for *any* [italics added] state or
local public benefit for which such alien would otherwise be
ineligible . . . only through the enactment of a State law after
August 22, 1996, which affirmatively provides for such eligibility.[16]

Section 1621 was clearly an exclusionary measure, yet it recognized that states still had the right to implement laws that provide undocumented immigrants with certain benefits.[17] In spite of this language, the plaintiffs claimed that the Kansas in-state tuition law could
not benefit from such a provision because it did not "contain the express statutory language required by federal law."[18]

The second count also alleged a violation of federal law, this time
of the 1996 IIRIRA, Section 505.[19] FAIR claimed that Section 505
precludes states from using undocumented students' residence in a
given state to grant them higher education benefits such as in-state tuition, on the grounds that doing so would be detrimental to U.S. citizens
paying out-of-state fees. However, as explained in Chapter Four, undocumented students' classification as in-state is based on their high
school attendance and graduation, and not on their residence. In addition, most of the in-state tuition bills have raised the bar by requiring

---

[16] TITLE 8. CHAPTER 14. SUBCHAPTER II. § 1621 (d) formally PRWORA
(1996).

[17] As stated by the sponsor of the in-state tuition law, Representative Sue
Storm, "The state Legislature is a policy-making body, and one of its preroga-
tives is a policy on how to set tuition requirements" (quoted in Adamson and
Moon, 2004).

[18] Complaint for Injunctive and Declarative Relief, *Day v. Sebelius*, p. 7.

[19] In this claim, plaintiffs also referred to U.S. Code TITLE 8. CHAPTER 14.
SUBCHAPTER II. § 1623, which limits undocumented immigrants' eligibility
for higher education benefits based on residency in a state. The U.S. Code is
the "official compilation of most general and permanent public laws of the
United States that are currently in force, organized by subject matter into 50
titles. The U.S. Code collates the original law with subsequent amendments and
deletes language that has been repealed or superseded, so as to provide the
current text of the law" (www.genome.gov/15014431).

undocumented students to have three years of high school attendance in the state, as opposed to the twelve months' in-state residence required of most U.S. citizens from out of state.

The third count alleged a violation of regulations governing alien students. In this claim, plaintiffs referred to the Student and Exchange Visitor Information System (SEVIS), a computerized database instituted as part of the USA PATRIOT Act, to track the admission and enrollment of international or nonimmigrant students who come to the United States for the sole purpose of studying or conducting research. Plaintiffs argued that the Kansas statue "frustrates this federal purpose by allowing aliens to illegally pose as students at Kansas institutions of higher education while remaining outside the SEVIS registration system."[20]

The fourth claim alleged issues of preemption.[21] Plaintiffs argued that the Kansas in-state tuition law is preempted by federal policies regulating immigration and the provision of public benefits to undocumented immigrants. They portrayed the Kansas law as attempting to regulate immigration and therefore as unconstitutional: Kansas law "is preempted because it is impossible for a person who is an illegal alien . . . to both receive postsecondary education . . . and to comply with federal immigration law."[22]

The fifth claim referred to the creation of a residency status contrary to federal law. Plaintiffs alleged that the Kansas law contradicts federal law by allowing undocumented students to be classified as residents for tuition purposes. Specifically, they asserted: "Congress has created a legal disability under federal law that renders illegal aliens incapable of claiming bona fide legal domicile in Kansas, notwithstanding the fact of physical presence or a subjective 'intent' to remain indefinitely in the jurisdiction."[23]

The sixth claim referred to an infringement on powers reserved exclusively to the federal government by the Constitution. Plaintiffs

---

[20] Complaint for Injunctive and Declarative Relief, *Day v. Sebelius*, p. 8.

[21] In general terms, the question of preemption deals with the fact that "by virtue of the Constitution, Congress has exclusive power to establish a uniform rule of immigration and naturalization" (Maxwell, 1979, p. 514).

[22] Complaint for Injunctive and Declarative Relief, *Day v. Sebelius*, p. 8.

[23] Ibid., p. 9.

claimed that the Kansas bill "violates Congress' power over the regulation of interstate commerce and foreign affairs."[24]

The seventh and last claim alleged a violation of the equal protection clause of the Fourteenth Amendment to the Constitution. Specifically, the plaintiffs alleged that the Kansas in-state tuition law "unlawfully and unfairly" allowed undocumented immigrants to attend Kansas
universities and be classified as residents for in-state tuition purposes.[25]
Their main goal here was to demonstrate that federal law does not enti-
tle undocumented students to postsecondary education benefits. Further, they claimed that by establishing an in-state tuition policy, "defendants have further denied nonresident U.S. citizens plaintiffs the
identical postsecondary education benefits to which they are expressly
entitled by federal law."[26]

The defendants and interveners, on the other hand, argued that the
plaintiffs lacked standing (that is, the legal right to bring a lawsuit); that
"the statutes and regulations relied upon by the plaintiffs do not create
private causes of action"; that the in-state tuition law is not pre-empted
by federal law; that "plaintiffs have not pled an equal protection violation"; and that Kansas Governor Sebelius should not be included as a
party in the lawsuit.[27]

Court deliberations began on May 10, 2005. On July 5, 2005, the
judge dismissed the FAIR lawsuit. The dismissal was based primarily
on FAIR's lack of standing to challenge the policy, but it also addressed two other complaints raised by the plaintiffs: the supposed violation of federal immigration law and private right of action; and the
alleged infringement on the equal protection clause. These three key
aspects of the ruling are reviewed below. In general terms, the judge
found that the plaintiffs did not have a case. More important, he ruled
that students who are U.S. citizens are not harmed in any way by in-
state tuition laws that provide access to higher education to undocumented residents. As an activist who advocated on behalf of the in-state
tuition law explained, "the issue of standing is not a procedural detail; it
is a fundamental problem that demonstrates a key policy contention—

---

[24] Ibid.

[25] Ibid. p. 1.

[26] Ibid., p. 10.

[27] Ibid., pp. 14–15.

that plaintiffs are not negatively impacted by the law."[28] In its decision, the court alluded to the constitutional standing required of a plaintiff in order to pursue an action.[29] As stated by the interveners, the plaintiffs lacked such standing with respect to the in-state tuition law:

> [it] only affects the price certain students pay to attend a regents school. Thus, the only people affected by the amount of tuition charged to certain students under [the in-state tuition law] are the students who satisfy each of its requirements—and plaintiffs are not among them. Plaintiffs do not have personal rights which are affected.[30]

The defendants' argument refers to the fact that annulling the in-state tuition law does not change the classification of the plaintiffs as out-of-state residents. Moreover, those filing the lawsuit were out-of-state students and therefore, unlike most undocumented students of Kansas, had not graduated from a Kansas high school, thus did not meet one of the law's key requirements. In addition, the cost of their tuition had not been an issue prior to the passage of the in-state tuition law. Therefore, one must conclude that the plaintiffs' arguments are a sophism aimed at hiding their real concern, that of denying access to education to certain eligible undocumented students.

In response to the defendants' argument that the plaintiffs lacked standing, the plaintiffs alleged that postsecondary education "is a scarce

---

[28] Lewis (2005). Lewis is director of policy, advocacy and research at El Centro Inc., one of the agencies that provided support for the passage of in-state tuition legislation.

[29] "A party raising only a generally available grievance about government—claiming only harm to his and every citizen's interest in proper application of the Constitution and laws, and seeking relief that no more directly and tangibly benefits him than it does the public at large—does not state an Article III case or controversy" (*Lujan v. Defenders of Wildlife*, as cited in *Day v. Sebelius*, p. 17). As explained by the court in its ruling, "there are three requirements to Article III standing: (1) injury in fact, (2) causation and (3) redressability" (*Day v. Sebelius*, p. 18).

[30] *Day v. Sebelius*, p. 19.

resource and that competition for that resource gives them standing."[31] The court found that the plaintiffs had failed to demonstrate the ways in which the in-state tuition law injured them. Further, they had not provided support for their contentions that they had a "property right in in-state tuition rates" or that the in-state tuition bill had led to tuition increases.[32] The court added that the impact of the in-state tuition bill had been minimal given the negligible enrollment. Figures from the Kansas Board of Regents for the first year of the law's implementation showed only 30 students benefiting.[33] That figure represented only 0.01 percent of total enrollment in the Kansas higher education system, and, as determined by the court, most of the beneficiaries were not even undocumented immigrants.[34] The court found that the plaintiffs were not affected by such regulations and that they had been unable to prove injury resulting from the alleged violation of immigration law.

With respect to violation of federal law, the plaintiffs claimed that the in-state tuition bill violated Section 505 of the IIRIRA and that they had a private right of action to redress violations of federal law. In other words, the plaintiffs interpreted the language of the federal statute as granting them the right to remedy the so-called injury caused by state law providing undocumented students access to in-state tuition. They argued that

> the language of the [federal] statue makes the U.S. citizen or national who is granted eligibility for a state postsecondary education benefit, beneficiary of the provision even if he or she is *not* [italics added] a resident of the state.[35]

The court found that the application of immigration laws is a matter reserved to immigration authorities. In addition, the court added that "no support can be found for the idea that Congress intended to grant enforcement rights to any private citizens for the alleged violation."[36]

---

[31] Complaint for Injunctive and Declarative Relief, *Day v. Sebelius*, p. 20.

[32] Ibid.

[33] Sullinger (2005).

[34] As one newspaper commentator put it: "Such a lot of fuss for such a small number of kids" (Hendricks, 2004).

[35] Complaint for Injunctive and Declarative Relief, *Day v. Sebelius*, p. 29.

[36] Ibid., p. 28.

Regarding the plaintiffs' adduced relationship between immigration violations and civil remedies, the court found that Section 505 targets undocumented immigrants and not U.S. citizens. Thus, there is "no implication of intent to confer rights on [the plaintiffs]."[37]

The court ruling also addressed the supposed violation of the Fourteenth Amendment's equal protection clause. The plaintiffs claimed that the in-state tuition law discriminated against them by creating "two classes of non-Kansas residents: illegal or undocumented aliens and United States citizens,"[38] and providing in-state tuition to the former group while denying it to the latter. However, a careful reading of the Kansas provision demonstrates that it does not apply solely to the undocumented but to any student who meets the criteria, "regardless of whether the person is or is not a citizen of the United States of America."[39] As supporters of the law have pointed out, advancing an equal-protection argument is a flawed approach because the Kansas law makes "no classification based on alienage, [it] applies to all individuals, aliens or U.S. citizens."[40] The court dismissed this challenge as well, finding that the plaintiffs lacked legal standing to assert an equal protection claim.

Finally, the court ruled that allowing undocumented immigrants to be classified as residents for tuition purposes did not preclude the admission of or alter the tuition rates charged to the plaintiffs. The nonresident tuition exemption created by the Kansas law does not differ from similar waivers that allow other classes of individuals, such as members of the military, to pay in-state tuition. And those other waivers have no impact on the tuition rates paid by the nonresident plaintiffs. To prove a denial of equal opportunity, the plaintiffs would have had to show that they met the requirements set forth in the in-state tuition law. Given that they all were out-of-state residents, their likelihood of having completed three years of high school in Kansas was improbable.

Historically, as previous chapters have shown, educational policy and control of educational resources have been used to achieve various

---

[37] Ibid., p. 30.
[38] Ibid., p. 32.
[39] Ibid., p. 1.
[40] Ibid., p. 32.

immigration-related goals.[41] Groups opposing in-state tuition policies for the undocumented have based their arguments on the premise that limiting these students' access to education is an effective way of deterring unauthorized immigration. Beyond charging that in-state tuition policies encroach on federal policies and arguing that the area of education is not reserved to the states, groups such as FAIR have tried to "dictate admissions policies at the state's colleges and universities."[42] The Kansas court decision reaffirms education as a prerogative of the states, while immigration remains regulated by Congress. By association, the court's ruling also reaffirms the fact that the in-state tuition policy is about education, not immigration. In response to its loss in *Day v. Sebelius*, FAIR filed an appeal before the Tenth Circuit. Almost three years after its passage, the in-state tuition statute was strengthened, because the "Tenth Circuit Court of Appeals affirmed the trial court decision."[43]

In bringing legal action against Kansas's in-state tuition policy, FAIR was aiming higher than this one state. As a spokesperson put it, "We expect that this case will set a legal precedent that will allow citizens and legal immigrants to challenge similar laws in other states."[44] Laws in California, New York, and Texas no doubt were high on the list, as these states are home to the bulk of the undocumented population.[45] Dismissal of the lawsuit, while undoubtedly a victory for supporters of undocumented students' access to higher education, should not be interpreted as a deathblow to FAIR's activity on this issue. Attempts to undermine legislative steps to open the doors of higher education to undocumented immigrants assuredly will continue.[46]

---

[41] For instance, in *Nyquist v. Mauclet* (see Chapter Two), New York State attempted to impose naturalization on foreign citizens as a requirement for financial aid eligibility.

[42] Hendricks (2004).

[43] See Olivas (2007c).

[44] FAIR (2004a), p. 2.

[45] Urban Institute (2004b).

[46] As one author noted, "the IIRIRA does not specify the sanctions or consequences of noncompliance, however most institutions consider themselves bound by its language because they wish to avoid the scrutiny of the Bureau of

Indeed, soon after the defeat in Kansas, Attorney Chris Kobach, who had represented the out-of-state plaintiffs, filed a class-action lawsuit in California, *Martinez v. Regents of the University of California.*[47] This lawsuit focused on the state's higher education system (namely the Regents of the University of California, the Trustees of the California State University System, and the Board of Governors of the California Community Colleges). Here the strategy was to recast the arguments against in-state tuition into a charge that California had illegally denied out-of-state residents the tuition waiver it makes available to both state residents and high school graduates. The suit, filed in state court, recited the same complaints expressed in the Kansas case and added a complaint against the California Unruh Civil Rights Act and the state constitution. It also referred to an "Illegal Alien Tuition Scheme" through which the defendants were alleged to have violated federal law by allowing undocumented students to enroll at in-state tuition rates and by creating protections within state law to preclude the recovery of damages in the case of litigation.[48]

In fall 2006, the court rejected the plaintiffs' arguments and upheld California's in-state tuition law. In doing so, it reinforced the same arguments that had been advanced in Kansas. It affirmed the law on the

---

Citizenship and Immigration Services (BCIS) and they fear losing federal financial student aid" (Yates, 2004, p. 597).

[47] No. CV-05-2064 (Yolo County Super. Ct. filed Dec. 14, 2005). Kobach has argued that FAIR did not fund his lawsuit in California (see Sullinger, 2005b). This lawsuit did not target the governor, as the Kansas one had, but instead named as defendants the Board of Governors and chancellor of the California Community Colleges, the University of California Regents and President Dynes and the California State University Trustees and chancellor.

[48] The protections within state law charge refers to AB 1543 (2001), passed soon after the in-state tuition law (AB 540, 2001) to protect the University of California, the California State University and the California Community Colleges from monetary damages in the event of a lawsuit. (See also Chapter Four.) Kobach's denunciation of this statutory protection was linked to the fact that his lawsuit sought "reimbursement of nonresident tuition fees resulting from the unlawful discrimination against them based on their status as out-of-state U.S. citizens." The remedies to plaintiffs were set at $25,000 each (*Martínez v. Regents of the Univ. of Cal.*, p. 3).

basis that (1) it does not regulate federal immigration law; (2) Congress and federal immigration authorities historically have not occupied the area of resident tuition determinations; and (3) the California Education Code dealing with in-state tuition does not conflict with federal law, nor does it create a private right of action.[49]

FILING COMPLAINTS WITH FEDERAL AGENCIES: THE CHALLENGE TO TEXAS LAW

In 2004, following their defeat in Kansas, in-state tuition opponents attempted to capitalize on the courts' holding that the enforcement of immigration law is the purview of federal authorities. A month after the dismissal of the FAIR-backed Kansas lawsuit, another anti-immigrant group, the Washington Legal Foundation (WLF), filed a formal complaint with the Department of Homeland Security (DHS) Office of Civil Rights and Civil Liberties (OCRCL) regarding the Texas in-state tuition bill.[50] The core of the foundation's complaint charges that Texas's implementation of its in-state tuition bill violates "the civil rights of U.S. citizens who live outside the State."[51] This allegation is similar to claims in the Kansas case, as it pertains to the rights of out-of-state students. As noted in the Kansas ruling, as well as in the subsequent ruling in California, applicants from other states do not meet the requirements of the in-state tuition law because they have not graduated from high schools within the state.

The Washington Legal Foundation bases its complaint on the *Day v. Sebelius* ruling that the application of immigration laws is a matter

---

[49] *Martinez v. Regents of the Univ. of Cal.* After its defeat in fall 2006, and as it had done in Kansas, FAIR filed an appeal. As of fall 2007, the appeal is still pending (see Olivas, 2007c).

[50] The OCRCL is responsible for investigating complaints of violations of rights arising from federal immigration laws (Howard Price, 2004).

[51] In line with other anti-immigrant groups, the WLF describes its objectives as "protecting the constitutional and civil rights of American citizens and aliens lawfully present in this country" (Popeo and Samp, 2005, p. 2). However, in the letter sent to the DHS, all references to those affected by in-state tuition laws are to U.S. citizens and nationals; there are none to permanent residents or to what they refer to as aliens lawfully present in this country. This kind of omission is indicative of the group's nativist rather than constitutional politics.

reserved to immigration authorities. The WLF demands that the federal government prosecute the violations that it asserts have been created by the Texas decision to allow certain undocumented students to qualify for in-state tuition. By filing against the DHS, the plaintiffs seek to satisfy that requirement and, further, to leave the matter in the hands of the Department of Justice. Specifically, the complaint demands that the Department of Justice file a lawsuit in order to achieve injunctive relief as well as monetary relief for "aggrieved nonresidents of Texas."[52]

Further, the WLF complaint requires the DHS to issue a "directive to Texas to cease further civil rights violations, withholding [DHS] funding until Texas brings itself into compliance, and referring this matter to the Department of Justice for appropriate enforcement action."[53] It demands that the state either offer in-state tuition to all U.S. citizens and nationals or stop making undocumented students eligible for in-state tuition on the basis of residency. The "all or nothing" language of these proposals is misleading. The real aim is not to achieve in-state tuition for "all," but rather to insure that undocumented students receive "nothing."[54] In an attempt to lend validity to their claims and deflect criticisms of anti-Latino racism, the complaint notes an exceptional case in which the WLF successfully challenged the University of Maryland's Bannerek scholarship program, which was available only to African Americans.[55] Pitting U.S.-born minorities against other disadvantaged groups is a common tactic. Indeed, FAIR portrays affirmative action measures as "weapons" used against what they describe as "native born minorities vs. imported minorities."[56]

The last important aspect of the WLF's lawsuit is the complaint that the Texas law violates Section 505 of the IIRIRA. As previously

---

[52] Popeo and Samp (2005), p. 9.

[53] Ibid., p. 1.

[54] See Yates (2004) for further discussion of the real goals of opponents' "either-or" proposals.

[55] The final decision from the U.S. Circuit Court of Appeals for the Fourth Circuit ruled that racially exclusive scholarships are unconstitutional, a decision that the Supreme Court let stand.

[56] FAIR (2002a), p. 1. Other organizations sharing FAIR views on matters of immigration and affirmative action include The Heritage Foundation where Kris Kobach served as visiting fellow.

explained, that provision, codified as United States Code Title 8, Section 1623, prohibits states from awarding postsecondary benefits on the basis of residence to undocumented immigrants if such benefits are not also awarded to out-of-state residents. However, the complaint also notes, "Section 1623 does *not* [italics added] prohibit a state from awarding postsecondary education benefits to an illegal alien, while denying similar benefits to nonresident citizens and nationals, where the basis for doing so is totally unrelated to residency."[57] This statement acknowledges that if eligibility is not based on an undocumented student's residence in the state but on any other requirement, nothing in the law precludes the state from offering the benefit to undocumented immigrants. In other words, the claimants recognize that undocumented students are eligible for in-state tuition, but not on the basis of residence in the state. Currently, the in-state tuition laws that extend benefits to undocumented students do so based on criteria other than residency. In-state tuition laws seek to benefit all high school graduates or GED recipients, without drawing distinctions based on immigration status. As even a cursory reading of existing laws shows, the critical criteria for eligibility apply to all college applicants and consist of school attendance and graduation (or GED completion), not residence in the state.

The WLF complaint anticipates this kind of rebuttal. It asserts that Texas cannot avoid conflict with the federal statutes "simply by amending the language of [its in-state tuition law] to offer lower in-state tuition rates to residents of Texas; or those who graduated from a Texas high school."[58] According to the WLF, high school attendance or GED receipt are invalid eligibility criteria. The use of high school graduation, the complaint argues, does not comply with Section 1623 because it is "a close proxy for physical presence within the state."[59] In that sense, the Texas in-state tuition law, according to the WFL, attempts to treat undocumented high school graduates as bona fide residents of the state, which is incompatible with federal regulations.

In the summary section of its complaint, the WFL repeats a common anti-immigrant mantra: unless the federal government steps in,

---

[57] Popeo and Samp (2005), p. 3.

[58] Ibid., p. 6.

[59] Ibid.

"immigration-rights groups may be emboldened to encourage yet other states to flout the federal law."[60] A month after submitting the complaint against Texas, the WLF filed a complaint against New York. As of fall 2007, the Department of Homeland Security had not taken action on either of these two complaints.[61]

STATE LEGISLATORS' EFFORTS TO OVERTURN IN-STATE TUITION LAWS

In addition to lawsuits against state officials or higher education systems and complaints filed with federal agencies, challenges to in-state tuition policies have taken the form of bills within state legislatures to overturn existing in-state tuition measures. In Utah, for instance, opponents have used this tactic in most legislative sessions.[62] Other attempts within state legislatures have taken place in California (see Chapter Four) and most recently, in Texas and Oklahoma. This final section of the chapter will review legislative attacks on in-state tuition laws.

In November 2006, soon after a California court had upheld that state's in-state tuition law, anti-immigrant forces in Texas filed five separate house bills aimed at overturning the gains codified in 2001.[63] One, HB 28, is of particular interest. Filed by a representative from Smith County, the same area in Texas where *Plyler v. Doe* (the Supreme Court decision allowing undocumented students K-12 access) had originated, the bill focused on the eligibility of individuals born in Texas, thus U.S. citizens, but whose parents are undocumented immigrant workers. Those U.S. citizens, HB 28 proposed, would not qualify for "any benefit provided by this state or a political subdivision of this

---

[60] Ibid.

[61] See Olivas (2007c).

[62] In 2005, the joint Education Interim Committee recommended repeal of the in-state tuition law. The most recent attacks include HB 7 (2006) and HB 224 (2007). In response to a request, and drawing on the Kansas ruling in *Day v. Sebelius*, the Utah Attorney General has indicated that the state law is valid (see Robinson, 2007; Stewart and Bulkeley, 2007; and Utah's Assistant AG opinion at Evans, 2006).

[63] All filed during the 80th legislative session, these bills are HB 28 (Berman), HB 104 (Riddle), HB 141 (Jackson), HB 39 (Paxton), and HB 159 (Zedler). The last two were companion bills.

state."[64] Thus, twenty-five years after the Supreme Court disagreed with the state's attempt to deny certain sectors of the population a primary and secondary education, efforts to revive racist education policies continue. Significantly, this latest attempt went even further than its predecessors. It targeted U.S. citizens, not undocumented students, and it limited access to a wide range of benefits, not education alone.[65] At the hearing before the House Committee on State Affairs, supporters of the existing law crowded the room and provided extensive testimony regarding the importance of preserving Texas' in-state tuition law. The anti-in-state tuition bills eventually died.[66]

---

[64] Berman (2006), p. 2. The bill went well beyond education, targeting ten areas (1) grant, contract, loan, professional license or commercial license provided by an agency of the state; (2) employment by the state; (3) state retirement; (4) public assistance benefits including welfare payments, food stamps or food assistance; (5) health care or public assistance health benefits; (6) disability benefits or assistance; (7) public housing or public housing assistance; (8) instruction in primary and secondary education; (9) instruction from a public institution of higher education; and (10) unemployment benefits.

[65] A somewhat similar case in California was filed in 2006. In *Student Advocates for Higher Education et al. v. Trustees, California State University et al.*, CPF-06-506755, Nov. 3, 2006, a U.S. citizen challenged the university's practice of denying residency status to students due to their *parents'* immigration status. The petitioner, a student at Cal State Los Angeles, had to apply to college under California's AB 540 in-state tuition law (see Chapter Four). However, because of the university's insistence that she was not able to claim residency, the student was unable to receive state financial aid in the form of Cal Grants. The case was settled in favor of the plaintiffs in 2007, and a consent decree order overturned the university's practice (Helwick, 2007). For more info see Superior Court of California, County of San Francisco at http://www.sftc.org/Scripts/Magic94/mgrqispi94.dll?APPNAME=IJS&PRGN AME=ROA&ARGUMENTS=-ACPF06506755.

[66] The anti-in-state tuition bills eventually were merged into one (HB 159). On May 11, 2007, a challenge to the bill was upheld on a technicality by the speaker of the House of Representatives. Aside from this, immigrant students and their supporters had been encouraged by the Texas governor's statement that he would veto the anti in-state tuition bill if it came to his desk. ``I'm for

None of the challenges described in this chapter has been successful in overriding the existence of in-state tuition policies. However, attempts at the state level to limit the impact of these policies continue, as experiences in Oklahoma make clear.[67] In 2007, the Oklahoma legislature passed House Bill 1804, sponsored by Representatives Randy Terrill (House) and James Williamson (Senate), to overturn the gains codified in the 2003 in-state tuition law. Section 11 of HB 1804, titled the "Oklahoma Taxpayer and Citizen Protection Act of 2007," specifies a "General prohibition on eligibility of Illegal Aliens for postsecondary education benefits," but it also contains an exception, "per the provisions of Section 13." Section 13 ("Specific Prohibition on eligibility of illegal aliens for postsecondary education benefits") limits the existing in-state tuition policy by (1) eliminating the GED diploma as part of the eligibility criteria for in-state tuition benefits; and (2) including a requirement that the student submit a copy of an application filed with the immigration service one year after enrolling in college. This new requirement will further reduce the already negligible number of undocumented students from pursuing a college education.[68]

Creating Hostile Environments

Another tactic (not examined in detail here) of those forces who oppose equal access to in-state tuition has been to pass legislation that explicitly makes undocumented students ineligible for in-state tuition. Arizona's Proposition 300, related to Public Program Eligibility and passed in 2006, "requires undocumented immigrants to pay out-of-state tuition

---

leaving the law like it is because I think it serves a good purpose," he said. (Robinson and Ratcliffe, 2007).

[67] For more information see Advancement of Hispanic Students in Higher Education Taskforce (2007).

[68] Section 13 also contains a provision for those who are not eligible to file paperwork with immigration authorities. As in the other states, the students must fill out an affidavit stating that they will file an application to adjust their immigration status as soon as they are eligible to do so. The new changes to the Oklahoma law require however that, once the U.S. Citizenship and Immigration Services provides an opportunity for such a formal process, the students file within a year and present copies of such paperwork to be kept in the institution's records.

at the state's public universities and colleges, prohibits students from receiving any type of financial assistance that is funded with state money, and requires schools to determine and report to the Legislature how many undocumented immigrants are attending their schools."[69] In addition to creating a climate of fear and hostility, the measure, enacted January 1, 2007, turns employees of the state's educational systems into immigration enforcement agents.[70] The climate of hostility has extended to those helping the affected students.[71]

Other states have created similarly hostile environments through constant legislative activity on the issue and through the actions of public officials. Nowhere has this been more evident than in Virginia and Colorado. In September 2002, the Virginia Attorney General's office issued an "Immigration Law Compliance Update," a memorandum addressed to education officials (from college and university presidents to registrars to the executive director of the State Council for Higher Education in Virginia) regarding the enrollment of undocumented stu-

---

[69] See Wingett and Benson (2007).

[70] The Joint Legislative Budget Committee's monthly fiscal highlights report indicates that 1,500 students from Arizona State University and the University of Arizona were denied classification as in-state students and state financial aid because they could not prove legal immigration status. That figure amounts to 1.9 percent of the 124,000 students enrolled at both universities. At the community-college level, 1,790 students statewide were prevented from enrolling as in-state (representing 1.1 percent of the total 124,000 enrollment) and another 320 were deemed ineligible for financial aid (which amounts to 0.78 percent of the 40,900 students who receive aid). In total, the measure, affected at least 5,000 people during its first seven months, including those now ineligible for government-assisted child care, state adult education and the Family Literacy Program. For more information see Joint Legislative Budget Committee Staff (2007) and Wingett and Benson (2007).

[71] The financial impact on the students prompted Arizona State University's president to award them private scholarships to help defray the cost of their education. The ASU president was accused by the principal sponsor of Proposition 300, State Treasurer Dean Martin, of breaking the law and violating the spirit of the law (see Roberts, 2007).

dents in institutions of higher education.[72] Although this memo did not constitute state law, it had the effect of discouraging the enrollment of undocumented students.[73] A year later, in 2003, House Bill 2339 was filed. This legislation would have prevented undocumented students from being eligible for in-state tuition rates or all other postsecondary benefits. The bill was eventually vetoed by Governor Mark Warner.[74]

---

[72] The memo included five recommendations: (1) prohibit the enrollment of undocumented students; (2) report students who are on campus (the memo included a form to be used by college and university employees); (3) adhere to the memo's interpretation of Virginia's Domicile Guidelines; (4) scrutinize students on tourist visas to prevent their full time enrollment and (5) inform the INS of the visa status of international students. The memo was presented as part of the "national response to the attacks of September 11" (Landry, 2002, p. 3).

[73] "Most Virginia community colleges have followed the guidance from the state attorney general's office not to admit students without documentation and to charge undocumented students who are admitted out-of-state tuition. However, Northern Virginia Community College and some of other large schools near Washington, DC, have been admitting these students" (Biswas, 2005, p. 5). As in Arizona, individual colleges have sought to ameliorate the excessive fees levied against undocumented students by providing private scholarships. In response to the obstacles created by the AG memo, the Mexican American Legal Defense and Educational Fund (MALDEF) "sued seven Virginia state colleges and universities on behalf of Latino undocumented students seeking entrance to the schools on the grounds that they were denied admission due to their legal status" (Melendez, 2004). In February 2004, in *Equal Access Education v. Merten*, the federal judge rule[d] that "institutions may, consistent with the U.S. Constitution, deny admission or enrollment to aliens unlawfully in this country. The court left this decision up to the individual colleges and universities" (Miksch, 2005).

[74] In his veto message, the governor reminded Virginia legislators that he was not signing the measure into law because it did not contain an amendment that he had proposed "which would have allowed a *small* [italics added] but deserving group of students to receive the benefit of in-state tuition only in those cases where they can show that: 1) they or their parents paid Virginia income taxes for three years; 2) they lived in Virginia for five years; 3) they are in the process of obtaining legal status; and 4) they graduated from a Virginia high

Since then, anti-immigrant forces have filed other legislative bills aimed at precluding undocumented students from college enrollment.[75]

A similar situation has taken place in Colorado. Since 2002, when Jesús Apodaca made the news with his story about college aspirations, there has been furious activity on this issue. Beginning in 2003, and continuing for the next three years, State Representative Val Vigil and State Senator Abel Tapia introduced in-state tuition legislation almost identical to the laws that have passed in the other ten states.[76] In 2005, the in-state tuition bill was introduced as House Bill 1124, but as with its predecessors, it did not pass out of the Senate Education Committee. The bill enjoyed the support of all of the higher education institutions and all but one of the members of the Colorado Commission on Higher Education (CCHE).[77] During 2005, the bill also gained support from

---

school. This amendment would have provided hope and opportunity to a small group of young people who were brought to this country by their parents through no fault of their own, and who are now—and who in all likelihood will continue to be—a part of our communities. The amendment was fully consistent with federal law, and *was more restrictive* [italics added] than measures adopted in several other states, including Utah, Texas, and California" (Warner, 2003, p. 1). See also Le Texier (2003).

[75] These restrictive bills include HB 156 (2004); HB 1798 (2005), titled Public Benefits—Proof of Legal Presence (signed by Governor Warner); HB 1050 (2006), In-state Tuition for Aliens (passed in the House, 76–23 but failed in the Senate); HB 262 (2006), Admission of Illegal Aliens to Public Institutions of Higher Education (passed in the House, 67–33 but failed in the Senate); and HB 2623 (2007), In-State tuition for Aliens. This last exclusionary bill included within it three others, HB 1961 (Hargrove), HB 2169 (Cline), and HB 2935 (Miller). As with all the other bills in previous years, this one passed in the House, 74–23, but failed in the Senate.

[76] In 2004, the Vigil's measure (HB 1178) was opposed by Rep. Ted Harvey (Highlands Ranch), who introduced HB 1187. Harvey's bill sought to make law a policy of the Colorado Commission on Higher Education that prevents immigrants from receiving in-state status (Henley, 2005).

[77] The 2004 bill (HB 1132) did not pass. In 2005, the vote in the Senate Education Committee was 7–5 (see Goodland, 2005). "The Colorado Commission on Higher Education was established in 1965 by the Colorado legislature. In 1985 the legislature gave the commission increased authority and specific directives

the Colorado Commission of High School Improvement, which recommended passage of the law.[78] Soon after the failure of House Bill 1124, questions were raised regarding whether CCHE had authority under existing law to "alter the state rules for tuition classification to allow undocumented aliens to qualify for in-state tuition without running afoul of federal law."[79] The question was directed to the Colorado Attorney General (AG). In his opinion, the AG reiterated that federal law allows states to make such determination, but he concluded that "CCHE lacks statutory authority to establish a policy or regulation granting in-state tuition status to undocumented aliens. Rather, such a determination would require an amendment to the Tuition Classification Act by the General Assembly."[80] This opinion effectively threw the issue back to the legislature. In 2006, during a special session called by Colorado Democrats, House Bill 1023 was passed.[81] That bill, co-

---

through the passage of House Bill 1187. Specific responsibilities include developing long-range plans for an evolving state system of higher education" (see History and Responsibilities of the Commission at http://www.state.co.us/cche/aboutus/history.html).

[78] One of the commission members made the following apt comment: "As a businessman, I see undocumented workers as a very important part of our economy. Until we are ready to repeal the laws of supply and demand, we are foolish from a selfish point of view not to have well trained, well educated workers . . . What's more they are taxpayers even if they are undocumented" (Protopsaltis, 2005, p. 4).

[79] Suthers (2006), p. 2.

[80] "In sum, federal law requires that, in order for states to grant in-state tuition status to undocumented aliens, they must first affirmatively provide for such eligibility, and do so on a residency-neutral basis" (Suthers, 2006, p. 3).

[81] Soon after the passage of the law, the executive director of the Department of Higher Education requested an opinion from the AG's office regarding whether HB 1023 applied to undocumented high school students who wished to pursue concurrent enrollment within institutions of higher education; the program is designated as the Postsecondary Enrollment Options (PSEO). A memo from the AG office reiterated that "all PSEO students, notwithstanding any other law to the contrary, are afforded in-state tuition at a public institution of higher education" (Dyl, 2007, p. 2). In his opinion, Dyl (2007) also added that PSEO students "are exempt from providing proof of lawful presence under

sponsored by Speaker of the House Andrew Romanoff, has been called one of the most draconian anti-immigrant measures enacted by any state.[82] The politics of bipartisan attacks against immigrant communities was once again in evidence.[83]

The tactic of using state legislatures as immigration battlefields, as occurred in Colorado, reached its zenith in Georgia. In 2006, the legislature passed the Georgia Security Immigration Compliance Act, which exceeds California's anti-immigrant Proposition 187 in both breadth

---

House Bill 06S-1023, because they are merely attaining a high school education, which is not a 'public benefit' under 8 USC 1621(c)(1)" (p. 3). During the same year when this opinion was made public, Governor Bill Ritter's P-20 Education Coordinating Council released its recommendations regarding educational issues from preschool to graduate school. In spite of the supportive AG's legal opinion, none of the council's recommendations dealt with undocumented students, and on the issue of concurrent enrollment, there was only a vague recommendation to expand the current program.

[82] "The new law, signed by Owens on July 31, requires 1 million people receiving state and federal benefits to prove they are legal residents of the United States. It is being described as one the toughest immigration laws in the country" (Siegel, 2006). Quoted in the Siegel (2006) article, John Straayer, a political science professor at Colorado State University stated: "The Republicans were hoping to pin the label of 'soft on immigration' on the Democrats, but it didn't work. . . . The Democrats saw it as a chess game, [and] for every move the Republicans made, they made adroit countermoves. . . . Many of Colorado's grassroots immigrant advocates say they feel betrayed by Romanoff. They lament legislation that they say will make it harder for the needy to access government services" (Siegel, 2006). "We were largely shut out of the process, we were shut out of much of the decision making, we were not present during many of the meetings," said Bill Vandenberg, executive director of the Colorado Progressive Coalition (ibid.).

[83] The bill has been opposed by a number of organizations, including those who sponsor the Latina/o Advocacy Day. They have called for a review and potential repeal of HB 1023 because of its potential for discrimination and racial profiling noting how, thus far, the law has affected U.S. citizens. Support for in-state tuition is represented, among many others, by Padres Unidos/Jovenes Unidos, the Colorado Federation for Community Integration, Metro Organizations for People and the Higher Education Access Alliance.

and harshness.[84] This act is an example of a tactic that involves incorporating educational restrictions into broader bills designed to limit immigrants' alleged use of social benefits. Georgia's legislation requires state and local government agencies to deny state and local benefits to people who are unable to verify legal residency and it deputizes local law enforcement officers to enforce federal immigration laws.[85] The Georgia law, referred to as SB 529, went into effect July 1, 2007 and added Chapter 36 to Section 9, Title 50 of the Official Code of Georgia Annotated, to read: "(7) For postsecondary education, whereby the Board of Regents of the University System of Georgia or the State Board of Technical and Adult Education shall set forth, or cause to be set forth, policies regarding postsecondary benefits that comply with all federal law including but not limited to public benefits as described in 8 U.S.C. Section 1611, 1621, or 1623."[86]

Until the passage of SB 529, the Board of Regents of the University System of Georgia allowed universities in the system to award out-of-state tuition waivers to international and superior out-of-state students "provided that the number of such waivers in effect does not exceed 2 percent of the equivalent full-time students enrolled at the institution in the fall term immediately proceeding the term for which the out-of-state tuition is to be waived."[87] This practice benefited some undocumented students. Soon after SB 529 was signed into law in April 2006, Burns Newsome, an associate vice chancellor who acts as the Board of Regents' attorney, sent a memo to the presidents of Georgia's public universities advising them "to stop granting so-called tuition 'waivers' to students who may have high grades but lack legal resident status."[88] Newsome's May 25, 2006 position paper did not circulate to the wider educational community. Instead, the Board of Regents delayed meetings on the matter in April 2007 and eventually

---

[84] See Chapter Two for an overview of Proposition 187.

[85] See Olivas (2007b).

[86] Senate Bill 529 (2006), p. 6. Also see Rogers (2007).

[87] Board of Regents (2007), p. 98.

[88] Feagans (2006). See also Watson (2007). Chip Rogers, author of the bill, stated that the intent of the legislature was to align Board of Regents policies with federal law because "it is not the right of the Board of Regents, or any public entity, to ignore federal law" (Rogers, 2007).

scheduled some "listening hearings" in May 2007 to purportedly hear from the students affected. During that period, arguments presented at these educational hearings sought to minimize the impact of SB 529's in higher education explaining that "the Georgia law, by directing the Board to comply with federal law, would enable public colleges affirmatively to enable the undocumented to establish residency. Had the Legislature wished to eliminate this option, it could have explicitly done so, as it did in a number of state benefits."[89]

Despite expert testimony clarifying the provisions of SB 529 during spring 2007, the Board of Regents moved to eliminate the availability of the out-of-state waivers to undocumented students regardless of the students' attendance and graduation from Georgia high schools. Community input was sought a year after the board had received Newsome's legal advice justifying educational limitations on this growing population and regardless of the voices of thousands of immigrants who demonstrated against SB 529 since its inception.[90]

In addition to the attacks on in-state tuition policies (both in states with in-state tuition laws and in those that have not enacted these measures), federal immigration law continues to present a significant obstacle for undocumented college graduates as they seek employment in their chosen fields. The next chapter examines the DREAM Act, a federal measure that would allow undocumented students who had been

---

[89] Olivas (2007a), p. 5. See also Watson (2007). Chip Rogers criticized these hearings arguing that the immigration law signed by Clinton already defined eligibility for tuition benefits. He stated: "Those who take issue with federal law, which defines benefits eligibility, should direct their concerns to the Congress of the United States not to the University System of Georgia" (Rogers, 2007).

[90] In Georgia, SB 529 spurred the creation of the March 17 Alliance, which organized to oppose the bill once it had passed the House and before it became law. On March 24, the Alliance organized a "Day of Dignity" where an estimated 80,000 immigrant workers stayed away from work sites (Abkowitz, 2006). On that same day an estimated 3,000 students in northeast Georgia did not report to school (Yee, 2006). On April 10, 2006, an estimated 60,000 immigrants marched in Atlanta against SB 529 and also as part of nationwide demonstrations against HR 4437, a federal proposal that would have made undocumented workers felons (Clermont, 2006).

in the United States for at least five years the opportunity to adjust their immigration status and to apply for cancellation of removal (i.e., nullification of deportation orders). This legislation addresses a deep injustice as well as a pressing need: Existing immigration law imposes severe penalties on undocumented students simply "for the crime of having been born somewhere else."[91]

---

[91] T. R. Mitchell (2001).

CHAPTER 6

Federal Initiatives and Student Advocacy

In 2001, as legislators in Texas were debating passage of HB 1403, a bill was introduced in the U.S. Congress to address the difficulties immigrant students like Jesús Apodaca and thousands of others face.[1] The bill sought (1) to eliminate provisions in existing federal law that have been interpreted as barring states from providing undocumented residents with access to in-state tuition; and (2) to allow certain immigrant students the opportunity to obtain permanent residency and thus be able to live and work legally in the United States.

Over the years since the bill's introduction, Congressional support for the measure, now known as the DREAM (Development, Relief and Education for Alien Minors) Act, has grown.[2] Although as of 2007, the act had not yet gathered enough votes to move forward in Congress, the prospect of legislation designed to improve the specific situation of undocumented youth has spurred the students themselves, the immigrant community, and local and national organizations to undertake various forms of advocacy. This chapter presents an overview of the DREAM Act's provisions, traces key aspects of its progress in Congress, and provides examples of the wide-ranging student advocacy that has coalesced around the act.

---

[1] The fate of this bill, HR 1918, and its subsequent iterations is discussed in this chapter.

[2] National Immigration Law Center (2006, 2007a).

OVERVIEW OF THE DREAM ACT

The basic provisions of the DREAM Act[3] would benefit those students who meet each of the following requirements:

1. They were brought to the U.S. more than 5 years ago;
2. They entered the country at age 15 or younger; and
3. They are able to demonstrate good moral character.

If passed, the DREAM Act would enable high school graduates to apply for conditional status, which would authorize them for up to six years of legal residence.[4] During this six-year period, individuals with conditional status would be required to attend an institution of postsecondary education and graduate from a two-year college or complete at least two years toward a four-year degree; alternatively, they could serve in the U.S. military for at least two years. Those who met these requirements would be granted permanent residency at the end of the six-year period.[5]

During the years that have elapsed since the first version of the act was introduced, undocumented students have begun graduating with college degrees, but they have little chance of successfully launching their careers. In the current legal framework, democratic and civil rights gains achieved at the state level are undermined by federal laws that make these students ineligible to receive federal aid, disqualify them from most scholarships because of their immigration status, and bar them from legal employment, even if they have graduated from a U.S. college or university.[6] The limitations imposed by immigration

---

[3] As explained further in this chapter, the act was refiled in 2007, as S. 2205. See also National Immigration Law Center (2007a).

[4] In 2006 the Migration Policy Institute estimated that if the DREAM Act were to become law, an estimated 360,000 students ages 18–24 would be immediately eligible for conditional permanent residency. The study also estimated that another 715,000 undocumented students ages 5–17 would eventually become eligible in the future under the proposed legislation (Batalova and Fix, 2006).

[5] National Immigration Law Center (2007a).

[6] Beginning in 2005, four years after the Texas legislature passed HB 1403, news stories began to appear about students who had graduated from college

law apply to undocumented college graduates even in areas of high demand and skilled employment, such as nursing, bilingual education, and engineering.[7] Given this catch-22, undocumented students in the ten states that provide equal access to college face a contradictory situation. On the one hand, the states where they have graduated from high school have recognized their right to continue their education. However, in the absence of change in federal policy, undocumented college graduates "will always live under the double threat of being ineligible to lawfully hold a job and possible removal from the United States."[8] Under current immigration law (IIRIRA), there are no practical legal avenues for granting immigration status to undocumented students. There are very few means by which undocumented persons can obtain permanent residency on their own, and many lack family members who would qualify as sponsors (a sponsor must be an immediate relative and able to demonstrate legal permanent residency or U.S. citizenship) who could petition on their behalf.[9] As a result, these students often face the threat of deportation. Even those who have a relative who could qualify as a sponsor face additional hurdles in their quest to attain permanent resident status.[10]

In the years since the passage of in-state tuition policies in various states, local immigrant communities have expressed concern over re-

---

but could not work. For a sample story, see the *Wall Street Journal*'s coverage of two University of Texas at Austin graduates (Jordan, 2005).

[7] In the event that U.S. companies are interested in hiring these graduates, they must "sponsor" them. This in turn requires that the potential employee leave the United States and apply for a visa from the U.S. consulates in their home countries. Under IIRIRA provisions, departing the U.S. triggers a bar against reentry. People who have been unlawfully present in the U.S. for more than 180 days but less than one year are subject to a three-year bar on admission, while those who have been unlawfully present for more than a year are inadmissible for ten years (http://www.visalaw.com/01nov3/12nov301.html). Many undocumented students are likely to be in the second category, since they first arrived as young children.

[8] Romero (2002), pp. 406–407.

[9] Alfred (2003).

[10] As explained in Chapter One, immigration law sets a high minimum income level the sponsoring family member must meet in order to qualify as a sponsor.

strictive federal employment regulations. And immigrant rights activists have drawn attention to the consequences of the clash between state policies that are expanding the rights of undocumented students and federal immigration law, which currently bars them from practicing their professions. Houston-based activists referred to this problem shortly after the passage of the Texas in-state tuition law in 2001:

> . . . we are concerned about the future of these students once they graduate and have not been given the opportunity to legalize their status at the time of their graduation. It would be fitting to consider future actions to help these students be able to [practice] their profession.[11]

In the spring of 2001, organizations across the country began pressing members of Congress for a federal proposal that would reaffirm states' rights to implement in-state tuition bills while allowing undocumented students to obtain permanent residence and receive the necessary legal status to secure employment after graduating from college. The first attempt, filed in the House of Representatives by Howard Berman (CA), Chris Cannon (UT), and Lucille Roybal-Allard (CA) during the first session of the 107th Congress, was part of HR 1918, the Student Adjustment Act.[12] The Senate version of the bill, filed as the Children's Adjustment, Relief and Education (CARE) Act, was introduced by Senator Orrin Hatch (UT) and co-sponsored by Senator Richard Durbin (IL).[13]

The Student Adjustment Act was touted as a bill that would (1) benefit undocumented students already enrolled in school and those applying to college; (2) lift federal restrictions prohibiting states from providing undocumented students with in-state tuition; and (3) make students eligible for federal financial aid under programs such as the Pell grant. The Subcommittee on Immigration was to vote on the bill on September 12, 2001. Statements were to be made by members of Congress, the secretary of education, educators from school districts and universities, employers, members of organizations promoting col-

---

[11] Aguiluz and Reyes (2001).

[12] Kim (n.d.).

[13] See Appendix C for details on both measures and related legislation.

lege attendance, and most important, the affected students. The events of September 11 sidelined the effort. The possibility of repealing the federal prohibition on postsecondary education benefits for undocu- mented immigrants disappeared from public discussion. In the after- math of September 11, discussion of pro-immigration legislation virtu- ally ceased, and anti-immigrant regulations, such as the USA PATRIOT Act, gained prominence.[14]

While momentum for the Student Adjustment Act weakened in the House, during the spring of 2002, the DREAM Act, which included similar proposals, gained support in the Senate. The DREAM Act passed the Senate Judiciary Committee in June 2002, but it went no further. This time it was the war against Iraq that derailed the effort. Undaunted, supporters continued their nationwide activities. On April 9, 2003, during the first session of the 108th Congress, and within weeks of the start of the Iraq war, the DREAM Act was reintroduced, with bipartisan support.[15] In November 2003, the Senate Judiciary Committee approved the measure, with a 16 to 3 vote. However, the proposed legislation now contained problematic amendments intro- duced by Senators Diane Feinstein (CA) and Charles Grassley (IA). These included making undocumented immigrant students ineligible for federal financial aid programs (e.g., Pell grants), a revision that would seriously curtail access for these students, since most have only limited means. An even bigger blow to democratic and immigrant rights was a proposed amendment that threatened to track undocu- mented students, using the Student and Exchange Visitor Information System (SEVIS), a database originally established to monitor interna- tional students. Proposals of this nature were touted by some as a way to overcome opposition from anti-immigrant sectors. The inclusion of such amendments did not result in passage of the DREAM Act. How- ever, such proposal ended up strengthening the anti-immigrant camp by repeating arguments that favor governmental surveillance of immi- grants who are portrayed as potential threats.

---

[14] The Uniting and Strengthening America by Providing Appropriate Tools Required to Intercept and Obstruct Terrorism Act is discussed in Chapter One. See also Badger and Yale-Loehr (2002).

[15] The measure was co-sponsored by 17 Republicans and 18 Democrats (see Appendix C).

By late 2003, when the Senate Judiciary Committee passed the DREAM Act, the bill enjoyed the support of 48 sponsors in the Senate and 150 in the House. In spite of this initial victory, the measure was not scheduled for a vote in the Senate. During 2004, the presidential elections led to an abandonment of efforts to pass the bill. No legislative activity was reported in support of the DREAM Act during the second term of the 108th Congress (2004), or during the first term of the 109th Congress (2005). The end of 2005 was marked by intense controversy over the passage in the House of the Border Protection, Anti-Terrorism, and Illegal Immigration Control Act of 2005 (HR 4437) filed by Representative James Sensenbrenner (WI). During the second session of the 109th Congress (2006), amid the largest mobilization by immigrants in the history of the United States, the Senate passed the DREAM Act, as part of CIRA, the Comprehensive Immigration Reform Act of 2006 (S. 2611). Neither CIRA nor HR 4437 became law, however, because the House and Senate were unwilling to reconcile differences between CIRA's provisions and the extreme anti-immigrant aspects of HR 4437. During the first session of the 110th Congress (2007), the DREAM Act was reintroduced.[16] Later, it was attached to the STRIVE Act of 2007 (HR 1645), a proposal that several immigrant rights organizations opposed, on various grounds.[17]

In a major shift, the original intent of the DREAM Act was now being perverted. When the strategy of including the DREAM Act in the Senate's immigration reform bill failed, its main sponsor, Senator Durbin, introduced the measure as an amendment to the Department of Defense authorization bill. In doing so, the Illinois senator explicitly

---

[16] Representatives Lincoln Diaz-Balart (FL), Howard Berman (CA), and Lucille Roybal-Allard (CA) reintroduced the act. In the Senate, the proposal was supported by Richard Durbin (IL), Chuck Hagel (NE), and Richard Lugar (IN).

[17] Critics argue that this proposal offers a precarious legalization process that penalizes families by limiting their ability to sponsor others. It also imposes a "merit point system" that limits immigration to those with specific skills and levels of education and imposes a temporary worker program. For a more extensive discussion of the limitations of this proposal, see the National Immigration Law Center's statement at http://www.nilc.org/immlawpolicy/CIR/cir028.htm.

acknowledged that the offer of citizenship would be used as a military recruitment strategy. The DREAM Act, Durbin noted, would help solve the "recruitment crisis we face today."[18] The amendment won prompt support from the Pentagon.[19] A number of critics asserted that this strategy of tying citizenship to military service constitutes a draft of undocumented immigrants. [20] The original intent of opening up educational opportunities and a path to citizenship, was now warped to satisfy the needs of the military. Thus, for a portion of students, in order to qualify under the act's provisions and thus overcome the government's denial of their legal status, they would have to "volunteer" as what some commentators have described as "cannon fodder."[21] This ap-

---

[18] Jordan (2007).

[19] Bill Carr, acting deputy undersecretary of defense for military personnel policy, explained that the Pentagon supported the DREAM Act because it would be "good for readiness. . . . The government estimates that there are at least 750,000 undocumented youths of military age in the United States. Only some of them would meet the standards of the DREAM Act, but even 10 percent would equal a typical full year's worth of new recruits. The Migration Policy Institute . . . estimates that as many as 280,000 illegal immigrants between 18 and 24 would qualify for the program" (Bender, 2007).

[20] Fernando Suarez del Solar, director of the Guerrero Azteca Peace Project in Escondido, California, argues that the "bill amounts to an aggressive draft of Hispanics" (Jordan, 2007). Suarez's son died in the military after being recruited in Tijuana, Mexico under questionable circumstances (D. Davis, 2007). Besides sending recruiters to Mexican border towns, other recruitment techniques include targeting students who will not receive a regular high school diploma, visiting high schools with high minority (and Latino) population, and paying those who have enlisted to recruit their friends (D. Davis, 2007). These predatory practices, which take advantage of the students' poverty, immigration status, and family situation, have prompted the organization of counter recruitment groups, such as Gold Star Families for Peace, Military Families Speak Out, Committee Opposed to Militarism and the Draft, and the Coalition Against Militarism in Our Schools (ibid.). In some instances, students have protested the recruiters' presence in their schools during career fairs by organizing under the slogan "students not soldiers."

[21] Gumbel (2003). The need for expendable recruits to fight the U.S. government's wars is exemplified by a remark from Michael O'Hanlon, a military

proach is a far cry from the DREAM Act's original goal of expanding educational and legal opportunities. However, some have asserted that young undocumented immigrants would have embraced the military service option, seeing it as an opportunity.[22]

When the strategy of including the DREAM Act in the Department of Defense authorization legislation also failed, the bill was gutted. The original 2001 provision that had reaffirmed that states can offer in-state

---

scholar at the Brookings Institution: "I would set up some recruiting offices in Manila and maybe some areas of Sub-Saharan Africa where English is spoken and al-Qaeda is not present . . . Like Ghana, Namibia, Zimbabwe. Congo, even, but with intensive language training" (Schulte, 2007). Air Force Lieutenant General Thomas McInerney, another opponent of proposals to grant status to undocumented immigrants comments, comments: "It is not perfect, but it is far better than some of the ways they are talking about to grant illegals new status here" (Bender, 2007). Anti-immigrant commentators such as Mark Krikorian of the Center for Immigration Studies, while trying to deny the relationship between citizenship and recruitment strategies, give an implicit nod to the idea: "I'm happy to have the military work that out however they want to. My concern is when people see service in the military and immigration as having some kind of synergy, as though we can offer citizenship as a way to fill out our recruiting quota" (ibid.). As Schulte (2007) points out, that relationship has always been there as immigrants, documented and not, have served in the U.S. military since the American Revolution, with an estimated 40,000 noncitizens (holding permanent residency) currently on duty. Indeed, one of the first casualties of the Iraq war was Lance Cpl. José Gutiérrez, 27, an orphan and undocumented immigrant from Guatemala, who received citizenship posthumously (Weiner, 2003). At his funeral in Guatemala, few of his countrymen attended. The head of Casa Alianza orphanage explained: "One group felt that these young Hispanic men were being sent as cannon fodder into the battlefield . . . That created a big question here. Are young Hispanic men who go up to the United States looking for future, for education? Are they being sent to the front because they're dispensable?" (*60 Minutes*, 2003).

[22] A *Boston Globe* article quoted an observation made by Josh Bernstein of the National Immigration Law Center that "most illegal immigrants who would be eligible for military service under the law come from a demographic group that is already disposed toward voluntary military service. Many of them would naturally otherwise go into it" (Bender, 2007).

tuition was dropped from the version presented to the Senate in September 2007.[23] A subsequent unfavorable vote there stopped the progress of the proposal. The DREAM Act will likely see very little progress in 2008 given the presidential elections. On the other hand, the political debates will continue to witness candidates from both parties intensify even harsher attacks on undocumented immigrants.[24] Unfortunately, many immigrant-oriented organizations will continue to subsume the fight for the undocumented to their electoral efforts. This will mean that the DREAM Act must likely wait until the first session of the 111th Congress (2009) before it will be reintroduced.

In spite of these challenges, and of the fact that the bill has significantly changed since it was first introduced, support for the DREAM Act continues to be in the forefront of immigrant student advocacy, as the next section details.

---

[23] See Herms (2007) and Zehr (2007). An October 24, 2007 Senate vote to move the DREAM Act forward to the next stage had bipartisan support, but it fell short of achieving the 60 votes necessary to permit "senators to begin debating and amending the DREAM Act before voting on its final passage" (American Immigration Lawyers Association, 2007).

[24] During CNN's November 26, 2007 Republican debate, presidential candidate Tom Tancredo observed, in reference to the exchange on immigration issues between frontrunners Rudy Giuliani and Mitt Romney, that "All I've heard is people trying to out-Tancredo Tancredo. It is great" (Blumenthal, 2007). See also Berger (2007). The Democrats confronted the issue during a December 2007 presidential debate aired by National Public Radio. While the frontrunners stated their condemnations of vigilantism, Senator Barak Obama referred to common anti-immigrant propaganda stating, "I will make sure that the federal government does what it's supposed to do, which is to do a better job of closing our borders and preventing hundreds of thousands of people to pour in, have much tougher enforcement standards when it comes to employers, and create a pathway of citizenship for the 12 million people who are already here" (Washington Post, 2007). Senator Hillary Clinton has voted to increase enforcement along the Southern border and has supported legislation to obtain a continuous flow of cheap immigrant labor for U.S. agrobusinesses, while at the same time dangling vague promises of comprehensive immigration reform. See also Nagourney and Zeleny (2007).

IMMIGRANT STUDENT ADVOCACY

The issue of undocumented students' access to college has generated a multilayered response among advocates. One approach has been the formation of coalitions fully dedicated to this access issue. These groups are composed primarily of immigrant students and supporters concerned with the need to take a more active stance and to garner support for legislative changes that will open the doors of higher education to this population. The earliest example is the Leticia "A" Network, formed in California in the mid-1980s.[25] The AB 540 Network, the Coalition of Student Advocates, and People United for the Legalization of the Students are some of the recently formed California-based groups. Elsewhere, examples of similar, focused advocacy organizations include the Houston-based Coalition of Higher Education for Immigrant Students,[26] Access to Higher Education Coalition of Minnesota, Arizona's Comité de Apoyo para el Desarollo Estudiantil de la Nación Americana, and the Colorado Higher Education Access Alliance Coalition. In addition, in some states, some organizations that traditionally have been dedicated to immigrant advocacy now have embraced the issue of equal access for undocumented students or have encouraged the inclusion of youth components within their coalitions.[27]

---

[25] See Chapter Four for details.

[26] See Chapter Three for details.

[27] These include WISE UP, a student subset of the year-old Coalition for Humane Immigrant Rights of Los Angeles (see Chapter Four); Jovenes Unidos, the student arm of Padres Unidos in Colorado; the Coalition for Immigrant and Refugee Rights in Illinois; the Immigrant Rights Network of Iowa-Nebraska; Sunflower Community Action: Hispanos Unidos Chapter and El Centro in Kansas; the Immigrant Rights Advocacy Coalition in Massachusetts; the Immigrant Policy Network in New Jersey; Somos un Pueblo Unido in New Mexico; and the Young Korean-American Service & Education Center Inc, among many others across the United States. In new immigration areas, supportive organizations include the Student Action with Farmworkers in North Carolina; the Northwest Tree Planters & Farm Workers Unions (PCUN) of Oregon; and Immigrant Rights of Tennessee. As noted in previous chapters, some national advocacy organizations that provide legal support include the Mexican American Legal Defense and Educational Fund (MALDEF), the National Immigra-

Another layer of advocacy is provided by local and national entities that have joined this cause and now contribute direct or indirect support. These groups include associations of educators, labor leaders, and civic organizations, as well as traditional advocacy entities.[28]

Perhaps the most remarkable impact of the DREAM Act is the degree to which it has galvanized immigrant students to organize under a common banner. A number of immigrant-student-led groups have appeared nationwide. Their main goals are to win the right to remain in this country, to go to school, and to obtain employment. Some groups are based on college and university campuses in order to provide a voice for undocumented college students and to serve as a support network. All, though, address issues specific to this population, particularly their lack of access to financial aid (particularly in states like California) and their ongoing struggle for equal treatment when applying for state financial aid in states where they are eligible (such as Texas).

In southern California, where there has been a long history of advocacy, examples of student-organized groups include Espíritu de Nuestro Futuro (Spirit of Our Future), founded at California State University Dominguez Hills; Improving Dreams, Equality, Access and Success (IDEAS), founded at the University of California at Los Angeles; Voces de la Mañana, founded at Glendale Community College; and the Orange County Dream Team, whose members are drawn from both the University of California at Irvine and the Santa Ana Community

---

tion Law Center, the National Council of La Raza, and the American Immigrant Lawyers Association.

[28] Supportive educational organizations include the Latino/a Educational Achievement Project in Washington State. In New York, Global Kids Inc., an education-oriented organization, has established a human rights activist project that supports youth involvement in issues surrounding undocumented students and college access. Supportive national educational associations include the American Council on Education, the National Association for Bilingual Education, the American Association of Community Colleges, the National Association for College Admissions Counseling, and the College Board. A more comprehensive list of the nearly 1,000 organizations that support in-state tuition and the DREAM Act is available at http://democracyinaction.org/dia/organizations/NILC/images/DREAM%20Endorsers.htm.

College.[29] Many of these groups, along with their Northern California counterparts, also are part of the California DREAM Act Network, which encompasses dozens of campus-based organizations.[30] In Texas, immigrant students' struggle has been spearheaded by Jóvenes Inmigrantes por un Futuro Mejor (JIFM), founded in 2003 as a student group at Houston's Lee High School.[31] JIFM soon expanded to the campuses where Lee High's graduating seniors were enrolling. There are chapters at the University of Houston-Downtown, the University of Houston-Central, Texas A&M, and University of Texas at Arlington. JIFM is supported by other organizations whose membership also includes some undocumented immigrant students.[32]

---

[29] There are many student groups on the campuses of the California State University system. Some of these are De Pie (Standing), based at CSU Pomona; Dreams to be Heard, at CSU Northridge; and SURGE, at CSU Los Angeles. Student Advocates for Higher Education and Equality is located at East Los Angeles Community College. In Northern California, the groups include Student Advocates for Higher Education at San Jose State University, Rising Immigrant Scholars through Education at UC-Berkeley, and Disclosing Resources through Education, Advising, and Mentoring for Students at Santa Clara University. For 2008, these groups have called for the creation of a Bay Area immigrant rights student coalition to "create a way for immigrant students, regardless of legal status, and their allies to find ways to move forward issues that will benefit them though awareness and social activism" (Mendoza, 2007). Other organizations that support immigrant student advocacy include MEChA at San Francisco State University and the Puente Program at West Valley Community College. For more information on these groups see Baskin (2007) and López (2007).

[30] This is a "statewide network of existing and emerging college campus organizations who actively address undocumented student issues and who work to create broader social change around immigration reform and access to higher education." See http://www.chirla.org/CADREAMNetwork for further details.

[31] The name of this group translates to Immigrant Youth for a Better Future. Lee High's student body has the highest number of pupils born outside the U.S. of any school in the Houston Independent School District.

[32] Examples of youth groups that support JIFM's mission include Amigas Latinas for College (http://www.amigaslatinas4college.org) and League of United Latin American Citizens (LULAC) Chapter #4765 at Prairie View A&M Uni-

Although students of Latin American descent have been especially active in forming these advocacy organizations, group membership is not limited to Latinos. Moreover, in recognition of the fact that many different groups of students face barriers to higher education, other organizations, such as the National Korean American Service & Education Consortium (NAKASEC), its members and their respective student affiliates, have been at the forefront of those advocating on behalf of the DREAM Act.[33]

An important aspect of the student advocacy groups' efforts has involved educating the public about the benefits of the DREAM Act. Students have organized and participated in conferences; taken part in newspaper, radio, and television interviews; and traveled across the country to disseminate information about their fight, holding press conferences, giving speeches, and participating in community-based meetings. The wide spectrum of these activities attests to the vibrancy of the immigrant community as a whole. Students' commitment to outreach activities (e.g., conferences to keep school counselors well informed, individual consultations with parents, and workshops within high schools to inform the immigrant community about their higher education opportunities), the distribution of bilingual information on the DREAM Act, and the creation of college guides specifically designed

---

versity. On April 19, 2007, US.-citizen members of the latter group provided supporting testimony before the Higher Education Committee of the Texas legislature when the in-state tuition law was in danger of repeal. Their collective efforts were successful: the law remained intact (see also Chapter Five). A new group in Texas is FIEL (Familias Inmigrantes y Estudiantes en la Lucha— Immigrant Families and Students in the Struggle), "an immigrants' rights activist organization with the purpose of upholding this community's family unity, culture, values, and supporting education" (http://www.my-space.com/ fiel_2007).

[33] NAKASEC's affiliates include the Korean American Resource & Cultural Center in Chicago, the Korean Resource Center in Los Angeles, and YKASEC-Empowering the Korean American Community in New York. Each has a youth component dedicated to advocating for the DREAM Act and related issues. See NAKASEC's website for further information (http://nakasec.org/bbs/ view.php?id=alert&no=20). Other Asian groups that support the DREAM Act include Samahang Pilipino at the University of California Los Angeles.

for undocumented students are all a testament to the breadth of their struggle.[34] To call attention to the plight of undocumented youth, student groups have also incorporated strategies used effectively during the civil rights movement and the protests against the war in Vietnam, such as hunger strikes, visits to and marches on Washington, mock graduations, national summits, and rallies. And, to defray the costs of their activism and generate money for scholarships, the students have organized various fundraisers.[35] Finally, their activism on U.S. campuses has generated support and research interest from academia.[36]

The extent of activism by undocumented students and its significant impact is more than a testimony to these students' ability to galvanize large and varied sectors of the public. It is also a remarkable, on-

---

[34] Recent examples of guides include California's "College and Financial Aid Guide for AB 540: Undocumented Immigrant Students" (2006), discussed in Chapter Four, and "Policies and Procedures of Texas Colleges and Universities for Immigrant Students" (2007), produced by David Johnston and this author on behalf of the Texas-based Coalition of Higher Education for Immigrant Students. A new resource aimed at immigrant youth in general is "Living in the United States: A Guide For Immigrant Youth," a publication by the Immigrant Legal Resource Center.

[35] These range from traditional activities such as car washes and food sales to rock concerts and theater productions. Increasingly, student groups have begun organizing large-scale fundraisers, such as the banquet sponsored by IDEAS members that raised over $40,000 to fund 38 scholarships for undocumented students at UCLA. Students with Espíritu de Nuestro Futuro at CSU Dominguez Hills organized a similar activity, on a smaller scale (Carrión, 2007).

[36] The Labor Center at UCLA offers a course titled "Immigrant Rights, Labor and Higher Education" that focuses specifically on the plight of undocumented students at UCLA. At California State University Dominguez Hills, the Chicana/o Studies Department has created The Immigration and Citizenship Program, which provides instruction and counseling regarding the citizenship process to students, their families, and the overall immigrant community. The inspiration for this program came from the student members of Espíritu de Nuestro Futuro. At the University of Houston, students from JIFM as well as participants in the Academic Achievers program take part in a study funded by the Center for Mexican American Studies.

going act of courage. They face numerous forms of discrimination based on their skin color, national origin, and, in some cases, limited English language proficiency, all of which might easily dissuade them from speaking in public about their status.[37] Moreover, the risks associated with their precarious legal position, and the routine and dehumanizing references to their families and themselves as outlaws or "illegal aliens," make their public advocacy still more impressive. Students are well aware that peers who have publicly advocated for the DREAM Act have been harassed by public officials and federal agents with Immigration and Customs Enforcement (ICE).[38]

As they have successfully sought supporters for their fight for educational rights, undocumented immigrant students have developed a new sense of empowerment. This has contributed to their interest in participating in broader activism to address additional issues of importance to immigrants and other marginalized groups in U.S. society.[39]

---

[37] In May 2006, students from JIFM in Houston organized a press conference titled "Defending Our Right to Speak: Students & Community Leaders Defend the Rights of Immigrants to Speak Out Without Fear of Harassment and Intimidation." In the aftermath of the successful marches for immigrant rights, the president of one of the JIFM chapters had received anonymous hate e-mail and phone calls threatening her with deportation (See Jóvenes Inmigrantes por Un Futuro Mejor, 2006).

[38] The most recent and infamous case involves three undocumented students who attended a press conference at the White House only to be harassed by Representative Tom Tancredo (CO), who demanded their deportation (Preston, 2007d). One of the students, Tam Tran, has been the subject of intimidation by ICE agents, who arrested her father, mother, and brother after conducting a predawn raid on their home in Orange County in October 2007. Tran, a recent UCLA graduate, is an outspoken advocate for undocumented students. The agency charged her family members with being fugitives from justice even though the family had been reporting to immigration officials annually to obtain work permits (Huang, 2007).

[39] Taking on new issues has drawbacks, however. Immigrant-established organizations sometimes divert the students' energy and enthusiasm toward "related matters," such as citizenship and voter registration drives, arguing that more minority voters are needed. This kind of sidetracking is problematic, par-

An area of particular concern is the plight of individuals facing deportation. Remarkably, the pressure of organized undocumented students and their supporters has been credited as a significant factor in preventing several impending deportations. Arguably, this achievement demonstrates that, while relentless anti-immigrant campaigns have generated hostility toward the undocumented in the abstract, there continues to be support for immigrant neighbors, co-workers, and classmates. This is why despite virulent anti-immigrant discourse, there is considerably less support for the enforcement of severe, discriminatory, and undemocratic provisions in federal immigration laws. As the examples given later in this chapter show, outreach and education by student advocacy groups, particularly when they focus on real-life situations, can generate a strongly positive response from the general public.

From 2002 to 2005, while the DREAM Act was being widely promoted, several cases involving students who had come to the United States as minors focused national attention on the draconian impact of existing immigration law. The first case to catch the attention of the advocacy community involved four Phoenix, Arizona students, dubbed the Wilson Four (from the name of their high school). After attending an academic competition in New York, the students wanted to visit Niagara Falls. At the U.S.-Canada border, they were asked for their immigration status, then detained; soon after, deportation proceedings were initiated against them. Following their release from immigration detention, the students participated in activities to support the DREAM Act. In the summer of 2002, they joined activists in Washington for a national day of action to demand passage of the DREAM Act. On July 2005, after a three-year campaign, an immigration judge threw out their cases on the grounds that their arrests had been based on racial profiling.[40]

The story of Jesús Apodaca also illustrates the high stakes in public efforts to increase understanding of the plight of the undocumented. In his case, after Representative Tancredo demanded that deportation proceedings be initiated, various individuals and organizations, including Denver's Latino Campaign for Education and Padres Unidos, spoke

---

ticularly when undocumented students' key cause becomes diluted by partisan politics.

[40] Melendez (2005).

in support of the Apodaca family.[41] Ultimately, Senator Ben Nighthorse Campbell introduced private legislation that prevented the family from being deported and extended the possibility of their becoming permanent residents.[42] Jesús Apodaca's dream of going to college, which was what first brought to light his undocumented status, was achieved: An anonymous donor paid his out-of-state tuition at the University of Colorado, Denver, where he enrolled while awaiting resolution of his immigration case.[43]

Because the DREAM Act has not been passed, a few undocumented students facing deportation and permanent exclusion have been protected by public campaigns of support that have resulted in the introduction of private legislation. A case in point is that of Majan Jean, an undocumented Haitian resident of Norwich, Connecticut, whose plight made the news in 2004. In the wake of unrest in Haiti, her mother had unsuccessfully applied for asylum in the United States. When the student and her mother were subsequently arrested and ordered deported, immigrant advocates organized to pressure then-Senate Majority Leader William Frist (TN) to support the DREAM Act. Advocates with the Tennessee Immigrant and Refugee Rights Coalition invited Ms. Jean to speak at a rally outside an event honoring Frist. This strategic use of public space paid off. Senator Christopher Dodd (CT) granted Majan Jean a private bill that prevented her deportation.[44]

Two other cases that came to national attention in 2004 are noteworthy. One was that of Griselda Lopez Negrete, an undocumented Mexican orphan living in South Carolina. The student's undocumented status was revealed while she was translating for a family member at an immigration office. While some of her immediate relatives were documented, they had not adopted her until she was threatened with depor-

---

[41] Padres Unidos (United Parents) is an immigrant advocacy group in the Denver area (Ochoa, 2002). The group was born in the early nineties "out of a struggle at Valverde Elementary School in Denver where parents removed a principal for refusing to stop the practice of forcing Mexicano children to eat their lunches from the cafeteria floor as a form of punishment" (http://www.padresunidos.org/node/4).

[42] Denver Channel (2002).

[43] Florio (2002).

[44] American Immigration Lawyers Association (2004b).

tation.[45] In light of her unusual circumstances, friends and advocates organized to raise funds to send her to Washington. There, she met with Senator Lindsey Graham (SC), who sponsored a private bill that made it possible for her to finish high school.[46] The other representative private bill issued in 2004 was for Venezuelan immigrant Heilit Martinez, a student at Utah State University. An undocumented Utah student, Martinez had participated in a conference in New Mexico and then joined others in a daytrip across the U.S.-Mexico border. When she attempted to return to the U.S., she was detained. Deportation proceedings were initiated when her immigration status could not be verified. Senator Hatch, an original sponsor of the DREAM Act, filed a private bill to provide Martinez relief.

Perhaps the most prominent case appeared in 2005. It involved Marie Gonzalez, a Costa Rican student raised in Jefferson City, Missouri. After ten years' residence in the United States, the Gonzalez family was subjected to deportation proceedings in 2002.[47] The community response illustrates the power of advocacy on behalf of the undocumented. Friends of the family formed the Gonzalez Group, a community effort that involved neighbors as well as Marie's teachers and the parents of her classmates. Throughout the next three years, as the family engaged in legal appeals, the Gonzalez Group undertook fundraising and other forms of support, including collecting hundreds of letters and thousands of signatures in support of the family.[48] Marie Gonzalez received further attention and support in April 2004, when she addressed a DREAM Act rally organized by immigrant students and their supporters. This national day of action included a mock graduation and the delivery of over 65,000 petitions to the Department of Education, one for each of the estimated number of high school students graduating every year without the opportunity to attend college, because of their immigration status. During 2005, Gonzalez's plight and that of the

---

[45] In the months leading up to her deportation, she was adopted by her U.S. citizen uncle. See Markoe (2004).

[46] Barra (2004).

[47] "Gonzalez's father was working as a courier and mail opener in the governor's office when he was fired in 2002 after an anonymous tip about his status. News coverage of the case led to deportation proceedings" (Hananel, 2006).

[48] Meyerson (2005).

thousands of students she represents gained more attention as advocates organized for her defense under the "I am Marie" campaign. In an indication of the increasingly collaborative approach being adopted by immigrant rights advocates, undocumented students with JIFM in Texas supported the "I am Marie" campaign, strengthening all of the students' ties as members of an informal national network. Despite all the efforts, in 2005, Gonzalez's parents were deported to their native Costa Rica; however, Marie was granted a one-year stay by the Department of Homeland Security so that she could begin her college education.[49] Since 2005, her deferral of deportation has been renewed twice, each time for a year. Her current deferral will expire in June 2008. Congress holds the key to Marie Gonzalez's future. "If the DREAM Act does not pass by then," she explains, "I will have to leave."

THE ONGOING ROLE OF ADVOCACY

Many of the cases reviewed here originated in states without in-state tuition laws, where students continue to face unequal access to education. This persistent inequality highlights the importance of the passage of federal legislation like the DREAM Act that would give at least some undocumented students the opportunity to attend college, to achieve legal immigration status, and to pursue their careers. The cases of successful fights against student deportations are also an important indication of the power of organized resistance. They demonstrate, as well, the importance of reaching out more broadly to the nonimmigrant community, because the inevitable commingling of native-born individuals and immigrants—in the workplace, at school, and in other daily, routine activities—tends to break down the dehumanizing stereo-

---

[49] She attends Westminster College in Fulton, Missouri, and is majoring in political science and international business, with a focus on communication and leadership. A similar case is that of brothers Alejandro and Juan Sebastián Gómez, born in Colombia, whose parents and grandmother were deported October 30, 2007, from Miami, where the family had been living. As with some other undocumented students, private bills were filed on the brothers' behalf, resulting in suspension of their deportations until 2009. The bills came about as "classmates of Juan's at Miami Killian Senior High School, citing his exceptional academic performance, rallied the support of federal lawmakers, winning a temporary retrieve from deportation" (Aguayo and Preston, 2007).

types promoted by those who oppose immigration. Bonds of human solidarity forged by these shared experiences counteract the effects of campaigns designed to instill fear and resentment. Several of the cases described here, and particularly the community effort on behalf of Marie Gonzalez and her family, confirm the reality of this process. In a February 2005 letter to then-Secretary of Homeland Security Tom Ridge, Jefferson City Mayor John Landwehr described the Gonzalez family as "de facto citizens."[50] Community actions and statements of this nature speak to the difficulties immigration opponents face in their efforts to demonize "illegals," other than in the abstract, and they provide evidence that some citizens recognize and accept the fact that this population is here to stay.

Finally, the efforts on behalf of students threatened with deportation bring to light a troubling dichotomy in advocates' arguments. Commonly, undocumented students' supporters argue that these young people should not be penalized for the actions of their parents. But the underlying logic of this kind of defense portrays the parents as criminals who have victimized their own children. It is a rationale that presumes the validity of the entire framework advanced by anti-immigrant forces and simply seeks exception for the students as "innocent bystanders"—a notion that by definition casts their parents as guilty parties. Blaming adults who have left behind their homes, friends, and extended family to immigrate precisely in order to provide a better life for their children may be expedient, but ultimately it is self-defeating. Aside from ignoring the social and economic conditions that force millions to immigrate, this approach also leaves the U.S. immigration system unchallenged. It overlooks the fact that the INS, aside from being a callous and humiliating bureaucracy, is rooted in discredited nineteenth-century ideas of eugenics and racism and that the agency (renamed and now located within the Department of Homeland Security) continues to discriminate against people of color and those with low incomes.[51] Rather than rebutting anti-immigrant attacks with argu-

---

[50] Fisher (2005).

[51] Many immigrant families have incomes too low to legally permit them to act as sponsors, and existing law discourages even those who do qualify financially from acting as sponsors (see Alfred, 2003). Given that most poor immigrants are people of color, requirements like this also appear to continue the tradition

ments that parents are to blame for their children's status, student advocates should point to the myriad ways in which this country systematically denies democratic, civil, and human rights to millions of its undocumented but indispensable immigrants. The next and last chapter addresses some of the reasons that arguments advancing this fight as a question of civil rights are needed.

---

of race-based immigration policies aimed at restricting nonwhite immigration (Tienda, 2002).

CHAPTER 7

Conclusion: *¡Sí se puede!*

Twenty-five years ago, the Supreme Court affirmed undocumented students' right to a public education in the *Plyler v. Doe* (1982) decision. Since then, there have been repeated efforts to curtail educational guarantees for students in grades K-12 and beyond. This book's history of the development of legislation that supports immigrant students' right to attend institutions of higher education at in-state tuition rates has demonstrated the crucial role of advocacy. Immigrant students and their supporters have mounted campaigns to educate the public, pressure school administrators, lobby legislators, and legally challenge discriminatory laws. Their efforts, which are ongoing, have helped bring about the passage of unprecedented state-and national-level legislative initiatives creating greater equality for all in access to higher education.

Thus far, the undocumented immigrant student advocacy movement has won victories in ten states and continues to push other state legislatures to address the question of the students' access to institutions of higher education at in-state tuition rates. In each state, advocacy has invariably begun as undocumented students have graduated from high school or completed their secondary studies and, poised to enter college, have discovered the door to higher education closed. This was the case, for instance, for Leticia "A" and four other high school students who applied for admission to the University of California (UC) in 1984. They were effectively denied entry by UC administrators, who classified them as out-of-state students, refusing to recognize that they had graduated from high school in the state and had met all other requirements. A decade and a half later, this was also the plight of Rosendo Ticas in Texas. The Houston Community College System told

Ticas that because of his immigration status, he had to pay out-of-state fees, even though he had complied with all other requirements. While students and their supporters in Texas and California successfully campaigned in the court of public opinion and eventually achieved legislative victories, others, such as Jesús Apodaca in Denver and the student advocacy movement in Colorado, have not yet attained an equal application of the state's higher education laws.

The issue of in-state tuition, as this book has shown, is far from settled. There are states where individual universities or college systems have adopted nondiscriminatory policies; however, these policies have not culminated in the passage of in-state tuition laws.[1] On the other hand, victories in ten states have signaled a new phase of the movement. In these states, advocates have reached for a wider public and have sought to build relationships with those responsible for implementing the laws. As experiences in California and Texas show, passing laws is only the first step. In most cases, state entities have done little or nothing to inform students, parents, and educators about the provisions of the new state policies. Thus, in these and other states, implementation of immigrant students' new statutory rights continues to require the active involvement of teachers, high school counselors, community activists, government employees, university researchers, university admissions staff, financial aid representatives, and on several occasions, high-level community college and university administrators who have gone on record advocating for these measures.[2] In California, the AB 540 College Access Network and the student-based California

---

[1] For instance, in Indiana several institutions of higher education accept undocumented students (for details, see www.elpuenteproject.com). Yet, the 2006 Indiana legislative session considered a proposal, House Bill 1383, that "would have barred undocumented children from public schools, prohibited public hospitals from treating certain immigrants, and required local law enforcement requirements to report "suspected" undocumented immigrants to federal authorities" (Broder, 2007, p. 2). The House ultimately rejected HB 1383.

[2] Examples include the presence of former chancellor of the Dallas County Community College District, Dr. William Wenrich, during one of the hearings that led to the passage of Texas House Bill 1403, and the 2002 testimony of University of Utah President Bernie Machen in support of Utah's in-state tuition measure, House Bill 144.

DREAM Act Network provide a forum for these parties, channeling important information and providing effective outreach. In Texas, the Houston-based Coalition of Higher Education for Immigrant Students is one of the organizations that accomplishes this work, in conjunction with the student chapters of Jóvenes Inmigrantes por un Futuro Mejor (JIFM).

Whether or not states have passed in-state tuition laws, the critical importance of advocacy groups is indisputable. These formal and informal groups of students and their diverse individual and organizational supporters continue to be the cornerstone of efforts to open the doors of higher education to undocumented immigrants. In California, advocates are not only working actively to guide implementation of the law, they are also undertaking efforts to pass a complementary bill that would make these students eligible for state financial aid. While the efforts have not been successful so far, a wide array of organizations, particularly in the Los Angeles area, are continuing to work with some members of the California State Legislature to provide equal access to state financial aid.[3] In Utah, concern over possible conflict with federal law initially slowed efforts to implement the state's new tuition policy, but advocates remained active and watchful, and the law's provisions are now being implemented. In general, it is through the ongoing efforts of advocacy groups that the issue of equal access to higher education is being brought to public light. Advocates also play a key role working with others in support of legislative bills and maintaining the momentum needed to ensure their passage and actual implementation.

Defending existing in-state tuition laws is another critical challenge for the student equal rights advocacy movement. Both past and present experience show that legal and political challenges to equal educational access will continue. For over a decade and a half, one organization in particular, the Federation for American Immigration Reform (FAIR) has mounted sustained attacks against undocumented students' right to a postsecondary education.[4] In recent efforts, FAIR has

---

[3] See Chapter Four for details.

[4] FAIR's activity on this issue extends back to their support in the lawsuit brought by the California-based American Association of Women in the 1990s (*AAW v. California State University*, 1995). The AAW challenged the rights

either brought or supported challenges in federal court (Kansas, 2004) and state court (California, 2005). These suits assert that federal policy trumps states' right to legislate their own educational policies, including equal access to college for all of their high school graduates, regardless of their immigration status.[5] To bolster their legal challenges, FAIR and other anti-immigrant forces resort to scare tactics. Two recurring themes are the threat of an "invasion" of "illegals" who will overwhelm states' higher education systems, and the equally far-fetched prediction that lifting restrictions on undocumented students' access to higher education will cause increased numbers of unauthorized entrants into the country.[6]

Opponents of in-state tuition laws do not restrict their efforts to court challenges. New bills designed to undermine or fully override these laws are regularly introduced within state legislatures. This has been the case in Kansas (HB 2615, 2006), Utah (HB 224, 2007), and Texas (HB 159, 2007), among others. While thus far all proposals have been defeated, these attacks indicate how tenuous and in flux students' rights to in-state tuition remain.[7] Indeed, while most states continue their de facto prohibitions by imposing discriminatory out-of-state tuition rates on impoverished undocumented students, some go further, creating a de jure system of exclusion by enacting legislation that ex-

---

undocumented students achieved under the 1985 Leticia "A" ruling (see Chapter Two).

[5] FAIR filed a lawsuit seeking to prevent implementation of Kansas's in-state tuition law (*Day v. Sebelius*, 2005). When this challenge failed, FAIR filed an appeal. The group also targeted California's in-state tuition law (*Martinez v. Regents of the Univ. of Cal.*, 2005). See Chapter Five for details.

[6] The notion that in-state tuition legislation increases unauthorized immigration ignores the reality that, unfortunately, only a small number of students have been able to enroll, even with these policies in place. It also ignores the continued validity of the point the Supreme Court made in *Plyler v. Doe* (1982, p. 228): "the dominant incentive for illegal entry is the availability of employment; few if any illegal immigrants come to this country, or presumably to the State of Texas, in order to avail themselves of a free education."

[7] Oklahoma House Bill 1804, dubbed the Oklahoma Taxpayer and Citizen Protection Act of 2007, limits the impact of the state's 2003 in-state tuition bill (see Chapter Five).

plicitly bans undocumented students from qualifying for in-state tuition or waivers of out-of-state tuition. Georgia's SB 529 (2006), for instance, attempts to exclude undocumented students from higher education as part of a sweeping bill aimed at limiting immigrant access to most public benefits. Arizona, on the other hand, has achieved the same exclusionary goal through a single-purpose measure, Proposition 300 (2006). Both approaches underscore the need for advocates' continued vigilance and pressure at the state legislative level.[8]

ARGUMENTS FOR IN-STATE TUITION: EFFECTIVE OR COUNTERPRODUCTIVE?

In examining the merits of the various arguments for allowing undocumented students to attend college at the same in-state tuition rates as every other high school graduate, it would seem relevant to consider what exactly is at issue. Is the demand for in-state tuition for the undocumented a matter of economics, fiscal policy, social planning, and the like, or is it a demand for equality, equity, and civil rights? Looking at it from the perspective of the students themselves, and in light of similar issues through history, it would seem clear that this is a matter of equality and fairness.

In chronicling the history of in-state tuition measures, the preceding chapters have highlighted some of the key arguments for and against undocumented students' presence in institutions of higher education. These arguments fall into three broad categories: economics, cultural assimilation, and crime deterrence. Versions of all three are frequently used by opponents and by many supporters of in-state tuition policies. Here each type of argument is reviewed briefly.

EDUCATING UNDOCUMENTED STUDENTS: WHO PAYS?

The defense of and the opposition to in-state tuition policies, and to the federal DREAM Act, have centered predominantly on arguments based on economics. These arguments have been touted mainly by organizations whose focus is lobbying politicians or enlisting the support of the business community. Opponents typically argue that immigrants are a drain on the economy or an additional burden, particularly at the state

---

[8] See Chapter Five for more details.

level. Supporters typically respond in kind, pointing out that, if educated, immigrants do provide additional resources, to the benefit of state and federal treasuries.

The use of economic arguments and strategies to bar disenfranchised populations from access to social services and democratic rights has a long history. Discriminatory tuition requirements (from K-12 to higher education) that exclude the undocumented bear a striking resemblance to Jim Crow techniques, such as poll taxes and literacy tests, designed to disenfranchise Chicanos and Blacks.[9] As in the Jim Crow South, today most states do not explicitly prohibit undocumented students from accessing higher education. Instead, they present immigrants who have recently graduated from high school or earned GED diplomas with the impossibly high hurdle of paying annual out-of-state or international tuition fees. This constitutes a de facto ban, since the great majority of these college aspirants come from impoverished conditions and simply cannot afford the higher fees.

Fiscal-economic arguments generally focus on immigrants' positive or negative budgetary impact on the economy. Nativist forces assert that immigrants are a drain on economic resources because they are being educated without the participating institutions receiving enough resources to bear the alleged additional costs.[10] They argue that giving this population access to in-state tuition rates amounts to a special subsidy or discount for immigrants, extends a privilege not available to U.S. citizens while limiting citizens' access to the same resources, and is likely to cost states substantial sums.[11] Here, as in other areas of the overall immigration debate, nativist forces can be counted on to present calculations that simply ignore the fact that immigrants are taxpayers themselves and that their labor adds greatly to employer profits and to government coffers.[12]

---

[9] See Hendricks (2004).

[10] See Federation for American Immigration Reform (2004c).

[11] See Federation for American Immigration Reform (2004b) and Friends of Immigration Law Enforcement (2004).

[12] The undocumented pay sales taxes, and their paychecks reflect the mandatory withholding of federal and state payroll taxes, as well as deductions for unemployment insurance, workers' compensation, retirement, disability, and

Proponents of in-state tuition often have simply accepted the terms of the debate as set by anti-immigrant opponents and have responded in kind. As a result, in-state tuition laws frequently have been defended simply as mechanisms that would allow undocumented students to add to the economy by increasing employers' profits and contributing to the overall soundness of state and national budgets.[13] Some proponents point out that allowing these students to attend college and legalizing their status would turn them into "productive citizens" who would repay society's "investment" in them. A related argument calls for lifting state and federal restrictions on tuition fees because these provisions "are merely creating a subclass of citizens who otherwise are fully capable of becoming successful individuals—i.e. skilled professionals and thus, significant taxpayers."[14] Although well intended, such logic accepts the misrepresentation that millions of working undocumented immigrants—the overwhelming majority of whom lack a college education—are not productive and are a burden on society.

Resisting the impulse to respond to anti-immigrant arguments using the same cost-benefits language and framework these groups favor does not mean leaving their many inaccuracies unanswered. It is significant that in the *Plyler* ruling, the Supreme Court did more than affirm the importance and applicability of the Fourteenth Amendment's equal protection clause to the arena of education. The Court also explicitly recognized that undocumented workers are "encouraged by

---

survivor benefits. Chapter One addresses these tax contributions and the annual Social Security system surplus they generate.

[13] Speaking at a May 18, 2007 hearing of the House Judiciary Committee's Subcommittee on Immigration, Citizenship, Refugees, Border Security and International Law, Diana Furchtgott-Roth, senior fellow, Hudson Institute, supported the DREAM Act by saying that students with college degrees "produce streams of income taxes and Social Security payments to bolster our fiscal position." In Texas, the Harris County tax office estimated that over a lifetime, "a college educated person is likely to earn approximately $620,000 more than a person with only a high school diploma" (Harris County Tax Office, 2000, p. 2). In Illinois, officials estimated that undocumented workers increase their wages by 5 percent for every additional year of college education (Mehta et al., 2003, as cited in Mehta and Ali, 2003).

[14] Alfred (2003), p. 618.

some to remain here as a source of cheap labor, but nevertheless [are] denied the benefits that our society makes available to citizens and lawful residents."[15] Today, that same "cheap labor" accounts for billions of dollars in surplus value and millions more in the taxes paid by those exploited women and men who provide the nation's cheap labor.

Ultimately, economic arguments in support of undocumented students' access to higher education are doomed to fail. They are fundamentally beside the point. U.S. immigration and economic policy is designed to create and sustain the economic, social, political, and military conditions that drive the immigration flows that underpin the U.S. economy. Immigrants are denied legal status precisely because their caste-like condition as undocumented is what is most profitable for business interests. Likewise, this precarious status makes immigrants politically and socially useful as scapegoats for ever-growing problems ranging from health care to unemployment. The idea that the economic contributions of college graduates whose degrees have been attained through in-state tuition legislation will be sufficient to persuade government and business interests to support such measures, which contradict the core reasons for the current immigration policy, fails to grasp the hard realities that underlie the whole debate.

IN-STATE TUITION AND POLICIES OF CULTURAL ASSIMILATION

In addition to economic arguments, some proponents of in-state tuition policies emphasize the importance of assimilation. They note that having grown up in this country, many undocumented students already are culturally assimilated, as measured by their English-language proficiency as well as the abandonment of their national heritage. Providing access to college, these supporters maintain, will facilitate even greater assimilation and adherence to the status quo. From this perspective, in-state tuition laws are a matter of good social policy—a means of preserving "American culture" and "sound values." The form assimilationist arguments take varies with the degree of the proponents' own assimilation and level of participation in mainstream political activities, as well as the type of audience being addressed.

---

[15] *Plyler v. Doe* (1982), p. 219.

For example, in response to accusations that the DREAM Act would confer blanket amnesty, the Senate Judiciary Committee rushed to assure opponents that in reality the act would simply allow some immigrants "who have been acculturated in the United States the privilege of earning the right to remain."[16] Placating nativists' fears that immigrants do not assimilate is a priority for some supporters of undocumented students.[17] Thus, they describe as the most important contribution of the DREAM Act that "it would provide a means for marginalized youth all across the country to assimilate into mainstream American society."[18] Similarly, others, in citing reasons that an in-state tuition law should pass, emphasize the essential "American-ness" of some potential beneficiaries of the bill, noting that the students "speak *unaccented* [italics added] English [and] consider themselves Americans."[19] Arguments like these make the mistake of presenting equal access to higher education as a "reward" that is "deserved" by students who demonstrate a high degree of assimilation.

Another attempt to gather support for undocumented students has led to an overemphasis on the alleged willingness of this population to be productive and patriotic in exchange for eligibility for benefits like higher education or legal status. The presentations of these students as uniformly talented, assimilated, academically gifted, English speaking, and flag weaving is problematic and reinforces the idea that only those who meet these criteria are deserving of benefits. What about those students whose English is still far from impeccable and those who do not aspire to be their high school's valedictorian? Should they not be allowed the same opportunity? What about those who have not grown

---

[16] Stevenson (2004), p. 574.

[17] House Representative Tom Trancredo (CO), whose callous response to the college dreams of an undocumented student in Denver is discussed in Chapter One, summed up this longstanding nativist fear succinctly when speaking to New York Times reporter Kirk Johnson, "'The impact of immigration—legal and illegal—on jobs, schools, health care, the environment, national security, are all very serious problems," he said. 'But more serious than all of them put together is this threat to the culture. I believe we are in a clash of civilizations'" (Johnson, 2007).

[18] Stevenson (2004), p. 555.

[19] Yates (2004), p. 601.

up in this country but were forced to come because of dire economic and political circumstances in their countries of origin? What about students who were not able to attend college upon graduation from a U.S. high school, or those who retain a strong sense of membership in their home countries? How does one evaluate which students *merit* adjustment of their status, and upon whom do we confer the right to make such determinations?

Criteria based on assimilationist views run far too close to the nativist waters of historically anti-immigrant groups. Indeed, arguments made under the aegis of Americanizing undervalue immigrant cultures and ultimately fail to recognize the degree to which immigrants enrich the cultural, political, and social experience of life in the United States.[20] By implication, these arguments also reinforce the idea that those immigrants who are not assimilated are themselves responsible for their caste-like condition (a position more in line with arguments set forth by nativist groups such as FAIR). In the end, assimilation-based arguments flounder because they are neither inclusive nor democratic propositions but rather are measures that "identify aliens who are likely to fit in."[21] The goal then becomes to legalize the cream of the crop.

This strategy has a corollary favored by a number of advocates for undocumented student access to higher education who focus their efforts on policymakers. These advocates increasingly have sought to make their argument more attractive by stressing that only a few such students would have access under the proposed legislation they support,

---

[20] One example arose during the first wave of marches in opposition to HR 4437 (the 2005 federal legislation aimed at criminalizing immigrants and all those who associated with them) in the spring of 2006. During the first mobilizations many immigrants proudly marched with their national flags. This prompted a virulent response from jingoist forces, as well as chiding from much of the mainstream media. During subsequent rallies immigrants were specifically discouraged by a number of organizers from carrying the Mexican flag. Referring to the work of the "ethnic media," one commentator noted: "They publicized the rallies and, among other things, advised listeners to wear white shirts, downplay the Mexican flag in favor of the American flag, and present a *dignified* (italics added) image to the rest of America" (Wang and Winn, 2006, p. 6).

[21] Aleinikoff (1989), p. 15.

and that access would be conditional.[22] To call for limited access to education, under the delusion that this would be more palatable to the very authorities that have denied such access, is both an erroneous and a self-defeating proposition. This strategy is mistaken in that it fails to understand that calls for equal educational access can be attractive and have successful only to the degree that they appeal to a sense of fairness that in turn is predicated on its universality.[23] Rights and equity are premised precisely upon their availability to all, not simply to a privileged few.[24]

UNEDUCATED UNDOCUMENTED STUDENTS: AN IMPENDING THREAT?

The third and perhaps the most extreme type of argument brought to bear on the question of in-state tuition laws casts education as a form of crime prevention, promoting the shocking proposition that it is cheaper to educate undocumented youth than it is to incarcerate them. In this

---

[22] Seeking to downplay the potential numerical impact of in-state tuition, some supporters reassure the opposition that the number of students who are likely to enroll under these policies is minuscule. See, for instance, the statement of the Austin-based University Leadership Initiative, which includes the following: "Less than 2 percent of this year's national high school graduating class is undocumented immigrants, and *only a fraction* [italics added] of these will attend college even if they are able to pay the in-state rate." Available at http:// criminaljusticecoalition.org/university_leadership/in-state_tuition.

[23] The focus on a "selected few" opposes education as a universal right. As Petronicolos and New (1999) argue, "those who would deprive certain classes of prospective students of educational opportunities do not question the value of education per se; they question the need for it to be universal and equal, and given this necessary limitation on its availability and quality, the right remains conditional rather than fundamental" (p. 403).

[24] An analogy with the Civil Rights movement is instructive. It is absurd to imagine that Jim Crow segregation could have been overcome by calling for only some Blacks to be granted access to education or equal treatment. Indeed, this is not a matter of conjecture. Championed by Booker T. Washington, the limited, cream-of-the-crop, gradualist approach for Black equality and advancement was put to the test for several decades—and it failed. The success of the Civil Rights movement was predicated on its universality.

"last resort" form of argument, proponents raise the menacing specter of potential criminality and position young immigrants as a possible threat to the U.S. social system. They are presented as "criminals to be," unless educated. This is a modern incarnation of nineteenth-century "criminal class" theories in which all working-class people, including the native born, but immigrants in particular, were considered likely to engage in criminal behavior. Education-as-crime-deterrence arguments echo the questionable logic of the assertion that the death penalty should be abolished because it is more expensive to execute than to incarcerate.[25] Arguments based on "cost effectiveness" are de-humanizing and are not likely to generate a laudable response, such as humanitarian sympathy. More important, these arguments sharply contradict the experience of the students and the immigrant community, who tend to view the issue as a matter of fairness, equality, and equity based on their arduous labor and poor working conditions.

The use of the specter of criminality as justification for educating the underserved is not new. Here, too, the Supreme Court's *Plyler* ruling is relevant. The Court's view that not educating undocumented children would promote the "creation and perpetuation of a subclass of illiterates within our boundaries, surely adding to the problems and costs of unemployment, welfare and crime" was part of its argument for including undocumented immigrants in public schools.[26] This reasoning, though, also appeals to the same fears of a "criminal class" that many supporters *and* opponents of immigration hold with respect to people of color.[27] This is clear in the language of some current sup-

---

[25] Some death penalty opponents readily reduce the question of life itself to a budgetary matter: "Over two-thirds of the states and the federal government have installed an exorbitantly expensive system of capital punishment which has been a failure by any measure of effectiveness. Literally hundreds of millions of dollars have already been spent on a response to crime which is calculated to be carried out on a few people each year and which has done nothing to stem the rise in violent crime." See Richard Dieter's report on the high costs of the death penalty at http://www.deathpenaltyinfo.org/article.php?scid=45&did=385.

[26] *Plyler v. Doe* (1982), p. 230.

[27] A similar reasoning marked the Proposition 187 debate. Opponents of the provision to exclude undocumented children from K-12 argued that "leaving

porters of in-state tuition policies who, regrettably, use age-old portrayals of working-class immigrants as "alien, uncouth, menacing"[28] as a warning for the need for equal access to higher education.[29] A memorandum circulated during the first hearing on the Texas policy stated that banning these students from college was the equivalent of "creating a second class of citizen who would be a burden on *our* [italics added] social services and criminal justice systems."[30]

The overall framework of the arguments surrounding the issue of access to education for undocumented immigrants emphasizes "investment" and "profits." Supporters and opponents debate the question of whether in-state tuition bills represent a useful investment that would yield greater economic profits, and most address their arguments to policymakers and powerful private interests. Rarely is it argued that equal access to higher education is a matter of civil or democratic rights and that its ultimate benefit is to the young people themselves and society as a whole. In light of the history of the movement for civil rights in this country and elsewhere, the issue is not a matter of economics, fiscal policy, or social planning. It is a question of equality, equity, and civil rights, with implications for society as a whole.

The challenge facing immigrant students is to remain at the center of their own fight as the protagonists of the modern civil rights movement. History would indicate that in order to succeed, immigrant students must reject persistent efforts to frame the debate in economic terms and, instead, present their case as a matter of equality, stressing the principles of basic fairness and democratic rights. In rejecting arguments that the opportunity to attend college should be available only

---

them on the streets to make trouble . . . would do nothing to reduce crime and graffiti" (Cooper, 2004, p. 348). Or, as another commentator put it, "not educating *these people* [italics added] will not diminish the problems but will likely exacerbate them" (Casey, 1996, p. 140).

[28] Katz (1987), p. 17.

[29] A 1999 RAND corporation study's concluded that "the average 30-year-old Mexican immigrant woman who graduated from college rather than dropping out of high school would pay $5,300 more in taxes every year while costing the criminal justice and welfare systems $3,900 a year less" (cited in Galindo, Medina, and Chavez, 2006, p. 97).

[30] Garcia (2001b), p. 2.

for those who will guarantee maximum profits and minimal dependence on social services, the students should affirm the demand for universal access to education. As they have become active, the students have rejected the distorted characterization of the undocumented population as economically dependent and potentially criminal as not only inaccurate but deeply offensive. The massive mobilizations in the spring of 2006 were an expression of the vehement objections by undocumented students and the immigrant community as a whole to the current tenor of the debate.[31] The next section explains how the marches signal both the need for and the shape of new arguments.

MOVING FORWARD

During the spring of 2006, student advocacy for the right to attend college and acquire legal immigration status intersected with the more critical issue of documentation affecting the lives of as many as 12 million people in the United States. The mobilizations that took place across the country signaled a historic moment for the immigrant community as a whole. While the legislative offensive that propelled the massive demonstrations was not surprising, given the ongoing bipartisan attacks on immigrants over the past decade, the response by the undocumented community and its supporters was unprecedented. Equally important was the role of the Latino community at the forefront of these efforts and the active involvement of large numbers of students. In certain cities, such as Houston, the protests were organized by undocumented students in college and high school and promoted widely by the overall immigrant community as well as by supporters in the education and labor sectors.[32] In other areas, such as Los Angeles,

---

[31] Throughout the marches, immigrants loudly rejected being likened to criminals. Signs carried by protesters illustrate this point: "Immigrant not criminal"; "I am not a criminal. I am a dishwasher at a restaurant"; "We are hard workers, not criminals"; "After I built your home and grow your food, why do you treat me like a criminal?"; "Immigrants are workers and human beings"; "People are not illegal: Denying workers' rights is illegal."

[32] JIFM (University of Houston Main campus chapter) organized a march in Houston on March 25, 2006, titled "Walk for a Dream" to express support for the DREAM Act. As happens frequently, this kind of public event also galva-

the marches were organized by wider coalitions where immigrant students played an important role as participants. Whether they were acting as organizers or as participants, this opportunity for intense involvement gave the students strength, encouragement, and increased confidence. Indeed, although federal immigration legislation (both the DREAM Act and any new immigration reforms) has stalled, immigrant students' activism has continued, as evidenced by the growing number of student groups formed to support demands for equitable and inclusive legislation.

Some of the signs carried by protesters proclaimed that "Immigrant rights are human rights," "We all have the right to a future," and "Equal rights for all." These placards make clear that the demonstrations were also addressing the questions of legalization and access as matters of civil rights and equality, and not simply as the source of economic benefits. As one organizer explained, "'This [the mobilization] is so effective because this is really a new civil rights movement reborn in this country . . . Remember, back in the '50s, the huge civil rights movement in this country was primarily about the blacks, but also about other minorities . . . This is not just about the immigrants . . . It's about human and civil rights, it's about all marginalized, underprivileged people in the United States.'"[33] The immigrant rights marches address universal rights and in this sense are a continuation both of the Civil Rights movement of the late fifties and sixties and of the efforts of the Chicano/a movement of the late sixties and seventies. Each of these movements dealt with myriad issues, but a central tenet in both was equal access to public education at all levels, including graduate and professional schools.[34]

---

nized others in the immigrant community to demand a regularization of their immigration situation.

[33] *Asheville Global Report* interview with Partha Banerjee, executive director of the New Jersey Immigration Policy Network. For the full article, see Kyriakou (2006, no. 376).

[34] Between 1936 and 1948, the National Association for the Advancement of Colored People championed three cases dealing with the admission of Blacks to segregated law schools. After years of litigation, their efforts paid off. All three students were admitted, but at great personal cost. In each case, the stu-

The historic decision in *Brown v. Board of Education* (1954) that no group be denied an equal right to an education was preceded by important, although less known efforts, within the Latino community. The *Mendez v. Westminster* case (1947) dealt with the state-sanctioned segregation of children of Mexican ancestry in a California public school district.[35] The case was eventually decided in favor of the Mexican plaintiffs, on the grounds that the state's arbitrary discrimination violated the rights of the students under the Fourteenth Amendment.[36] Today, more than sixty years since this historic ruling, the words of the young woman whose father fought to secure her and others' access to elementary school, resonate with immigrant students seeking access to higher education: "My father did not want us to grow up thinking that we were not equal."[37]

With the birth of the Chicano/a movement in the late sixties, activism spearheaded by young people across the southwest included, among many other demands, calls for an end to segregated schools, full participation in all school-related activities, school-based recognition of

---

dents faced incredibly harsh conditions that, for two, affected their ability to continue their studies (Patterson, 2001).

[35] *Mendez v. Westminster School Dist. of Orange County*, (1946). Beginning in 1911, public schools in Orange County maintained a dual school system, separating Mexican from Anglo children. The Mendez children were denied access to a local school on the basis of their alleged language deficiencies. Outraged, family head Gonzalo Mendez organized a group of parents who eventually petitioned the school board "requesting doing away with segregation . . . as their children were . . . all American born and it does not appear fair nor just that our children should be segregated as a class" (Ferg-Cadima, 2004, p. 17). In 1945, Mendez and others filed the lawsuit that was decided in their favor in 1946. An earlier case also dealt with the issue of segregated school facilities in California. See *Alvarez v. Owen* (1931).

[36] The case was supported by various civil rights organizations, including "the NAACP, Japanese American Citizens League (JACL), American Jewish Committee (AJC) and others" (Ferg-Cadima, 2004, p. 19).

[37] Events in 2007 held across the country to commemorate this case are described in Hendricks (2007).

Chicano/a students' cultural heritage,[38] school board representation, bilingual education,[39] access to higher education, an end to discriminatory hiring practices at universities, and a push for the establishment of Chicano studies departments at colleges and universities. Many of the activities in the spring of 2006, when thousands of Latino and immigrant students walked out of their schools, were reminiscent of this earlier Chicano/a activism.[40] Indeed, many of the long-time activists who have supported immigrant students in their quest for higher education are veterans of the Chicano/a movement.[41]

The legacy of the educational struggle of Chicanos and other minorities is important for immigrant students. Furthermore, the increasing attacks against affirmative action during the past decade and a half provide a basis for undocumented students to reach out to other stu-

---

[38] This recognition was a key demand in school boycotts in Texas organized by the Mexican American Youth Organization (MAYO). See Navarro (1995).

[39] For information on efforts to establish bilingual education programs in Texas, see Trujillo (1998).

[40] The largest student boycott began on March 3, 1968, at Lincoln High School in Los Angeles, to protest school conditions. The student strike (eventually known as the LA Blowouts) grew to incorporate 10,000 high school students across the city (see Seattle Civil Rights and History Project at www.civilrights.washington.edu). In Texas, a similar fight was developing in the high schools located in border areas, to protest the schools' "No Spanish Rule" that prohibited students from speaking their native language. In November 1968, students in Ed Couch Elsa Independent School District organized a boycott with MAYO members from Pan American University; this initial action was followed by other boycotts in Kingsville, and a year later in Crystal City. For more information, see Navarro (1995).

[41] This is especially evident in the role that organizations originally rooted in the Chicano/a movement, such as the Movimiento Estudiantil Chicano de Aztlán (MEChA), have played in the passage of in-state tuition policies. For example, the MEChA chapter at the University of Washington supported the passage of House Bill 1079 in 2003 (see Seattle Civil Rights and History Project at www.civilrights.washington.edu); UCLA's MEChA chapter has supported immigrant student organizations there that advocated for California's in-state tuition law; and the University of Houston chapter of JIFM and MEChA worked together in defense of the in-state tuition law in Texas.

dents. The fight against anti-affirmative action propositions presents an important point of convergence for undocumented immigrant students, students of color who are U.S. citizens, and all supporters of equal access to higher education.[42] From a civil rights perspective, these connections are of particular significance, especially as they increase the solidarity between immigrants and Blacks, groups that nativist forces frequently try to pit against one another. FAIR, for instance, asserts that "the cruelest effects of our current policy of mass immigration is [*sic*] the impact it has had on already struggling black communities."[43]

In general terms, anti-immigrant forces seek to undermine immigrants' struggle for equal access to institutions of higher education because they recognize a basic truth: All measures tending toward equal rights for immigrants are apt to strengthen their sense of worth and equality, with broader implications for the labor market and society as a whole. Indeed, the controversy over in-state tuition bills is not merely a difference of opinion about access to a specific benefit, or right, but rather involves a debate over the conditions that the larger population is willing to accept for one group of people, and the impact this has on society as a whole.

In light of the historical exclusion of underrepresented populations, the cause of immigrant youth would be more effectively advanced by defending access to higher education for all, and in particular for minorities and underrepresented youth. In addition to building coalitions with other minority youth, undocumented students could also establish common ground with students who are not affluent and who also face limitations.[44]

---

[42] Examples of anti-affirmative action decisions in the nineties include Proposition 209 in California (1996); the 1997 Hopwood decision in Texas; and the I-200 initiative (1998) in Washington. One decade later, the push continues, as exemplified by the passage of Proposition 2 in Michigan on November 7, 2006.

[43] See "How Mass Immigration Affects American Minorities" at http://www.fairus.org/site/PageServer?pagename=iic_immigrationissuecenters1609.

[44] Attacks on affirmative action affect many different groups, including immigrant students, minority youth, and those who live in rural areas. In Texas, a law that allows the top 10 percent of graduates of any state high school to gain automatic admission to any public university in the state has been met with efforts to restrain such access under the guise of limited capacity at the state's

Reframing the issue also requires finding a way to extend constitutional protections based on the equal protection clause of the Fourteenth Amendment to the undocumented, particularly youth who are seeking access to institutions of higher education.[45] The Supreme Court's ruling in *Plyler v. Doe* applied to undocumented children in grades K-12, but it reverberated far beyond public primary and secondary schools.[46] The Court recognized that the exclusion of children from public education reinforced their minority status. Most important, the justices acknowledged that although the undocumented were not authorized to be in the United States, they were nevertheless protected under the provisions of the Fourteenth Amendment by their very presence in the country. By allowing undocumented students to pay in-state tuition rates, even with the arbitrary restrictions that some of the bills contain, the states have extended this constitutional guarantee of equal protection for all to include laws pertaining to postsecondary education. In-state tuition policies also function as an extension of the ideals inherent in *Brown v. Board of Education*. They aim to make education

---

flagship institution. In 2007, SB 10, which sought to limit access, was defeated. "Top Ten Percent" proponents understood that, given the segregated nature of state high schools, current law provides access to minority and other students. In explaining the defeat of the bill, MALDEF attorney Luis Figueroa said, "It was about rural, border and inner-city members versus suburbanites" (see Haurwitz, 2007).

[45] Despite the importance of the Fourteenth Amendment in this area, little has been written about its specific application to higher education (an exception is Petronicolos and New, 1999). Some authors argue that constitutional guarantees have not been extended because the nativist view that "there is of course, a significant difference between an elementary education and a university education" (Yates, 2004, p. 594) has prevailed. Others have pointed out the legal impediment that, unsurprisingly, in the Supreme Court's view, the undocumented are not a suspect class and that education is not a fundamental right (see Pabón-López, 2005). See also Galassi (2003).

[46] Washington Governor Gary Locke described his state's in-state tuition bill as "a logical extension of the constitutional right to a K-12 education for all students residing within our borders" (LEAP Educator, 2003, p. 1). For additional discussion of the impact of *Plyler*, see Olivas (1995) and Pabón-López (2005).

equal and available to all students. In that sense, in-state tuition policies represent another step toward the even larger goal of equal opportunity for all.

Advocates for in-state tuition have yet to make full use of these constitutional guarantees. Doing so is imperative in order to defend existing gains and advance the educational cause of immigrant youth. Civil and democratic rights codified in law and supported in the court of public opinion as aspects of fundamental human dignity, and rights are more likely to endure than promises of aggrandizement for business interests. Significantly, referencing these kinds of principles also tends to break down rather than reinforce the caste-like status imposed on the undocumented.

The fight of the undocumented today is for equality. As the current expression of the long struggle that minorities have waged to secure their right to attend public postsecondary institutions, the in-state tuition movement is part of the broader issue of civil rights. This is why, as some authors have suggested, immigrant rights advocates are obliged to examine the similarities between these struggles:

> Today a growing number of labor, immigrant rights and Black political activists recognize the similarity between the denial of civil rights to African Americans and the second-class status of immigrants in the [United States]. U.S. Congresswoman Jackson Lee looks at the situation of immigrants, and sees the historic discrimination against people of color, especially Black people, and women. "I had the benefit of the 13th, 14th and 15th Amendments, the 1964 Civil Rights Act and the 1965 Voting Rights Act, and the executive order signed by Richard Nixon on affirmative action. Without them, I would never have seen the inside of the United States Congress," she declares, while cautioning, "the rights of minorities in this country are still a work in progress. Nevertheless, someone recognized that the laws of America were broken as they related to African Americans—that we had to fix them. Now we

have to fix other laws to end discrimination against immigrants."47

Principles of equality and human dignity, as well as constitutional
guarantees, form the most basic rationale for all formal and informal
efforts to extend to undocumented immigrant students the right of equal
access to higher education. Ultimately, these principles and democratic
protections will prove the most persuasive criteria, as well. In the words
of José López, the foundry worker whose family became one of the
plaintiffs in the *Plyler* case: "School is very important for all children,
and they should not be discriminated against because they are Mexican
or white or black. They should be equal."[48]

---

[47] Bacon (2005), p. 4.
[48] Leal Unmuth (2007).

Appendixes

Admission of Students to Public Schools in Texas Provisions of Section 21.031 (1975)

(a) All children who are citizens of the United States or legally admitted aliens and who are over the age of five years and under the age of 21 years on the first day of September of any scholastic year shall be entitled to the benefits of the available fund for that year.

(b) Every child in this state who is a citizen of the United States or a legally admitted alien and who is over the age of five years and not over the age of 21 years on the first day of September on the year on which admission is sought shall be permitted to attend the public free school of the district in which he resides or in which his parents, guardian or the person having lawful control of him resides at the time he applies for admission.

(c) The board of trustees of any public free school district of this state shall admit into the public free schools of the district free of tuition, all persons who are either citizens of the United States or legally admitted aliens who are over five years and not over 21 years of age at the beginning of the scholastic year if such person or his parent, guardian or person having lawful control resides within the school district.

Appendix B: Overview of In-State Tuition Policies 2001–2006, in Order of Passage

State / Date Enacted	Bill number, sponsor, amendments (if any), and *higher education oversight entity*	Summary of language of in-state bill	Yrs in HS	GED	Fin Aid
TX 6/16/01	**HB 1403** –Representative Rick Noriega **SB 1528 (2005)** – Amends Section 54.052 of TEC, *Texas Higher Education Coordinating Board*	Relating to the payment of tuition and fees at public institutions of higher education and the **determination of Texas residency** for that purpose (as revised under SB 1528, 2005).	3	Yes	Yes
CA 10/12/01	**AB 540** –Assemblyman Marco Firebaugh, Assemblyman Abel Maldonado, *No oversight entity*	A student, other than a nonimmigrant alien within the meaning who meets certain re-quirements shall be **exempt from paying nonresident tuition**	3	Yes (except from adult schools)	No
UT 3/6/02	**HB 144** –Representative David Ure, *State Board of Regents*	Allows a student who meets certain require-ments to be **exempt from paying nonresi-dent tuition.**	3	Yes	No
NY 6/25/02	**SB 7784** – Assemblyman Peter Rivera, Assemblyman Adriano Espaillat	In relation to payment of tuition and fees charged to **nonresident students** of the state university of NY, the City University of New York and Community Colleges	2	Yes (but applying to college in 5 yrs)	No
WA 5/7/03	**HB 1079** – Representative Phyllis Gutierrez-Kenney, Senator Don Carlson *Higher Education Coordinating Board*	An Act Relating to **resident tuition** at insti-tutions of higher education	3	Yes	No

(Continued...) Appendix B: Overview of In-State Tuition Policies 2001–2006, in Order of Passage

State / Date Enacted	Bill number, sponsor, amendments (if any), and *higher education oversight entity*	Summary of language of in-state bill	Yrs in HS	GED	Fin Aid
OK 6/12/03	**HB 1559** – Kevin Calvey, Senator Keith Leftwich **HB 1804 (2007)** – Amends Sec. 1 of State Leg. (2003), *Oklahoma State Regents for Higher Education*	Provides in-state tuition to **qualified immigrants** who graduate from Oklahoma high schools after at least two years of attendance.	2	No	Yes
IL 5/18/03	**HB 60** - Representative Edward Acevedo, Representative Mark H. Beaubien, Representative Antonio Muñoz, *Illinois State Board of Higher Education*	Requires an individual who is not a citizen or permanent resident of the United States to be **classified as an Illinois resident** if the individual graduated from a high school in IL.	3	Yes	No
KS 5/20/04	**HB 2145** – Representative Sue Storm *Kansas Board of Regents*	**Extends in-state tuition** to all Kansas high school graduates or GED recipients regardless of their residential status.	3	Yes	No
NM 4/5/05	**SB 582** (admissions) and **SB 482** (financial aid), Senator Cynthia Nava, *Commission on Higher Education*	Establishes a policy for the purpose of **determining resident and nonresident tuition classifications** for students enrolling at public postsecondary institutions.	1	Yes	Yes
NB 4/13/06	**LB 239** - Schimek, DiAnna, (carry-over legislation, 2005), *Coordinating Commission for Postsecondary Education*	Would allow aliens to attend state-supported public institutions for resident tuition if the student has graduated from a Nebraska high school and resided in Nebraska for at least three years.	3	Yes	No

Appendix C: Chronological Review of Federal Legislation for Undocumented Students

Introd.	House Legislation _Sponsors_	Language	Status
2001	Student Adjustment Act (HR 1918) _Howard Berman (CA) Chris Cannon (UT) Lucille Royball-Allard (CA)_	(1) Amend IIRIRA to permit states to determine residency for higher education (2) Amend the INA to cancel the removal and allow for the adjustment of status of certain college bound students who are long term U.S. residents (3) Make these students eligible for federal financial assistance	
2002	Student Adjustment Act (HR 1918) _Total sponsors: 62_	Same language as above	Received little attention in the 107th Congress
2003	Student Adjustment Act (HR 1684) _30 co-sponsors: Total sponsors: 66_	Same language as above	
2006	American DREAM Act (HR 5131) _Lincoln Diaz-Balart (FL), Howard Berman (CA), and Lucille Roybal-Allard (CA)_	This is the House version of the DREAM Act S. 2075	

(continued...) **Appendix C: Chronological Review of Federal Legislation for Undocumented Students**

Introd.	House Legislation _Sponsors_	Language	Status
2001	DREAM Act (S. 1291) _Orin Hatch (UT)_	(1) Eliminate federal provision that discourages states from providing in-state tuition (2) Permit certain students to adjust their immigration status to permanent residents	Voted on June 20,2002 but not considered on Senate floor
2002	DREAM Act (S. 1291) _Richard Durbin (IL) Orin Hatch (UT) 18 other co-sponsors_	(1) Eliminate federal provision that discourages states from in- state tuition (2) Permit eligible immigrant students to adjust their immigration status to that of permanent residents	
2003	DREAM Act (S. 1545) _Richard Durbin (IL) Orin Hatch (UT) 48 co-sponsors_	Same language as above but introduces two stage process to adjust status: (1) Conditional resident status for 6 years is tied to college enrollment, community or military service (2) Upon completion of requirements, students are eligible for adjusting status An amendment to this bill limited the financial aid eligibility	Voted out of Senate Judiciary Committee by 16-3 vote, October 23, 2003
2003	Educational Excellence for All Learners Act (S. 8) _Thomas Daschle (SD)_	(1) Restoration of state option to determine residency for Higher Education benefit (2) Cancellation of removal and adjustment of status of certain alien high school graduates who are long-term residents of the United States	

(continued...) **Appendix C: Chronological Review of Federal Legislation for Undocumented Students**

Introd.	Senate Legislation *Sponsors*	Language	Status
2004	DREAM Act (S. 1545) *48 co-sponsors*	Same language as DREAM Act (S. 1545)	Voted out of Senate Judiciary Committee by 16-3 vote
2005	DREAM Act (S. 2075) *Durbin (IL), Chuck Hagel (NE), Richard Lugar (IN)*	Same language as DREAM Act (S. 1545)	Introduced November 18, 2005
2006	DREAM Act (S. 2075) *Durbin (IL), Chuck Hagel (NE), Richard Lugar (IN)*	Same language as DREAM Act (S. 1545)	May 2006 – Passed Senate as part of Comprehensive Immigration Reform Act of 2006 (S. 2611). Bill was not brought to House for vote.
2007	DREAM Act (S.2205) *Durbin (IL), Chuck Hagel (NE), Richard Lugar (IN)*	Same language as DREAM Act (S. 1545)	In the Senate, 52 voted in favor of allowing debate on the DREAM Act. The final vote did not gather the necessary 60 votes that would have allowed the legislation to proceed.

Photographs

In 1944, Gonzalo and Felicitas Méndez sought to enroll their children at Westminster Elementary School in Orange County, California. However, the school district enforced segregation and sent them to a "Mexican school." Outraged, they organized a group of parents, and on March 2, 1945 Mr. Méndez became the lead plaintiff in *Mendez v. Westminster*. Ultimately prevailing, the case served as a precedent for *Brown v. Board of Education* in 1954. (*Courtesy of Sylvia Méndez*)

Sylvia Méndez (*second row, third from left as indicated by arrow*), plaintiff's daughter, at Westminster Elementary School. She recounted decades later, during the 50 anniversary of the case: "My father did not want us to grow up thinking that we were not equal." On September 14, 2007, The United States Postal Service honored the 60th anniversary ruling of *Mendez v. Westminster* with a commemorative stamp. (*Courtesy of Silvia Méndez*)

Members of the Houston Coalition of Higher Education for Immigrant Students (CHEIS) speak at the 15th Annual Career & Education Day organized by the Houston Hispanic Forum, February 24, 2001. From left: Art Murillo, University of Houston-Downtown; State Representative Rick Noriega; Felipe Reyes, Houston Community College; and Jeff Fuller, University of Houston, Main Campus. (*Photo by author, February 2001*)

Education supporters rally at the Texas capitol in Austin, in April 2001, to support passage of legislation allowing undocumented immigrants to enroll in college and obtain drivers' licenses. (*Photo by author, April 2001*)

Beginning in 2001, thousands of immigrant students gained the right to complete their college studies and obtain a degree. Soon after the passage of HB 1403, Jay Pennywell, director of the Pre-College Institute at Prairie View A&M University, welcomes immigrant students to the university's summer programs. (*Photo by author, June 2001*)

Jay Pennywell thanks Dulce Ibarra following her talk to immigrant students to encourage them to attend college. Ms. Ibarra also testified in the initial hearing that led to the passage of HB 1403. (*Photo by author, June 2001*)

Original members of the Leticia "A" Network. Taking its name from the student plaintiff in the successful class action lawsuit for in-state tuition, it advocated for undocumented students in California. (*Top row from right to left: Alfred Herrera, Dennis López, Ramón Muniz, Betsy Regalado. Front row from left to right: Patricia Portillo and Irma Archuleta*) With the founding members are students from pro-immigrant group IDEAS at UCLA. *(Photo by author, November 2007)*

Washington State Governor Gary Locke signs House Bill 1079 on May 7, 2003. He is flanked by LEAP director Ricardo Sanchez and bill sponsor Representative Phyllis Kenney Gutierrez. *(Courtesy of Pedro Perez)*

In New York students, advocates, and members of the Mexican American Student Association (MASA) protest against the decision of the City College of New York (CUNY) post 9-11 to charge out-of-state tuition to undocumented immigrants. (*Courtesy of MASA, 2002*)

State Assemblyman Adriano Espaillat (*second from left*) joins students from the Mexican American Student Alliance in their protest against CUNY's decision to exclude undocumented students by raising their tuition. (*Courtesy of MASA, 2002*)

Students and educators from Houston and Prairie View A&M University hold press conference at Texas Capitol building in Austin, with State Rep. Scott Hochberg (*center with tie*) to support passage of the DREAM Act. Co-founder of the Coalition of Higher Education for Immigrant Students, David Johnston is on the far left. (*Photo by author, June 2004*)

State Representative, Rick Noriega, (*third from left*), sponsor of Texas HB1403, after a hearing to defend the bill. In the background is State Rep. Roberto Alonzo (*third from right*). The bill survived the attempts to repeal it. (*Photo by author, April 2007*)

Members of the League of United Latin American Citizens (LULAC) Council 4765 at the historically Black Prairie View A&M University attend the Houston "Walk for a Dream" immigrant rights march, organized by Jóvenes Inmigrantes por un Futuro Mejor (JIFM) on March 25, 2006. Sign in Spanish reads: "Prairie View also has a dream DREAM Act." (*Photo by author*)

Students demonstrate in front of Horlick High School in Racine, Wisconsin, in 2005, in favor of granting in-state college tuition to undocumented immigrants. (*Courtesy of Al Levie*)

Students with the California Dream Act Network protest in front of the federal building in San Francisco over failure of U.S. Senate to approve the DREAM Act in 2007. (*Photo by author, November 2007*)

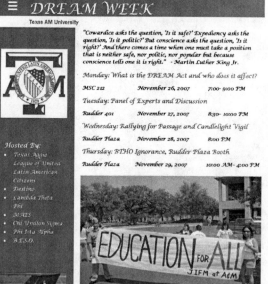

A number of student organizations at Texas A&M University organized a "Dream Week" of educational events and a rally in November 2007, to support passage of the DREAM Act. (*Courtesy Cinthya Álvarez*)

The American Youth Policy Forum at Capitol Hill on March 22, 2002 titled "Equal Access to Postsecondary Education: The Case of Undocumented Alien Students." The forum was organized to inform government staff, congressional aides, and community workers about changes in state laws in Texas and California that allowed immigrant students to attend college and to hear opposing views from anti-immigrant forces. Participating in the debate, and pictured above from left to right are Dan Stein, Executive Director of the Federation for American Immigration Reform (FAIR); this author; and Josh Bernstein with the National Immigration Law Center (NILC). *(Courtesy of Aaron Ruby)*

Flyer with drawing of U.S. soldiers shooting immigrants crossing the U.S.-Mexico border, including an image of a pregnant woman, and skeletons, reads, "The only way to stop a flood is to cut off the flow!" Distributed by Tyler Joseph Froatz, a reported member of the Minutemen, arrested and charged with assaulting a woman organizer at a May 1, 2007 immigrant rights march in Washington, D.C. Police later found an arsenal in his car and home. The increasingly inflammatory language by more mainstream anti-immigrant organizations and the media has emboldened more violent elements. *(Reproduction courtesy of Mexicanos Sin Fronteras)*

The GREAT AMERICAN BOYCOTT 2006!
"A DAY WITHOUT AN IMMIGRANT" May 1, 2006

Hotline: 1-(800)598-6379   Web: www.NoHR4437.org

No Work
No School
No Selling
No Buying

No Consumption On This Day
Wear White T-Shirt at May 1

- Yes To Immediate Amnesty
- Yes To Family Unity
- No To Criminalization
- No Border Fences and Racism
- No Increased Enforcement

On May 1, we are calling No Work, No School, No Sales, and No Buying, and also to have rallies around symbols of economic trade in your areas (stock exchanges, anti-immigrant corporations, etc.) to protest the anti-immigrant movements across the country.

On May 1, we will wear "white" a T-Shirt and/or white arm bands, we can paint and write our political demands (and creative arts) at the T-shirt go to rally, protest, strike, vigil, work or school—we will have a ocean of white T-shirts with our political demands from east coast to west coast, at the street, work place, school, bus station & store... and our voice will be LOUD AND CLEAR AND CANNOT BE SILENT FOR EVER!!

We will settle for nothing less than full amnesty and dignity for the millions of undocumented workers presently in the U.S. We believe that increased enforcement is a step in the wrong direction and will only serve to facilitate more tragedies along the Mexican-U.S. border in terms of deaths and family separation.

March Begins at 12:00 PM @ Olympic & Broadway
Ending @ Los Angeles City Hall

Leaflet announcing immigrant rights march in Los Angeles on May 1, 2006. The series of protests around the country during the spring of 2006 were reported to be the largest in U.S. history, both in numbers and geographic distribution. Following the series of demonstrations, the authorities unleashed the largest wave of raids and deportations. (*Author's collection*)

Massive protest on May 1, 2006 of around one million persons in Los Angeles, the largest in the history of the city and one of the largest in the United States. An estimated 600,000 marched in Chicago, 400,000 in Dallas (the largest ever in Texas). Rural towns in nearly every state reported immigrant marches and rallies. (*Courtesy Madeline Rios*)

At nearly every immigrant rights protest are handmade signs reading, "No human being is illegal," showing an understanding of the issue as a matter of fundamental human rights. (*Courtesy Madeline Rios*)

References

Abkowitz, A. (2006, March 29). 80,000 immigrants strike in Georgia. Creative Loafing Atlanta. Retrieved December 16, 2007 from http://atlanta.creativeloafing.com

Abrego, L. J. (2002). Beyond the direct impact of law: Is Assembly Bill 540 benefiting undocumented students? Unpublished manuscript. Los Angeles: University of California.

Acuña, R. (1996). Anything but Mexican: Chicanos in contemporary Los Angeles. New York: Verso.

Adams, J. (1995, March). Proposition 187 lessons. Applied Research Center. Retrieved September 10, 2005 from http://www.arc.org

Adamson, E. (2005, March 23). Dreams hang in balance: Immigrants would benefit from House bill now in Senate committee that would lower cost of tuition state education more affordable. The Topeka Capital-Journal. Retrieved November 3, 2007 from http://cjonline.com

Adamson, E., & Moon, C. (2004, July 20). Out-of-state students protest tuition break. Suit says law violates U.S. Constitution. The Topeka Capital-Journal. Retrieved November 3, 2007 from http://cjonline.com

Advancement of Hispanic Students in Higher Education Taskforce. (2007, February). Annual Report. Oklahoma City: Oklahoma Legislature.

Aguayo, T., & Preston, J. (2007, October 31). Students' family members are deported. New York Times. Retrieved November 22, 2007 from http://www.nytimes.com

Aguiluz, T., & Reyes, N. (2001, July 11). Letter from Central American Resource Center and Gulfton Area Neighborhood Organization to members of the Texas Legislature in re: HB 1403.

Alanis, J. (2004, March 4). Making it count. Gulfton group to lobby for education bill. Houston Chronicle. Retrieved March 4, 2004 from http://www.chron.com

Alarcon, R. (1994, October). Proposition 187: An effective measure to deter undocumented migration to California? San Francisco: Multicultural Education, Training and Advocacy.

Aleinikoff, A. (1989). Federal regulations of aliens and the Constitution. The American Journal of International Law, 83(4): 862–871.

Alexander, J. (2001, May 31). Houston immigrant students and English language learners are performing well in HISD. Memo from Director of Immigrant/Refugee Programs to Carmen Abascal/Heather Brown.

Alfred, J. (2003). Denial of the American Dream: The plight of undocumented high school students within the U.S. educational system. New York Law School Journal of Human Rights, 19, 615–650.

Amaya, L., Escobar, W., Gonzalez, M., Henderson, H., Mathay, A., Ramirez, M., Viola, M., & Yamini, N. (2007). Undocumented students: Unfulfilled dreams. Los Angeles: UCLA Center for Labor Research and Education.

American Civil Liberties Union. (2007, April 26). Civil rights groups sue immigration officials for unlawfully detaining six-year-old U.S. citizen. Retrieved June 16, 2007 from http://www.aclu.org

American Immigration Lawyers Association. (2004a). Five immigration myths explained. Retrieved September 28, 2004 from http://aila.org

American Immigration Lawyers Association. (2004b). DREAM Act event: Connecticut teenager facing deportation calls for passage of DREAM Act. Retrieved November 4, 2005 from http://www.aila.org

American Immigration Lawyers Association. (2007, Oct. 25). InfoNet Doc. No. 07102560. Cloture vote on DREAM Act (S. 2205) fails. Retrieved November 17, 2007 from http://www.aila.org

Anton, N. (2007). California SB 160. Senate Committee on Education. 2007-2008 Regular Session. Official California Legislative Information. Retrieved October 22, 2007 from http://www.leginfo.ca.gov

Archie-Hudson, M. (1993, April 27). California AB 2114—Student Residency. Bill analysis. Assembly Committee on Higher Education. Retrieved October 21, 2005 from http://info.sen.ca.gov

Archie-Hudson, M. (1994, April 5). California AB 3380—Student Residency Status. Bill analysis. California Assembly Committee on Higher Education. Retrieved October 21, 2005 from http://info.sen.ca.gov

Assessing Immigration Changes. (1996). Migration News. Information retrieved October 31, 2005 from http://migration.ucdavis.edu

Axtman, K. (2002, July 25). A diploma: new ticket for immigrants? Proposed law would give illegal-immigrant minors permanent residency if they finish US high school. The Christian Science Monitor. Retrieved October 2, 2005 from http://www.uh.edu

Bacon, D. (2005, Summer). Uniting African-Americans and immigrants. The Black Scholar. Retrieved June 29, 2007 from http://dbacon.igc.org/index.htm

Badger, E., & Yale-Loehr, S. (2000). They can't go home again: Undocumented aliens and access to U.S. higher education. Bender's Immigration Bulletin, 5(10), 413–423.

Badger, E., & Yale-Loehr, S. (2002, Winter). Myths and realities for undocumented students attending U.S. colleges and universities. The Journal of College Admission, pp. 10–15.

Bailey, T., & Weininger, E. B. (2002). Performance, graduation and transfer of immigrants and natives in City University of New York community colleges. Educational Evaluation and Policy Analysis, 24(4), 359–377.

Baker, A. (2001, July 6). A rising Long Island voice in immigration debate. The New York Times. Retrieved April 29, 2007 from http://www.nytimes.com

Barnard News Center. (2002, June 10). Barnard sociology professor Robert Smith urges Governor Pataki to adopt the most inclusive Assembly Bill 9556 concerning undocumented immigrant students. Retrieved November 2, 2007 from http://www.barnard.edu

Barra, P. (2004, April 22). Aiken student update: Sen. Graham will sponsor bill to help Negrete. The Catholic Miscellany. Retrieved November 4, 2005 from http://www.catholic-doc.org

Barrera, L. (2002). AB 540—Train the trainers: How immigrant students can achieve a higher education. Office of Assembly Member Firebaugh. PowerPoint presentation.

Baskin, T. (2007, April 13). Voces del Mañana supports undocumented students. El Vaquero. Retrieved May 30, 2007 from http://www.elvaq.com

Batalova, J., & Fix, M. (2006). New estimates of unauthorized youth eligible for legal status under the DREAM Act. Migration Policy Institute. Retrieved July 20, 2007 from http://www.migrationpolicy.org

BCIS. (2007). Education and resources: Glossary: Refugee. Bureau of Immigration and Citizenship Services Retrieved October 20, 2007 from http://www.uscis.gov

Beirich, H. (2007, December 11). The Teflon nativist: FAIR marked by ties to white supremacy. Intelligence report. Southern Poverty Law Center. Retrieved December 20, 2007 from http://www.splcenter.org

Belejack, B. (2007, July 13). A lesson in equal protection: The Texas cases that opened the schoolhouse door to undocumented immigrant children. The Texas Observer. Retrieved July 14, 2007 from http://www.texasobserver.org

Bender, B. (2007, June 16). Immigration bill offers a military path to U.S. dream. Boston Globe. Retrieved November 17, 2007 from http://www.boston.com

Berger, E. (2001a, March 14). Plan would offer in-state tuition for visa students. Houston Chronicle, p. A19.

Berger, E. (2001b, May 21). Undocumented students may get big tuition break. Houston Chronicle. Retrieved July 26, 2001 from http://www.chron.com

Berger, J. (2007, December 12). Debates persist over subsidies for immigrant college students. New York Times. Retrieved December 20, 2007 from http://www.nytimes.com

Berman, L. (2007). Relating to the eligibility of an individual born in this state whose parents are illegal aliens to receive state benefits. Filed November 13, 2006 Texas Legislature. Retrieved January 8, 2007 from www.capitol.state.tx.us

Bernstein, N. (2007a, April 16). Tax returns rise for immigrants in U.S. illegally. New York Times. Retrieved April 16, 2007 from http://www.nytimes.com.

Bernstein, N. (2007b, September 21). Immigration raids single out Hispanics, lawsuit says. New York Times. Retrieved October 16, 2007 from http://www.nytimes.com.

Biswas, R. (2005, January). Access to community college for undocumented immigrants: A guide for state policymakers. An Achieving the Dream policy brief: Community Colleges Count. Boston: Jobs for the Future.

Black, R. (2001, June 29). Letter from General Counsel of the California Community Colleges Chancellor's Office to Lynn Neault, Assistant Chancellor for Student Services at San Diego Community College District Re: the extent to which no-resident students can be counted for purposes of claiming state apportionment in noncredit courses. Sacramento.

Blauner, R. (1987). Colonized and immigrant minorities. In R. Takaki (Ed.), From different shores: perspectives on race and ethnicity in America (pp.149–160). New York: Oxford University.

Blumenthal, M. (2007, December 1). Tom Tancredo hired illegal laborers to renovate his McMansion. Retrieved December 1, 2007 from http://www.alternet.org

Board of Regents University of Georgia. (2007, April 17-18). Minutes of meeting. Retrieved November 4, 2007 from http://www.usg.edu

Boloorian, S., & Anton, N. (2001, June 20). California AB 540 (Firebaugh and Maldonado). Hearing before Senate Committee on Education, California State Legislature. Retrieved July 16, 2005 from http://www.leginfo.ca.gov

Bolson, B. (1995). Experts dissect federal judge's Proposition 187 ruling. Legal challenges expected to reach to Supreme Court. Retrieved June 28, 2005 from http://www-paradigm.asucla.ucla.edu

Border Patrol expands (2006). Transactional Records Access Clearinghouse. Retrieved June 16, 2007 from http://trac.syr.edu

Bosworth, M. (2006, February 22). The Earnings Suspense File: Social Security's "secret stash": "Money from nowhere" fattens government accounts. ConsumerAffairs.com. Retrieved June 10, 2007 from http://www.consumeraffairs.com.

Broder, T. (2007). State and local policies on immigrant access to services: Promoting integration or isolation? Updated by National Immigration Law Center (NILC). Washington, DC: .American Immigration Lawyers Association.

Brown, D. (2000a, July 21). Letter from Texas Commissioner of Higher Education to the Honorable Rick Noriega. Austin, Texas.

Brown, D. (2000b, August 11). Letter from Texas Commissioner of Higher Education to Registrars, Admissions Officers and Chief Fiscal Officers re: Policy guidelines for determining residency of aliens. Austin, Texas.

Bryant, S. (1997, February 22). Houston Livestock Show and Rodeo/Scholarship controversy is not expected to hurt Tejano Day. Houston Chronicle, p. 2.

Bustillo, M. (2007, November 24). Hold the tacos, New Orleans says. Mexican-food trucks are outlawed in a parish. Is it racism wrapped in a health issue? Los Angeles Times, p. A1.

Cabaldon, C. (2001, May 14-15). Positions on state legislation. Board of Governors. California Community Colleges Chancellor's Office. Retrieved July 19, 2005 from http://archive.cccco.edu

Caine, N., Torres, P., Walling, E., & Neilson, D. (1999, September). Citizenship and admission: Case study in admitting immigrant students in transition to citizenship. Presentation, National Association of College Admission Counseling (NACAC), Orlando, Florida.

Calderón-Barrera, D. (2003). Hoffman v. NLRB: Leaving undocumented workers unprotected under United States labor laws? Harvard Latino Law Review, 6, 119–143.

Caldwell, J. (2001, January 31). Letter from Director of Grants and Special Programs at the Texas Higher Education Coordinating Board to Cindy Gonzalez re: Residency and foreign students. Austin, Texas.

California Immigrant Welfare Collaborative, (2001, October 8). California update. Legislature passes immigrant rights bill: Higher Education—AB 540—Firebaugh and Maldonado. Sacramento.

Cano, G. (2006). Political mobilization of Mexican Immigrants in American cities and the U.S. Washington DC: Mexico-North Research Network, and Omaha: University of Nebraska.

Capps, R., Castañeda, R. M., Chaudry, A., & Santos, R. (2007). Paying the price: The impact of immigration raids on America's children. A report for the National Council of La Raza. Washington DC: The Urban Institute.

Carrión, A. (2007, April 20). Con todo el espíritu para salir adelante. Universitarios indocumentados venden pupusas y lavan autos para poder pagar sus estudios. Diario Hoy, p. 3.

Carter, L. (1997). Intermediate scrutiny under fire: Will Plyler survive state legislation to exclude undocumented children from school? University of San Francisco Law Review, 31, 345.

Casillas, L., & Punongbayan, C. (2006). National Network for Immigrant and Refugee Rights March Immigration Proposal Comparisons: Bush, Sensenbrenner, Specter. National Network for Immigrant and Refugee Rights. Retrieved June 16, 2007 from ww.nnirr.org

Castillo, J. (2007, May 10). After delay, bill challenging in-state tuition law all but dead. House legislation sought to overturn policy allowing undocumented students to get cheaper tuition at universities. Austin American-Statesman. Retrieved July 1, 2007 from http://www.statesman.com

Chapman, L. (2007, January 29). Immigrants to Nebraska now enjoy in-state tuition. The Daily Nebraskan. Retrieved June 2, 2007 from http//media.www.dailynebraskan.com

Chomsky, A. (2007). They take our jobs and 20 other myths about immigration. Boston: Beacon Press.

Clermont, B. (2006, April 11). 60,000 at Atlanta's immigrant march. Atlanta Progressive News. Retrieved December 16, 2007 from http://www.atlantaprogressivenews.com

Cohen, H. G. (2003). The (un)favorable judgment of history: Deportation hearings, the Palmer raids, and the meaning of history. New York University Law Review, 78(4), 1431–1474.

Commission on Higher Education. (2004, October 22). Revisions to the CHE Residency Regulation 5.7.18 NMAC. Santa Fe, NM.

Connerly, W. (2002, February 19). California is rewriting the Constitution: Why it must say no to subsidized education for illegal immigrants. [Op-ed] Washington Times. Retrieved March 22, 2002 from http://www.washingtontimes.com

Cooper, E. (2004). Embedded immigrant exceptionalism: An examination of California's Proposition 187, the 1996 welfare reforms and the anti-immigrant sentiment expressed therein. Georgetown Immigration Law and Journal, 18, 345–372.

Coutin, S. (2003). Legalizing moves: Salvadoran immigrants' struggle for U.S. residency. Ann Arbor: University of Michigan Press.

Crawford, J. (1996, March 21). Anatomy of the English-Only movement. Paper presented at conference, University of Illinois at Urbana-Champaign.

Davis, D. (2007, July 25). Illegal immigrants: Uncle Sam wants you. Latino teenagers including illegal immigrants are being recruited into the military with false hopes. In These Times. Retrieved September 22, 2007 from www.inthesetimes.com

Davis, G. (2000, September 29). California Assembly Bill No. 1197—Governor's veto message to California Assembly. Retrieved July 16, 2005 from http://www.leginfo.ca.gov

Davis, G. (2003, October 12). California Senate Bill 328—Governor's veto message to California Assembly. Information retrieved July 16, 2005 from http://www.leginfo.ca.gov

Davis, K. (2007, July 3). The founding immigrants. The New York Times. Retrieved July 3, 2007 from http://nytimes.com

De Cardenas, D. (2001, October 21). Champion of transfer students: He partners with community colleges. UCLA Today. Retrieved November 19, 2005 from http://www.today.ucla.edu

De los Santos, K. (2004, March 23). Texas colleges admit illegal immigrants. The Daily Texan. Retrieved March 25, 2005 from http://www.dailytexanonline.com

Democratic presidential candidates participate in NPR debate. (2007, December 4). Washington Post CQ Transcripts. Retrieved December 22, 2007 from http://www.washingtonpost.com

DeParle, J. (2007, November 22). A Western Union empire moves migrant cash home. The New York Times, p. A1, A6.

Dieter, R. (1994). Millions misspent: What politicians dont [sic] say about the high costs of the death penalty. Death Penalty Information Center. Retrieved June 30, 2007 from http://www.deathpenaltyinfo.org

Dinan, S. (2006, April 25). Bush rejects mass deportation of illegal aliens. Washington Times. Retrieved May 1, 2006 from http://www.washingtontimes.com

Dozier, S. (2001). Undocumented and documented international students: A comparative study of their academic performance. Community College Review, 29(2), 43–53.

Dyl, A. B. (2007, January 16). Memo from Colorado Assistant Attorney General, State Services Section, Education Unit to Executive Director, Department of Higher Education re: Effect of House Bill 06S-1023 on the Postsecondary Enrollment Options Act. Denver.

Eldridge, A. (2005, July 25). Study: Illegal immigrant enrollment up in state. The Daily Texan. Retrieved March 25, 2007 from http://www.dailytexanonline.com

Erisman, W., & Looney, S. (2007, April). Opening the door to the American Dream: Increasing higher education access and success for immigrants. Washington, DC: Institute for Higher Education Policy.

Espinosa, R. (2007). Tracking ICE's enforcement agenda. Detention Watch Network. Retrieved October 19, 2007 from http://www.ilw.com

Evans, W. T. (2006). Letter from Utah Assistant Attorney General Chief, Education Division to Richard E. Kendell, Commissioner of Higher Education Re: Validity of tuition statute. Salt Lake City.

Feagans, B. (2006, December 7). State's immigration law makes college enrollment harder for illegal immigrants. The Atlanta Journal-Constitution. Retrieved December 27, 2007 from http://www.ajc.com

Federation for American Immigration Reform. (2002a). How mass immigration affects American minorities. Retrieved June 24, 2007 from http://www.fairus.org

Federation for American Immigration Reform. (2002b, April). Immigration Report: New book exposes immigration's harm to American minorities. Retrieved October 10, 2002 from http://www.fairus.org

Federation for American Immigration Reform. (2004a, July 16). Lawsuit to be filed challenging constitutionality of Kansas Law granting in-state tuition to illegal aliens at public universities. Twenty-four Americans challenge law, claiming new policy discriminates against American citizens. FAIR News Release. Retrieved July 25, 2004 from http://www.fairus.org

Federation for American Immigration Reform. (2004b, July 22). Kansas Attorney General agrees with FAIR on tuition benefits for illegal aliens. FAIR News Release. Retrieved July 25, 2004 from http://www.fairus.org

Federation for American Immigration Reform. (2004c). Taxpayers should not subsidize college for illegal aliens. Retrieved July 25, 2004 from http://www.fairus.org

Ferg-Cadima, J. (2004). Black, white and brown: Latino school desegregation efforts in the pre- and post- Brown v. Board of Education era. Los Angeles: Mexican American Legal Defense and Educational Fund (MALDEF).

Fernandes, D. (2007). Targeted: National security and the business of immigration. New York City: Seven Stories Press.

Fernández-Kelly, P., & Massey, D. (2007). Borders for whom? The role of NAFTA in Mexico– U.S. migration. The ANNALS of the American Academy of Political and Social Science. 610 (1) 98–118.

Firebaugh, M. (1999, February 26). California Assembly Bill No. 1197—An act to amend Sections 76140 and 89706 of the Education Code, relating to public postsecondary education. Retrieved October 21, 2007 from http://www.leginfo.ca.gov

Firebaugh, M. (2000). California Assembly Bill No. 1197: Bill analysis. Public postsecondary education: Residency. Senate Rules Committee. Office of Senate Floor Analyses. Retrieved October 21, 2007 from http://www.leginfo.ca.gov

Firebaugh, M. (2002a). California AB 540: Assisting immigrant students to pursue higher education. Resource Manual. South Gate: Office of Assembly Member, 50th Assembly District.

Firebaugh, M. (2002b). California AB 540—An act to add Section 68130.7 to the Education Code, relating to Public Postsecondary Education. Retrieved February 15, 2003 from http://www.leginfo.ca.gov

Firebaugh, M. (2002c). California AB 1543—An act to add Section 68130.7 to the Education Code, and to amend Section 1 of Chapter 814 of the Statutes of 2001, relating to public postsecondary education, and declaring the urgency thereof, to take effect immediately. Retrieved February 15, 2003 from http://www.leginfo.ca.gov

Firebaugh, M., & Maldonado, A. (2001). California AB 540 – An Act to Add Section 68130.5 to the Education Code, relating to Public Postsecondary Education. Retrieved February 15, 2002 from http://www.leginfo.ca.gov

Fischer, K. (2004, December 10). Illegal immigrants rarely use hard-won tuition break. Some states offer in-state rates, but students still have trouble paying. Chronicle of Higher Education. Retrieved January 11, 2005 from http://chronicle.com

Fisher, W. (2005, June 30). Hoping for a miracle. CommonDreams.org. Retrieved November 4, 2005 from http://www.commondreams.org

Flores, Y. (1993). Texas House Bill 2510: An act relating to the tuition charged certain students at public institutions of higher education. Retrieved January 8, 2007 from www.capitol.state.tx.us

Florio, G. (2002, October 20). College dreams face harsh reality: Laws in several states hamper immigrants' quest for education. The Denver Post. Retrieved November 6, 2005 from http://www.denverpost.com

Franzoia, B. (2001). California AB 540 (Firebaugh): Appropriations Committee Fiscal Summary. California State Legislature. Retrieved February 15, 2002 from http://www.leginfo.ca.gov

Friends of Immigration Law Enforcement. (2004). In-state tuition. Retrieved July 6, 2007 from http://fileus.org

Furchtgott-Roth, D. (2007, May 18). Testimony on the future of undocumented immigrant students. House Judiciary Committee's Subcommittee on Immigration, Citizenship, Refugees, Border Security and International Law. Washington, DC.

Galassi, J. (2003). Dare to Dream? A review of the Development, Relief and Education for Alien Minors (DREAM Act). Chicano Latino Law Review, 24 (79).

Galindo, R., Medina, C., & Chavez, X. (2005). Dual sources of influence on Latino political identity: Mexico's dual nationality policy and the DREAM Act. Texas Hispanic Journal of Law and Policy, (11) 77-98.

Garcia, D. (2001a). Texas House Bill 158: A bill to be entitled an act: Relating to the eligibility of certain persons to qualify as residents of this state for purposes of higher education tuition and to qualify for higher education financial aid. Retrieved January 26, 2001 from http://www.capitol.state.tx.us

Garcia, D. (2001b, March 8). Texas Committee Hearing for 1403. Memorandum to witness for HB 1403. Austin, Texas.

Garcia, R. (1995). Critical race theory and proposition 187: The racial politics of immigration law. Chicano-Latino Law Review. 17(118), 1–28.

George, D. (1996, June 29). Legal immigrants say dreams at risk. Houston Chronicle. Retrieved June 30, 2006 from http://www.chron.com

Ghandi, P., Aguilar, A., & Santillán, R. (2002, March 27). Leavitt a strong backer of resident tuition bill. The Salt Lake Tribune. Retrieved March 27, 2002 from http://www.sltrib.com

Gill, M., Regalado, E., & Riegel, V. (2002, May). Revised guidelines on AB 540: Exemption from nonresident tuition. Sacramento: California Community College Chancellor's Office.

Glenn, E. (2003). New Mexico Assistant Attorney General opinion to Miguel Hidalgo, Acting Executive Director for the Commission on Higher Education in re: Undocumented immigrants' rights to attend state post-secondary educational institutions. Retrieved July 19, 2005 from www.ago.state.nm.us

Gonzales, R. (2007). Wasted talent and broken dreams: The lost potential of undocumented students. San Francisco: Immigration Policy Center.

González, A. (2004, April 29). Con título pero sin papeles. Al Día. Dallas Morning News, pp. 1A, 4A.

Goodland, M. (2005, February 17). Legislative resolution: Fire Churchill. SJR 10 says essay "strikes evil blow" on 9/11 healing process. Silver & Gold Record. Retrieved November 4, 2007 from https://www.cu.edu

Gorman, A. (2007, November 5). Immigration detainees are at record levels. Los Angeles Times. Retrieved November 23, 2007 from http://www.latimes.com

Graham, L. (2007, October 3). Graham Amendment providing $3 billion for border security passes Senate. Press release. Retrieved November 23, 2007 from http://lgraham.senate.gov

Guillen, L. (2002). Undocumented immigrant students: A brief overview of access to higher education in California. Public Advocates Inc. Retrieved July 16, 2005 from www.publicadvocates.org

Gumbel, A. (2003, 10 September). Pentagon targets Latinos and Mexicans to man the front lines in war on terror. CommonDreams.org. Retrieved November 17, 2007 from http://www.commondreams.org

Hallums, M., & Lewis, M. (2003, June). Welfare, poverty, and racism: The impact of race on welfare reform. Washington, DC: Lawyers' Committee for Civil Rights under Law.

Hananel, S. (2006, June 20). Student who fought deportation last year wants more time in U.S. The Associated Press. DREAM act list serve at NILC@democracyinaction.org

Harvard Educational Review. (2001). Immigration and education. Harvard Educational Review, 71(3).

Harvard Law Review Association. (2002, March). California extends in-state tuition benefits to undocumented aliens—Act relating to public post-secondary education. Harvard Law Review, 115(5), 1548-1554

Haurwitz, K. M. (2007, May 31). How minority, rural interests defeated top 10 percent changes. UT president calls House vote "a bad result" for the university. Retrieved June 29, 2007 from http://www.statesman.com

HB 144, allowing in-state tuition for illegals, is a feather in Ure's cap (editorial). (2002, March 5). The Park Record. Retrieved January 28, 2008 from http://www.parkrecord.com

Hebel, S. (2001, November 30). States take diverging approaches on tuition rates for illegal immigrants. Chronicle of Higher Education, p. A22.

Hebel, S. (2002, June 26). N.Y. Legislature passes bill to provide illegal immigrants in-state tuition rates. Chronicle of Higher Education. Retrieved October 12, 2002 from http://chronicle.com

Hebel, S. (2004, July 21). Opponents of lower tuition for illegal immigrants seek to strike down Kansas law. Chronicle of Higher Education. Retrieved June 15, 2005 from http://chronicle.com

Hegstrom, E. (2000a, May 11). Top student to be denied scholarships: Immigration status casts cloud on future. Houston Chronicle. pp. 1A, 14A.

Hegstrom, E. (2000b, May 12). Outpouring of help greets immigrant scholar. Houston Chronicle, pp. 1A, 18A.

Hegstrom, E. (2000c, May 25). HCC to admit immigrants at same tuition as Texans. Houston Chronicle. Retrieved May 25, 2000 from http://www.chron.com

Hegstrom, E. (2000d, November 26). Green card applicants face wait of 3½ years. Houston Chronicle. Retrieved December 10, 2000 from http://www.chron.com

Hegstrom, E. (2005, July 28). Head of Texas Minutemen quits, cites racism in group. Houston Chronicle, p. B1.

Helwick, C. (2007, March 13-14). General Counsel's Report. Minutes of the meeting of

Committee of the whole. Trustees of the California State University, Office of the Chancellor. Long Beach.

Hendricks, M. (2004, June 2). One issue, but many fictions. Kansas City Star, p. B1.

Hendricks, T. (2007, May 9). An early blow for equality: Case helped end separate but equal schooling. San Francisco Chronicle, pp. A1, A15.

Henley, K. (2004, February 20). Tuition restriction gets early OK. The Gazette. Retrieved November 4, 2007 from http://findarticles.com

Hermes, J. (2007, November). Legislative update: DREAM Act. American Association of Community Colleges. Retrieved November 17, 2007 from http://www.aacc.nche.edu

Hernandez, D. (2005). Undue process: Immigrant detention, due process, and lesser citizenship. Paper ISSC WP 06. Berkeley: University of California.

Herrera, A. (2007). Assisting undocumented students in higher education. Power point presentation. Counselor Conference, University of California, Los Angeles.

Herrera, L. (2000, August). Undocumented students. Southwest College News, pp. 1–3.

Hiltzik, M. (2004, May 24). Fabricating a statistic in the immigration debate. Los Angeles Times. Retrieved May 24, 2004 from http://www.latimes.com

Higher Education Committee. (2001). Texas HB 1403 witness list. House Committee Report. Retrieved July 7, 2005 from http://capitol.state.tx.us

Hispanic Forum. (2001, February 24). Higher education for immigrant students. Career & Education Day. Houston, TX.

Horwedel, D. (2007, October 1). Keeping the DREAM alive. DiverseEducation.com. Retrieved November 3, 2007 from http://www.diverseeducation.com

House, D. (2002, September 6). Leavitt seeks to implement tuition break. The Salt Lake Tribune. Retrieved February 3, 2004 from http://www.sltrib.com/

Houston Area Forum for Advisors to Internationals. (2001, February 7). Spring meeting. Prairie View A&M University, Prairie View, TX.

Houston Community College System. (2000a, February 24). Action item: Admission of undocumented students. Houston, Texas.

Houston Community College System. (2000b, May 22). Notice of a regular meeting of the Board of Trustees. Houston Community College System. Houston, TX.

Houston Community College System. (2000c, May 25). Policy to allow certain undocumented students to pay in-state tuition fees approved. Regular meeting of the Board of Trustees. Houston Community College System, Houston, TX.

Houston Community College System. (2000d, May 30). HCCS lowers tuition for undocumented students. Retrieved June 7, 2000 from http://www.hccs.edu

Houston Independent School District. (2000). Demographic overview of HISD population: Emergency immigrant education program. Multilingual Programs. Annual Report, 1999-2000. Houston, TX.

Howard Price, J. (2004, May 24). Kansas gives illegal aliens tuition break: Governor signs bill, joins seven other states. Washington Times. Retrieved July 6, 2007 from http://www.washingtontimes.com

Howard Price, J. (2005, August 24). Texas' tuition policy challenged: Complaint hits discount for illegal aliens denied to legal nonresidents. Washington Times. Retrieved August 24, 2005 from http://www.washingtontimes.com

Huang, D. (2007, October 17). Vietnamese immigrant activist threatened with deportation: Asian Pacific American Legal Center condemns ICE actions. Press release. Los Angeles: Asian Pacific American Legal Center of Southern California.

Hu-DeHart, E. (2003). Globalization and its discontents: Exposing the underside frontiers, Journal of Women Studies, 24 (2-3) 244–260.

Humphrey, K. (2007, May 16). Austin schools overlook 2,000 English language learners. New database created to improve system caught discrepancy. Austin American-Statesman. Retrieved November 11, 2007 from http://www.statesman.com

Huntington, S. (2004, March). The Hispanic challenge. Foreign Policy, pp. 1-12.

Hurdle, J. (2007, July 26). Judge strikes down town's immigration law. New York Times. Retrieved November 23, 2007 from http://www.nytimes.com

Illegal immigrants arrested in raids sue Wal-Mart. (2003, November 9). Associated Press. Retrieved June 17, 2007 at http://www.cnn.com

Illinois Government News Network. (2003, May 18). Blagojevich opens access to higher education for immigrant students: Governor signs in-state tuition bill. Retrieved November 3, 2007 from http://www.illinois.gov

Immigrant Legal Resource Center. (2007). Living in the United States: A guide for immigrant youth. Retrieved December 21, 2007 from http://static.scribd.com

Institute of Agriculture and Natural Resources. (2006, November 13). Rural poll reflects reservations about Latino immigration to Nebraska. Retrieved June 17, 2007 from http://ianrnews.unl.edu

Iwasaki, J. (2003, October 30). Tuition break has surprise beneficiaries: Undocumented students often unaware of benefit. Seattle Post Intelligencer. Retrieved October 30, 2003 from http://seattlepi.nwsource.com

Jarvie, J. (2007, July 29). Citizenship checks strain trust in police: Georgia law puts illegal immigrants at risk as victims of crime and racial profiling, Latino activists say. Los Angeles Times, p. A16.

Johnson, K. (1995). Public benefits and immigration: The intersection of immigration status, ethnicity, gender and class. UCLA Law Review, 42, 150–1575.

Johnson, K. (2004). The "huddled masses" myth: Immigration and civil rights. Philadelphia: Temple University Press.

Johnson, K. (2007, June 24). Anxiety in the land of the anti-immigration crusader. New York Times. Retrieved November 24, 2007 from http://www.nytimes.com

Johnston, D. (1999a). Letter to then-HCCS administrator Helga Mattei concerning undocumented students who have graduated from U.S. high schools. Houston.

Johnston, D. (1999b, September 1). New American Student Foundation. Unpublished manuscript. Houston, TX.

Johnston, D. (2000, October 5). Coalition of higher education for immigrant students. Unpublished manuscript. Houston, TX.

Johnston, D. (2001a, n.d). Letter to Texas Governor Rick Perry. Houston, TX.

Johnston, D. (2001b, February). Some questions and answers on House Bill 1403. Unpublished manuscript. Houston, TX.

Johnston, D. (2001c, April 24). Dear Texas Senator letter. Houston, TX.

Johnston, D. (2001d). HB 1403 – Immigrant tuition. Unpublished manuscript. Houston, TX.

Johnston, R. (2000, May 31). Talented but not legal. Los Angeles Times. Retrieved June 1, 2000 from http://www.latimes.com

Johnston, R. (2000). Guidance counselors often struggle to help undocumented students. Education Week 19 (38), 11.

Joint Legislative Budget Committee Staff. (2007, July 31). Monthly fiscal highlights. Report prepared for the Arizona Legislature. Retrieved November 4, 2007 from http://www.azleg.gov

Jonas, S., & Thomas, S. (1999). Immigration: A civil rights issue for the Americas. Wilmington, DE: Scholarly Resources.

Jones, B. (2003, February 12). Revisiting Farmingville: TV show recounts brutal attack on Latino day laborers. Newsday.com Retrieved April 29, 2007 from http://www.newsday.com

Jordan, M. (2005, April 26). Illegal immigrants' new lament: Have degree, no job. The Wall Street Journal. Retrieved May 5, 2005 from http://www.washingtontimes.com

Jordan, M. (2007, September 21). Bill offers U.S. citizenship for military service: Illegal immigrant act offering U.S. citizenship may fill military void. The Wall Street Journal, p. A8.

Jóvenes Inmigrantes por un Futuro Mejor. (2006, May 7). Defending our right to speak: Students and community leaders defend the rights of immigrants to speak out without fear of harassment and intimidation!! Press conference, Houston, TX.

Kaestle, C. (1983). Ins and outs: acquiescence, ambivalence and resistance to common-school reform. In Pillars of the republic: Common schools and American society, 1780-1860 (pp. 136–181). New York: Hill & Wang.

Kandula, N. R., Grogan, C., Rathouz, P., & Lauderdale, D. (2004). The unintended impact of welfare reform on the Medicaid enrollment of eligible immigrants. Health Services Research, 39(5), 1509–1526.

Katz, M. (1987). Reconstructing American education. Cambridge, MA: Harvard University Press.

Keel, J. (2001a, March 20). HB 1403 by Noriega: Relating to the eligibility of certain persons to qualify as residents of this state for purposes of higher education tuition. Austin: Texas Legislative Budget Board.

Keel, J. (2001b). SB 1526 by Van de Putte: Relating to the eligibility of certain persons to qualify as residents of this state for purposes of higher education tuition or to pay tuition at the rate provided to residents of this state. Austin: Texas Legislative Budget Board.

Kersten, E. (1994, September). Highlights of the legislative accomplishments of 1994: A summary of significant legislation that reached the governor's desk. California Senate Office Of Research. Retrieved October 21, 2007 from http://www.sen.ca.gov

Kim, L. (2004). Higher education of undocumented immigrants: The student adjustment Act. Unpublished manuscript. Wellesley, MA: Wellesley College.

Kinslow, S. (2004, March 25). Letter from Austin Community College interim president to Pat Forgione, Superintendent Austin Independent School District in reference to immigrant high school students. Austin, TX.

Ku Klux Klan rebounds. (2007). Anti-Defamation League. Retrieved June 17, 2007 at http://www.adl.org

Kyriakou, N. (2006, no. 376). "New civil rights movement" seen in immigration protests. Asheville Global Report. Retrieved June 24, 2007 from http://www.agrnews.org

Landry, A. (2002, September 5). Immigration law compliance update to presidents, chancellors, rectors, registrars, admissions directors, domicile officers, and foreign student advisors (INS designated school officials), and the executive director of the State Council for Higher Education in Virginia. Office of the Attorney General, Commonwealth of Virginia.

Leal Unmuth, K. (2007, June 14). Tyler case opened schools to illegal migrants. The Dallas Morning News. Retrieved June 30, 2007 from http://www.dallasnews.com

LEAP Educator. (2003, October). Students gain access to higher education: Legal residency is next hurdle. Des Moines, WA: Latino/a Educational Achievement Project.

LEAP Educator. (2004, September). State policies help "1079 students" aim for college, universities. Des Moines, WA: Latino/a Educational Achievement Project.

LEAP Educator. (2007). LEAP policy priority: Extend state need grant financial aid to undocumented students. Retrieved November 3, 2007 from http://www.leapwa.org

Legislative Education Study Committee. (2001, September 24). Access to higher education for undocumented immigrants. LESC meeting, Santa Fe, NM.

Legislative Counsel's Digest. (2006). California Senate Bill 160: An act to amend Section 76300 of, and to add Section 66021.6 to, the Education Code, relating to student financial aid. Retrieved June 2, 2007 from http://www.leginfo.ca.gov.

Leticia A Network. (1999). Immigrant students: rights and opportunities: How counselors can help students qualify for resident tuition. Los Angeles: Leticia A Network.

Lewis, M. (2005, July 6). Basic facts for state advocates re: Day vs. Sebelius, in-state tuition for immigrant students. DREAM act list serve at NILC@democracyinaction.org.

Lewis, R. (2005, November 9). In-state tuition not a draw for many immigrants. The Boston Globe. Retrieved November 27, 2005 from http://www.bostonglobe.com

Le Texier, E. (2003, May 9). The debate for in-state tuition fees regardless of immigration status: the right to education. La Prensa. Retrieved November 4, 2007 from http://www.laprensa-sandiego.org

Lipman, F. (2006). The taxation of undocumented immigrants: separate, unequal, and without representation. Harvard Latino Law Review, 9, 1–59.

Lipton, E. (2006, May 18). Bush turns to big military contractors for border control. The New York Times. Retrieved June 10, 207 from http://www.nytimes.com

Lomonaco, C. (2006, June 27). U.S. Mexico border: The season of death. Frontline World. Retrieved June 16, 2007 from http://www.pbs.org

López, L. (2007, March 9). Mujeres destacadas: Educación, la mejor herencia. La Opinion. Retrieved May 30, 2007 from http://www.laopinion.com

Los Angeles Community College District. (2007, October 17). Reports/recommendations: Proposed waiver of nonresident tuition for part-time students. Board of trustees. Planning and student success committee. Los Angeles: Educational Services Center.

Decade later, California's Proposition 187 is resurrected in Arizona. (2004, October 23). Los Angeles Times. Retrieved October 30, 2004 from http://www.latimes.com

Loya, L. (2002, September 27). Leticia "A" Network news regarding AB 540 students. Meeting at Rio Hondo College.

Luna-Torres, M. (2007, September 26). Texas application for state financial aid—new and improved! Presentation during National Association of College Admission Counseling pre-conference seminar: Increasing college-going rates among undocumented immigrant students. Austin, TX.

Markoe, L. (2004, March 21). Illegal is illegal: Time to take out the trash. Aiken, S.C., student must return to native Mexico. Retrieved November 4, 2005 from http://www.nnnforum.org

Martin, D., & Schuck, P. (2005). Immigration stories. New York: Foundation Press.

Massey, B. (2005, March 16). Tuition for immigrants in NM passes! College aid plan may grow; assistance could go to non-citizens. Associated Press. Retrieved March 15, 2006 from http://www.ap.org

Maxwell, J. (1979). An alien's constitutional right to loan, scholarship and tuition benefits at state supported colleges and universities. California Western Law Review, 14, 514–562.

McGee, P. (2004, June 14). Immigrants may get help for college. Fort Worth Star-Telegram, p. 1A.

Mehta, C., & Ali, A. (2003, March). Education for all: Chicago's undocumented immigrants and their access to higher education. Chicago: Center for Urban Economic Development and University of Illinois.

Mehta, C., & Hincapié, M. (2003). Social Security Administration's No-Match Letter Program: Implications for immigration enforcement and workers' rights. Retrieved November 23, 2004 from http://www.uic.edu/cuppa

Melendez, M. (2005, July 29). Sweet relief: Latinos rejoice at "Wilson 4" verdict, but officials plan appeal. The Arizona Republic. Retrieved November 13, 2005 from http://www.azcentral.com

Melendez, S. (2004, April 12). In-state college tuition for undocumented students continues to divide state, federal lawmakers and immigration groups. Hispanic Link Weekly. Retrieved November 4, 2007 from http://lideres.nclr.org

Mendoza, E. (2008, January 19). The creation of a Bay Area immigrant rights student coalition. Flier announcing meeting. Santa Clara, CA: Santa Clara University.

Meyerson, H. (2005, June 29). A deportation tragedy. Washington Post. Retrieved November 4, 2005 from http://www.washingtonpost.com

Mexican American Legal Defense and Educational Fund. (2006, February 9). Latino civil rights organizations file legal action to improve bilingual education programs in Texas. Press release. Retrieved October 3, 2007 from http://www.maldef.org

Mindiola, T., Salinas, L., & Eschbach, K. (2002). A profile of undocumented seniors in select Houston Independent School District high schools. Houston: Center for Mexican American Studies, University of Houston.

Miksch, K. (2005, October 1). Legal issues in developmental education: Immigrant students and the DREAM Act. Research & Teaching in Developmental Education. Retrieved November 4, 2007 from http://findarticles.com

Mitchell, P. (2001, April 17). California AB 540 (Firebaugh). Public postsecondary education: Residency. Hearing before Assembly Committee on Higher Education. Retrieved July 16, 2005 from http://www.leginfo.ca.gov

Mitchell, T. (2001, April 15). Busted from college because of where they were born. [Op-Ed]. Los Angeles Times. Retrieved October 1, 2001 from http://www.latimes.com

Mladinich, L. (1995). Falling through the cracks. Prism Online. Retrieved July 16, 2005 from http://www.journalism.sfsu.edu

Montemayor, S., Regalado, E. & Riegel,V. (2003). Revised guidelines and information on AB 540 exemption from nonresident tuition. California Community College Chancellor's Office. Retrieved June 29, 2005 from http://www.gwc.info

Morales, D. (2000). Undocumented Valedictorians: Problems, Solutions and Implications. Houston: Harris County Tax Office.

Morris, B. (2001, July 10). Letter to State Representative Rick Noriega re: Determining residence status. Project Grad. Houston, TX.

Mulay Casey, S. (1996). Dealing with confusion: Admission of undocumented aliens into public postsecondary institutions. Immigration Law Report, 15(2), 138–148.

Murdock, S., & Hoque, M. (1999). Demographic factors affecting higher education in the United States in the twenty-first century. New Directions for Higher Education, 108, 5–13.

Nagourney, A., & Zeleny, J. (2007, December 5). For Democrats, a strained debate on immigration in U.S. International Herald Tribune. Retrieved December 21, 2007 from http://www.iht.com

National Conference of State Legislatures. (2007). 2007 Enacted state legislation related to immigrants and immigration. immigrant policy project. Retrieved November 23, 2007 from http://www.ncsl.org

National Immigration Law Center. (2006). DREAM Act Summary. Retrieved May 31, 2007 from http://www.nilc.org

National Immigration Law Center. (2007a). DREAM Act: Basic information. Retrieved May 31, 2007 from http://www.nilc.org

National Immigration Law Center. (2007b, October 24). Statement on DREAM Act vote. Retrieved November 17, 2007 from http://www.nilc.org

Navarrete, R. (2007a, July 15). Border bullies of San Diego: Minutemen, other groups spread anti-immigrant invective. San Francisco Chronicle. Retrieved November 23, 2007 from http://www.sfgate.com

Navarrete, R. (2007b, July 29). Hate in the immigration debate. San Diego Union Tribune. Retrieved November 23, 2007 from http://www.signonsandiego.com

Navarro, A. (1995). Mexican American Youth Organization. Avant garde of the Chicano movement in Texas. Austin, TX: University of Texas Press.

Nerini, T. (2006, December 5). Letter from Tom Nerini, Director, Student Outreach Services to Dr. Eileen Coughlin, VP Student Affairs in re: Issues and implications of HB 1079 for Council of VP meeting. Seattle, WA: Western Washington University.

New York City Council Committee on Higher Education. (2004, March 3). Immigration law and obstacles faced by students pursuing a higher education. Retrieved March 15, 2004 from http://council.nyc.gov

New York State Education Department. (2005, April). Demographic changes in New York state schools 1993-94 to 2002-03. Retrieved November 2, 2007 from http://www.oms.nysed.gov

Newman, M. (2002, September 20). School district blocks 5 children of illegal immigrants from classes. The New York Times. Retrieved November 15, 2003 from http://www.nytimes.com

Nicholson, M. (2003, May 15). Outreach director honored for social work: Herrera placed in Congressional Record for effort in transfer students. The Daily Bruin Online. Retrieved May 15, 2003 from http://www.dailybruin.com

Nominees, problems with hired help. (2001, January 9). Associated Press. Retrieved November 6, 2005 from http://quest.cjonline.com

Noriega, R. (2000a, June 1). Letter to Commissioner of Higher Education. Austin, TX.

Noriega, R. (2000b, June 29). Letter to Chairman of the Texas Higher Education Coordinating Board. Austin, TX.

Noriega, R. (2000c, July). Barriers to higher education eased for some Texas immigrants. Release from Rick Noriega's office. Texas House of Representatives. Austin, TX.

Noriega, R. (2000d, August 4-10). Immigrants face barriers to higher education. Houston Business Journal, p. 5.

Noriega, R. (2001a). Texas HB 1403 introduced version: A bill to be entitled an Act: Relating to the eligibility of certain persons to qualify as residents of this state for purposes of higher education tuition or to pay tuition at the rate provided to residents of this state. Retrieved February 19, 2001 from http://www.capitol.state.tx.us

Noriega, R. (2001b, August 28). Draft letter to Texas Higher Education Coordinating Board Commissioner re: Implementation of House Bill 1403. Austin, TX.

Noriega, R. (2001c, August 30). E-mail correspondence from State Representative Rick Noriega Chief of Staff re: Coordinating Board rules proposed to implement House Bill 1403. Austin, TX.

Noriega, R. (2002, August 27). Letter to Don Brown, Commissioner of the Texas Higher Education Coordinating Board (THECB) regarding changes in the policies and procedures of the Immigration and Naturalization Service [that] will seriously affect the enrollment of undocumented students in higher education. Austin, TX.

NYPIRG. (2002, February 19). Testimony of New York Public Interest Research Group before New York City Council Higher Education Committee. Retrieved August 2, 2005 from http://www.nypirg.org

Oakes, J. (2005). Keeping track: How schools structure inequality (2nd ed.). New Haven, CT: Yale University Press.

O'Brien, J. (2005, May 26). Texas SB 1528 by Zaffirini relating to the payment of tuition and fees at public institutions of higher education and determination of Texas residency for that purpose. Austin: Texas Legislative Budget Board.

Ochoa, J (2002, September 29). Teen sparks debate on immigrant rights. Greely Tribune. Retrieved November 4, 2005 from http://www.greeleytrib.com

Office of the Governor. (2002, August 9). Governor helps keep college affordable for immigrants. New York State. Retrieved October 17, 2002 from http://www.ny.gov/governor

Office of the Senate Floor Analyses. (2003). SB 328 Senate Bill Analysis: Student financial aid. California State Legislature. Retrieved July 16, 2005 from http://www.leginfo.ca.gov

Office of Senate Floor Analyses. (2007). SB 1: Student financial aid: California DREAM Act. Senate Rules Committee, California State Legislature. Retrieved October 22, 2007 from http://www.leginfo.ca.gov

Olivas, M. (1986). "Plyler v. Doe," "Toll v. Moreno" and postsecondary admissions: undocumented adults and "enduring disability." Journal of Law and Education, 15(1), 19–55.

Olivas, M. (1995). Storytelling out of school: Undocumented college residency, race, and reaction. Hastings Constitutional Law Quarterly, 22(4), 1019–1086.

Olivas, M. (2004). IIRIRA, the DREAM Act and undocumented college residency. The Journal of College and University Law, 30(2), 435–464.

Olivas, M. (2007a, April 17). Testimony before the Board of Regents of the University System of Georgia. Houston: Institute for Higher Education Law and Governance (IHELG), Law Center, University of Houston.

Olivas, M. (2007b). Immigration-related state statutes and local ordinances: Preemption, prejudice, and the proper role for enforcement. University of Chicago Legal Forum. Retrieved January 27, 2008 from http://papers.ssrn.com

Olivas, M. (2007c). Recent developments in undocumented college student issues (2005-present). Houston: Institute for Higher Education Law and Governance (IHELG), Law Center, University of Houston.

Olivérez, P. M. (2006, Spring). Too little but not too late: A discussion of policies and practices shaping college access for undocumented immigrants in the U.S. Association for the Study of Higher Education, 19(1), 4–6.

Olsen, J. (1998). Made in America: Immigrant students in our public schools. New York: The New Press.

Orozco, E. (2005). College program for immigrant students. Austin: Bilingual/ESL Education Department, Austin Independent School District.

Ortiz, M. L. (2002). College outreach campaign: Education at your reach! Educación a tu alcance. Powerpoint presentation by Director of Statewide Immigrant Outreach. Mexican American Legal Defense and Educational Fund (MALDEF).

Pabón-López, M. (2005). Reflections on educating Latino and Latina undocumented children: Beyond Plyler v. Doe. Seton Hall Law Review, 35(4) 1373–1406.

Paget-Clarke, N. (2002). CUNY undocumented students organize to stay in college. Interview with Angelo Cabrera, Mexican American Student Alliance. In Motion Magazine. Retrieved June 30, 2005 from http://www.inmotionmagazine.com

Paredes, R. (2004, November 12). Memo to registrars, admissions officers, and chief fiscal officers, all institutions of higher education in Texas regarding correction to 2004 update on visas for non-citizen students. Austin: Texas Higher Education Coordinating Board.

Parsons, P. (2007). U.S. immigration laws. Retrieved December 24, 2007 from http://www.immigrate-usa.com/mainweb

Parsons, R., & Ten Eyck, T. (2007). People stand up AGAINST inhumane raids: In critical moment: news, analysis and culture from the Southeast Michigan. Retrieved June 17, 2007 from http://criticalmoment.org

Passel, J. (2003). Further demographic relating to the DREAM Act. Population Studies Center. Washington, DC: Urban Institute.

Passel, J. S., Capps, R., & Fix, M (2004). Undocumented immigrants: Facts and figures. Washington, DC: Urban Institute Immigration Studies Program.

Perez, M., & Llorente, E. (2002, September 20) Illegal aliens' children regain right to schooling. North Jersey.com. Retrieved September 24, 2002 from http://www.northjersey.com

Peters, B., & Fitz, M. (2001). To repeal or not to repeal: The federal prohibition on in-state tuition for undocumented immigrants revisited. American Immigration. Retrieved October 4, 2002 from www.ilw.com

Petronicolos, L., & New, W. (1999, Fall). Anti-immigrant legislation, social justice and the right to equal educational opportunity. American Educational Research Journal, 36(3): 373–408.

Pew Hispanic Center. (2006a). Estimates of the unauthorized migrant population for states based on the March 2005 CPS. Retrieved June 16, 2007 from www.pewhispanic.org

Pew Hispanic Center. (2006b, October 10). From 200 million to 300 million: The numbers behind population growth. Fact sheet. Retrieved June 16, 2007 from www.pewhispanic.org

Pfaelzer, J. (2007). Driven out: The forgotten war against Chinese Americans. New York: Random House.

Pitzl, M., & Hansen, R. (2007, December 22). Judge: Employer-sanctions law stands. Ruling allows hiring law to take effect Jan. 1; opponents vow challenge. The Arizona Republic. Retrieved December 22 from http://www.azcentral.com

Plotkin, S. (1999). Assembly Bill 1197 Bill Analysis. Senate Committee on Education Hernandez, California State Legislature. Information retrieved July 16, 2005 from http://www.leginfo.ca.gov

Ponce de León, J. (2003). The underground of higher education. Voices That Must Be Heard. Retrieved August 2, 2005 from http://indypressny.org

Poole, H. (2006). Unlawful entry or unlawful overstay of a visa: Consequences of unlawful entry. Retrieved October 21, 2007 from http://www.humanrightsattorney.com

Popeo, D,. & Samp, R. (2005, August 9). Letter to the Office for Civil Rights and Civil Liberties of the Department of Homeland Security in re: Instate tuition for illegal aliens. Washington DC: Washington Legal Foundation.

Porter, E. (2005, April 5). Illegal immigrants are bolstering Social Security with billions. The New York Times. Retrieved April 5, 2005 from http://select.nytimes.com

Portes, A., & Rumbaut, R. (2006). Immigrant America: A portrait. Berkeley: University of California Press.

Preston, J. (2007a, August 3). In increments, Senate revisits immigration bill. The New York Times. Retrieved September 22, 2007 from from http://www.nytimes.com

Preston, J. (2007b, August 6). Surge in immigration laws around U.S. The New York Times. Retrieved November 23, 2007 from http://www.nytimes.com

Preston, J. (2007c, October 11). Judge blocks Bush measure on illegal workers. The New York Times. Retrieved October 10, 2007 from http://www.nytimes.com

Preston, J. (2007d, October 24). Candidate calls for raid on immigration bill event. The New York Times. Retrieved November 17, 2007 from http://www.nytimes.com.

Preston, J. (2007e, November 17). Immigration quandary: A mother torn from her baby. The New York Times. Retrieved November 23, 2007 from http://www.nytimes.com

Preston, J. (2007f, November 25). Revised rule for employers that hire immigrants. The New York Times, p. 24A.

Protopsaltis, S. (2005, April). Undocumented immigrant students and access to higher education: An overview of federal and state policy. Denver, CO: The Bell Policy Center.

Ramirez, B. (2001, August 10). La migra en la embajada de EE.UU. Vejaciones y despojos a la estudiante Tania Unzueta al tramitar una visa. La Jornada. Retrieved August 10, 2001 from http://www.jornada.unam.mx

Ramirez, D., & Dennis, D. (2004, March 22). International students part of UTEP history. 90th anniversary media news release. University of Texas at El Paso. Retrieved July 1, 2007 at http://www.utep.edu

Rangel, I. (2001, March 13). Public Hearing. HB 1403: Noriega et. al: Relating to the eligibility of certain persons to qualify for as residents of this state for purposes of higher education tuition or to pay tuition at the rate provided to residents of this state. Committee on Higher Education, Texas House of Representatives. Texas State Legislature. Austin, TX.

Reade, J. (2002, March 6-8). Rep Ure's bill narrowly passes Utah house. Exemption from non-resident tuition heads to the Senate, where proponents predict smoother passage. The Park Record, pp. A11-A12.

Reich, P. (1995). Environmental metaphor in the alien benefits debate. UCLA Review, 42, 1577.

Reid, G. (1995). Guardians at the bridge: Will immigrants maintain equal access? Community College Journal, 65(6): 14–19.

Riley, M. (2002, August 11). Immigrants shut out of colleges: Children of undocumented workers must pay out-of-state tuition. Denver Post, p. A-01.

Rincón, A. (1999, Fall). Bilingual youth at their best. Multilingual Programs Newsletter, Houston Independent School District.

Roberts, L. (2007, Sept. 12). ASU scholarships snub Prop. 300's intent. The Arizona Republic. Retrieved November 4, 2007 from http://www.azcentral.com

Robinson, J. (2007). In-state tuition for undocumented students in Utah: Policy Hernandez brief. Salt Lake City: Center for Public Policy Administration, University of Utah.

Robinson, C., & Ratcliffe, R. (2007, January 12). Perry to stick by law giving tuition breaks to illegal immigrants. Houston Chronicle. Retrieved March 1, 2007 from http://www.chron.com

Robledo, A. (1977). The impact of alien immigration on public policy and educational services on selected districts in the Texas educational system. Unpublished doctoral dissertation. Houston: University of Houston.

Rodriguez, L. (1998, January 12). Letter from Texas Higher Education Coordinating Board General Counsel to Dallas County Community College District General Counsel in re: Attorney General's Opinion on the question of tuition classification for undocumented immigrants to the United States. Austin, TX.

Rodriguez, N. (1992). Undocumented immigrant students and higher education: A Houston study. Monograph 90-10. Houston: Institute for Higher Education Law and Governance (IHELG), University of Houston Law Center.

Rodriguez, O. (1996). The politics of Chicano liberation. New York: Pathfinder Press.

Rogers, C. (2007). Letter from State Senator Chip Rogers to whom it may concern re: hearings on the decision to comply with federal law with respect to persons who do not qualify for taxpayer supported tuition benefits. Atlanta, GA.

Rojas, A. (2003, March 2). The publicizing of in-state fees for illegal immigrants at state colleges stirs a backlash. Sacramento Bee. Retrieved October 12, 2006 from http://www.sacbee.com

Rojas. A. (2006, October 12). Appeal planned on in-state tuition for illegal immigrants. Sacramento Bee. Retrieved October 12, 2006 from http://www.sacbee.com

Rojas, P. (2000, December 9). Immigrant students' aid in Viewpoints: Immigration Service leaves a lot to be desired. Houston Chronicle, p. 47A.

Romero, V. (2002). Post-secondary education benefits for undocumented immigrants: promises and pitfalls. North Carolina Journal of International Law and Commercial Regulation, 27, 393–418.

Ruiz de Velasco, J., Fix, M., & Chu Clewell, B. (2000). Overlooked and underserved: Immigrant students in U.S. secondary schools. Washington, DC: The Urban Institute.

Rumbaut, R. (2006). The making of a people, in M. Tienda and F. Mitchell (eds.), Hispanics and the future of America Washington, DC: The National Academies Press.

Russell, A. (2007, August 2007). In-state tuition for undocumented immigrants: States' rights and educational opportunity. Policy brief, American Association of State Colleges and Universities. Retrieved November 3, 2007 from http://www.aascu.org

Rush, S. (1998). The education of immigrant children. The competing goals of state sovereignty and racial equality. Rutgers Race & Law Review, 1, 155.

Salsbury, J. (2003). Evading residence: Undocumented students, higher education and the states. The American University Law Review, 53, 459.

San Jacinto Community College. (2000, August 8). VI-X: Policy on undocumented immigrants tuition. San Jacinto, TX.

San Miguel, G. (2001). Brown, not white: School integration and the Chicano movement in Houston. College Station: Texas A&M University Press.

Sandoval, C., & Tambini, C. (2004). Farmingville. Video. 74 min.

Schulte, B. (2007, June 3). Non-citizen soldiers: Why won't we let them fill the ranks? Washington Post, p. B1.

Schwarzenegger, A. (2006). SB 160 – Governor's veto message to California Assembly. Retrieved October 22, 2007 from http://www.leginfo.ca.gov

Sebastian, L. Y. (2002). Legislative branch developments: DREAM put on hold; Congress and in-state tuition for children of illegal immigration. Georgetown Immigration Law Journal, 16, 874.

See, L. (1996). On Gold Mountain: The one hundred odyssey of my Chinese-American family. New York: Vintage Books.

Selyee, K. (2002, September 22). Campaign season; Lawmaker's immigration views fall flat. New York Times. Retrieved May 30, 2007 from http://www.nytimes.com.

Senate Judiciary Committee. (2005, September 12–15). Confirmation hearing on the nomination of John G. Roberts, Jr. to be Chief Justice of the United States. Washington, DC.

Seper, J. (2004, December 7). Illegal aliens cost California billions. Retrieved September 17, 2005 from http://www.washingtontimes.com

Siegel, J. (2006, August 25). Colorado Speaker's bill saves Democrats. The Jewish Daily Forward. Retrieved November 4, 2007 from http://www.forward.com

Sifuentes, E. (2004, February 28). Echoes of Proposition 187 in Save our State initiative. North County Times. Retrieved November 25, 2007 from http://www.nctimes.com

Sifuentes, E. (2007, July 11). Protests at church spur reaction from Catholic League. Retrieved November 23, 2007 from http://www.nctimes.com

60 Minutes. (2003, August). The death of Lance Cpl. Gutierrez. CBS News. Retrieved December 27, 2007 from http://www.cbsnews.com

Smith, J. F., & Bustillo, M. (2001). Fox urges state to ease tuition residency laws: In address to Legislature, Mexican leader speaks bluntly on an issue opposed by Gov. Davis. Los Angeles Times. Retrieved March 28, 2001 from http://www.latimes.com

Smith, R. (1985). The meaning of American citizenship. Retrieved November 12, 2003 from American Political Science Association at http://www.apsanet.org

Solis, G. (2004, April). More than a diploma: Strategies to improve the educational attainment of Latino students. Report Prepared for Coalition of Humane Immigrant Rights of Los Angeles (CHIRLA).

Somos El Futuro. (2005). New York State Assembly Puerto Rican/Hispanic Task Force. Retrieved November 6, 2005 from http://www.somoselfuturo.org

Sonfield, A. (2006, Winter). The impact of anti-immigrant policy on publicly subsidized reproductive health care. Guttmacher Policy Review, 10, 1.

Southern Poverty Law Center. (2005). Immigration protesters joined by neo-Nazis in California. Intelligence report. Retrieved December 22, 2007 from http://www.splcenter.org

Spring, J. (2001). The American school 1642-2000. Boston: McGraw Hill.

State Board of Education hopeful: Stop teaching kids of illegals. (2002, November 4). Associated Press. Retrieved November 15, 2002 from http://www.ap.org

Stevenson, A. (2004). Dreaming of an equal future for immigrant children: Federal and state initiatives to improve undocumented students' access to postsecondary education. Arizona Law Review, 46, 551.

Stewart, E., & Bulkeley, D. (2007, Jan 29). Students fear repeal of the in-state tuition perk. Deseret Morning News. Retrieved November 4, 2007 from http://deseretnews.com

Stuart, B. (2002). The maize maze in Mexico: Environment and culture. Santa Cruz: University of California.

Suarez-Orozco, C. (2001). Afterword: Understanding and serving the children of immigrants. Harvard Educational Review, 71(3), 579–589.

Suarez-Orozco, M. (2001). Globalization, immigration and education: The research agenda. Harvard Educational Review, 71(3), 345–365.

Sullinger, J. (2004a, June 1). Rush to Kansas colleges not expected under immigration tuition law. The Kansas City Star. Retrieved June 7, 2004 http://www.kansascity.com

Sullinger, J. (2004b). Kansas tuition law under fire: Activist group vows suit over in-state rates for some immigrants. The Kansas City Star. Retrieved June 7, 2004 http://www.kansascity.com

Sullinger, J. (2005a). Judge hears tuition lawsuit: Immigration laws at issue in case. The Kansas City Star. Retrieved June 25, 2005 from http://www.kansascity.com

Sullinger, J. (2005b, December 16). Tuition lawsuit has roots in Kansas. The Kansas City Star. Retrieved July 6, 2005 from http://lawprofessors.typepad.com

Supinger, A. (1999). Assessment of non-resident tuition. AB 1197 (Firebaugh) bill analysis. May 28, 1999. Retrieved July 16, 2005 from http://www.leginfo.ca.gov

Sutherland, H. (2003) America Educating the world—at taxpayer expense. Retrieved November 12, 2003 from http://www.vdare.com

Suthers, J. (2006, January 23). Formal opinion of Attorney General, requested by Executive Director Rick O'Donnell, concerns the authority of the Colorado Commission on Higher Education ("CCHE") to grant in-state tuition status to undocumented aliens. Denver: Attorney General.

Szelenyi, K., & Chang, J. (2002). Educating immigrants: The community college role. Community College Review, 30(2), 55–74.

Tamayo, B. (1995, January/February). Proposition 187: Racism leads to deaths and more poverty. Poverty & Race Research Action Council. Retrieved June 7, 2005 from http://www.prrac.org

Texas Criminal Justice Coalition. (2007, April 19). Testimony provided to the Committee on State Affairs of the Texas House of Representatives. Austin, TX.

Texas Education Today. (2007). Federal court ruling: Judge finds TEA's bilingual monitoring system sound. Retrieved November 11, 2007 from http://www.tea.state.tx.us

Texas Higher Education Coordinating Board. (1987). Texas Charter for Public Education. Available at http://www.thecb.state.tx.us

Texas Higher Education Coordinating Board. (2000a). Chapter 21, Subchapter BB. Pilot program for enrolling students from Mexico. Retrieved March 6, 2000 from http://www.thecb.state.tx.us

Texas Higher Education Coordinating Board. (2000b). Residency determination for non-U.S. citizens (aliens). Austin, Texas.

Texas Higher Education Coordinating Board. (2000c). Closing the Gaps: The Texas Higher Education Plan. Retrieved November 11, 2000 from http://www.thecb.state.tx.us

Texas Higher Education Coordinating Board. (2001, August). Residency: Questions and answers generated from the June 19 and July 25, 2001 Residency Conferences. Division of Student Services. Austin, Texas.

Texas Higher Education Coordinating Board. (2005a). Chapter 21. Student Services Subchapter X: Determination of resident status and waiver programs for certain nonresident persons. Retrieved November 3, 2007 from http://www.thecb.state.tx.us

Texas Higher Education Coordinating Board. (2005b). A comparison of provisions of HB 1403 (77 Legislature, Regular Session) and Senate Bill 1528 (79 Legislature, Regular Session). Austin, TX.

Texas Higher Education Coordinating Board. (2006). Texas higher education facts. Retrieved November 11, 2007 from http://www.thecb.state.tx.us

Texas Higher Education Coordinating Board. (2007). Summary data of HB 1403: 2001-2006. Austin, TX.

Texas House of Representatives. (1976, September). Report of the Committee on Public Education. Austin, TX.

Tienda, M. (2002). Demography and the social contract. Demography, 39(4), 587–616.

Torres, C., & Van Ooyen, M. (2004, March 3). Oversight: Immigration law and obstacles faced by students pursuing higher education. Briefing paper of the Human Services Division and the Governmental Affairs Division before the Committees on Higher Education and Immigration. New York City Council. Retrieved November 3, 2007 from http://webdocs.nyccouncil.info

Treviño, A. (2002, June 26). Eligible immigrants unaware of affordable tuition. Houston Chronicle. Retrieved June 30, 2002 from http://www.chron.com

Treviño, R. (2003, February). Hereford, Texas to Harvard: Low income Mexican origin parents and high achieving bilingual children. Paper presented at the 2003 National Conference of the National Association of Bilingual Educators, New Orleans, LA.

Treviño, M. (2007, October 5). It's been a bad week to be an immigrant child in the U.S.A. The Huffington Post. Retrieved October 20, 2007 from http://www.latinalista.net

Trujillo, A. (1998). Chicano empowerment and bilingual education: Movimiento politics in Crystal City, Texas. New York: Garland Publishing.

University of California Office of the President. (2002). Letter to members of the Committee on Finance. Amendment of standing order 110.2—matters relating to residency: Proposal to establish new policy on tuition exemptions to conform to AB 540. Oakland, CA.

University of Texas at El Paso. (1997). Información para estudiantes Mexicanos. [Brochure]. El Paso, TX.

University of Texas at El Paso. (2000). Programa de Asistencia Estudiantil para Mexicanos. [Brochure]. El Paso, TX.

Van de Putte, L. (2001). SB 1526: A bill to be entitled an Act: Relating to the eligibility of certain persons to qualify as residents of this state for purposes of higher education tuition or to pay tuition at the rate provided to residents of this state. Retrieved April 26, 2001 from http://www.capitol.state.tx.us

Van Ooyen, M. (2005). Oversight: An overview of financial aid at CUNY: The impact of upcoming changes to Pell, Tap and Other financial aid vehicles. Briefing paper of the Human Services Division before the Committee on Higher Education. City Council. Retrieved November 2, 2007 from http://webdocs.nyccouncil.info

Visalaw. (2004). Kansas immigrants will receive in-state tuition rates. Visalaw Immigration Information. Retrieved June 7, 2004 from http://www.visalaw.com

Walth, B. (2001, Dec.10-15). Asylum seekers greeted with jail. The Oregonian. Retrieved December 11, 2007 from http://www.oregonlive.com/oregonian

Wang, T., & Winn, R. (2006). Groundswell meets groundwork: Preliminary recommendations for building on immigrant mobilizations. New York: The Four Freedoms Fund and, Sebastopol, CA: Grantmakers Concerned with Immigrants and Refugees.

Warner, M. (2003). Governor's veto: H.B. 2339 relating to in-state tuition for undocumented students at Virginia's colleges and universities. Retrieved November 2, 2007 from http://www.lva.lib.va.us

Washington State School Directors' Association. (2003). Locke signs tuition bill into law. Retrieved May 7, 2003 from http://wssda.org

Watson, S. (2007, April 20). Minutes, USG Committee on International Students and Scholars. Macon State College. Macon, GA.

Weiner, T. (2003, April 4). A Nation at war: Immigrant Marines; Latinos gave their lives to new land. New York Times. Information retrieved December 27, 2007 from http://www.nytimes.com

Weinstein, B., & Clower, T. (2007). Telling the truth: Dispelling the myths about the negative impacts of undocumented residents in Farmers Branch, Texas. Prepared for Let the Voters Decide. Retrieved October 20, 2007 from http://www.unt.edu

Wenrich, W. (1999, March 22). Letter to DCCCD personnel dealing with admissions of students having no legal status. Dallas County Community College District. Dallas, TX.

Wernick, A. (2004, Fall). The CUNY guide for international students. Retrieved November 3, 2007 from http://www.ccny.cuny.edu

Widess, S. (2007). Impact of the freeze on farm-workers and their families and opportunities for grantmaking. Rosenberg Foundation. Retrieved June 16, 2007 from http://www.ncg.org

Wilson, B. (1995). Bradford decision: "Leticia A." From the President's Desk. California State University, Northridge. Retrieved July 16, 2005 from http://www.csun.edu

Wingett, Y. (2007, January 3). Arizona's colleges struggle to enforce new tuition statute. The Arizona Republic. Retrieved May 28, 2007 from http://www.azcentral.com

Wingett, Y., Benson, M. (2007, August 2) Migrant law blocks benefits to thousands: Prop. 300 denying college aid, child care. The Arizona Republic. Retrieved August 2, 2007 from http://www.azcentral.com

Women's Commission for Refugee Women and Children. (2007, February). Locking up family values: The detention of immigrant families. Baltimore, MD: Lutheran Immigration and Refugee Service, and New York: Women's Commission for Refugee Women and Children.

Wong, J. (n.d.). City University hikes tuition for undocumented immigrants. GothamGazette. Retrieved November 2, 2007 from http://www.gothamgazette.com

Yachnin, J. (2001, April 13). Bills in 2 states would cut college costs for some illegal immigrants. The Chronicle of Higher Education. Retrieved June 12, 2001 from http://chronicle.com

Yates, L. (2004, Summer). Plyler v. Doe and the rights of undocumented immigrants to higher education: Should undocumented students be eligible for in-state tuition college tuition rates? Washington Law Quarterly, 82, 585.

Yee, D. (2006, March 25). Measure penalizes businesses employing illegals. Associated Press. Retrieved December 16, 2007 from http://www.mdjonline.com

Yñiguez, J. (2006). Providing support for California's undocumented students. California Chicano Latino Intersegmental Convocation. Retrieved November 2, 2007 from http://www.clic-policy.info

Young, J., & Noldon, D. (2002). AB 540—New law increases access to community college for non-resident students. Ijournal. Retrieved June 29, 2005 from http://www.ijournal.us

Zaffirini, J. (2005). Texas SB 1528: An act relating to the payment of tuition and fees at public institutions of higher education and determination of Texas residency for that purpose. Austin, TX.

Zehr, M. A. (2007). Defense authorization bill moves forward without "DREAM Act." Education Week. Retrieved November 17, 2007 from http://blogs.edweek.org

Zuniga, J. A. (1996, February 7). Rodeo's new citizenship rule angers some Go Tejano leaders. Houston Chronicle, p. 1A.

Index

LaVergne, TN USA
26 May 2010
184059LV00001B/1/P